HISPANIC AMERICANS:

A STATISTICAL SOURCEBOOK

2005 Edition

information
publications

Also from Information Publications, Inc.

State & Municipal Profiles Series™

Almanac of the 50 States

California Cities, Towns & Counties

Connecticut Municipal Profiles

Massachusetts Municipal Profiles

The New Jersey Municipal Data Book

Florida Municipal Profiles

American Profiles Series™

Asian Americans: A Statistical Sourcebook

Black Americans: A Statistical Sourcebook

Hispanic Americans: A Statistical Sourcebook

Printed in the United States of America

ISBN 0-929960-39-4

Hispanic Americans: A Statistical Sourcebook, 2005

Information Publications, Inc.
3790 El Camino Real #162
Palo Alto, CA 94306

(877)544-INFO (4636) • (650)851-4250

www.informationpublications.com • www.statebooks.us

Hispanic Americans:

A Statistical Sourcebook

Introduction

Introduction xi

Chapter 1 - Demographics 1

Table 1.01	Resident Population and Median Age, 1980 - 2002	3
Table 1.02	Resident Population, by Age and Sex, 2000 - 2003	4
Table 1.03	Hispanic Population, by Type of Origin, by Age, 2002	5
Table 1.04	Hispanic Population, by Type of Origin, by Sex, 2000 and 2002	6
Table 1.05	Population Projections, by Age, 2005 and 2010	7
Table 1.06	Population Projections, by Sex, 2000 - 2050	9
Table 1.07	Population Projections, 1999 - 2100 (revised)	10
Table 1.08	Resident Population, by State, 1980	11
Table 1.09	Resident Population, by State, 1990	13
Table 1.10	Population of Cities with 250,000 or More Inhabitants, 2000	15
Table 1.11	Resident Population, by State, Projections for 2020	17

Chapter 2 - Social Characteristics 19

Table 2.01	Marital Status, Persons 15 Years Old and Older, 1990 - 2003	21
Table 2.02	Marital Status, Men 15 Years Old and Older, 1985, 1990 - 2003	22
Table 2.03	Marital Status, Women 15 Years Old and Older, 1985, 1990 - 2003	23
Table 2.04	Marital Status of the Hispanic Population, by Type of Origin, 2000, 2002	24
Table 2.05	Characteristics of Married and Unmarried Male-Female Couples, 2000	25
Table 2.06	Hispanic Married Couple Households, by Type of Origin of the Husband and Wife, 1993	26
Table 2.07	Age, Educational Attainment, and Residence, 1985	27
Table 2.08	Age, Educational Attainment, and Residence, 1990	28
Table 2.09	Age and Residence, 2003	29

Chapter 3 - Household & Family Characteristics 31

Table 3.01	Selected Characteristics of Households, 1985	33
Table 3.02	Selected Characteristics of Households, 1990	35
Table 3.03	Selected Characteristics of Households, 2003	37
Table 3.04	Type and Tenure of Hispanic Households, by Type of Hispanic Origin, 2000 and 2002	39
Table 3.05	Selected Characteristics of Family Households, 1985	40
Table 3.06	Selected Characteristics of Family Households, 1990	42
Table 3.07	Selected Characteristics of Family Households, 2003	44
Table 3.08	Type and Size of Hispanic Family Households, by Type of Hispanic Origin, 2002	46
Table 3.09	Single Parents Living With Own Children Under 18 Years Old, 2000, 2003	47
Table 3.10	Living Arrangements of Children Under 18 Years of Age, 2000, 2003	48

Table 3.11 Primary Child Care Arrangements Used for Preschoolers by Families with Employed Mothers, Spring 1997 and Spring 1999   49

Chapter 4 - Education: Preprimary through High School   51

Table 4.01 School Enrollment by Age, 2000 and 2002   53
Table 4.02 School Enrollment by Level and Control of School, 2002   54
Table 4.03 Estimates of the School Age Population, by Age and Sex, 2002   55
Table 4.04 Preprimary School Enrollment of Children 3 - 5 Years Old, by Selected Characteristics of the Mother, 2002   57
Table 4.05 Enrollment in Public Elementary and Secondary Schools, by State, Fall, 1999   59
Table 4.06 Public Elementary and Secondary School Teachers, by Selected Characteristic, 1999 - 2000   61
Table 4.07 Private Elementary and Secondary School Teachers, by Selected Characteristic, 1999 - 2000   62
Table 4.08 Percent of Students At or Above Selected Reading Proficiency Levels, By Age, 1999   63
Table 4.09 Percent of Students At or Above Selected Science and Math Proficiency Levels, by Age, 1999   64
Table 4.10 Student Use of Computers at School, 1993 - 2001   65
Table 4.11 Labor Force Status of 2004 High School Graduates and 2003-04 High School Dropouts, October, 2004   66
Table 4.12 High School Dropout Rates, Grades 10-12, by Sex, 1975 – 2001   67
Table 4.13 SAT (Scholastic Aptitude Test) Scores, 1990 - 2003   68

Chapter 5 - Education: Postsecondary & Educational Attainment   69

Table 5.01 Enrollment in Institutions of Higher Education, by Type of Institution, 1980 - 2001   71
Table 5.02 Enrollment in Institutions of Higher Education, by State, Fall, 2001   72
Table 5.03 Enrollment Rates of 18 - 24 Year Olds in Institutions of Higher Education, 1975 - 2001   74
Table 5.04 Enrollment of Persons 14 - 34 Years Old in Institutions of Higher Education, by Sex, 1975 - 1999   75
Table 5.05 School Enrollment by Attendance Status, By Type and Control of the School, Fall, 2002   76
Table 5.06 College Enrollment, October 2000 and 2002   77
Table 5.07 Undergraduates Receiving Financial Aid: Average Amount Awarded per Student, by Type and Source of Aid, 1995-96 and 1999-2000   78
Table 5.08 Employment Status of Students 15 - 17 Years of Age, Enrolled in School, 1998 - 1999   79
Table 5.09 Enrollment in Schools of Medicine, Dentistry, and Related Fields 1980-81 and 2001-2002   80

Table 5.10 Earned Degrees Conferred, by Type of Degree, 1991 - 2002 ... 81
Table 5.11 Associate Degrees Conferred, by Major Field of Study, 2001 - 2002 ... 82
Table 5.12 Bachelor's Degrees Conferred, by Major Field of Study, 2001 - 2002 ... 83
Table 5.13 Master's Degrees Conferred, by Major Field of Study, 2001 - 2002 ... 84
Table 5.14 Doctor's Degrees Conferred, by Major Field of Study, 2001 - 2002 ... 85
Table 5.15 First Professional Degrees Conferred, by Field of Study, 2001 - 2002 ... 86
Table 5.16 Educational Attainment: Years of School Completed by Persons 25 Years Old and Older, 2000 and 2003 ... 87
Table 5.17 College Completion, Persons 25 Years Old and Older, by Sex, 1970 - 2003 ... 88
Table 5.18 Educational Attainment of the Hispanic Population, 25 Years Old and Over, by Type of Origin, 2000 and 2002 ... 89
Table 5.19 Highest Educational Level and Degree Earned, Persons 18 Years Old and Older, 2000 and 2002 ... 90
Table 5.20 Employment of 12th Graders, 1992 ... 91

Chapter 6 - Government & Elections ... 93

Table 6.01 Hispanic Elected Public Officials, by Type of Office Held, 1985 - 2003 ... 95
Table 6.02 Members of Congress, 1981 - 2005 ... 96
Table 6.03 Voting Age Population, Registration, and Voting, 1972 - 2002 ... 97
Table 6.04 Voting Age Population, Selected Characteristics, 1990 ... 99
Table 6.05 Selected Characteristics of Persons Registered to Vote, 1990 ... 100
Table 6.06 Selected Characteristics of Persons Voting, 1990 ... 101
Table 6.07 Voting Age Population, Selected Characteristics, 2000 ... 102
Table 6.08 Selected Characteristics of Persons Registered to Vote, 2000 ... 104
Table 6.09 Selected Characteristics of Persons Voting, 2000 ... 106
Table 6.10 Voting Age Population, Selected Characteristics, 2002 ... 108
Table 6.11 Selected Characteristics of Persons Registered to Vote, 2002 ... 110
Table 6.12 Selected Characteristics of Persons Voting, 2002 ... 112

Chapter 7 - The Labor Force, Employment & Unemployment ... 115

Table 7.01 Labor Force Participation of the Civilian Noninstitutional Population 16 Years Old and Over, by Age, 1985 - 2004 ... 117
Table 7.02 Labor Force Participation of the Civilian Noninstitutional Population 16 Years Old and Over, by Sex and Age, 1985 - 2004 ... 121
Table 7.03 Labor Force Participation of the Hispanic Civilian Noninstitutional Population 16 Years Old and Over, by Type of Hispanic Origin, 1990, 2000 and 2002 ... 125
Table 7.04 Civilian Labor Force and Civilian Labor Force Participation Rates: Projections for 2008 and 2012 ... 128
Table 7.05 Employed Members of the Civilian Labor Force, by Sex and Age, 1990 - 2004 ... 129
Table 7.06 Employed Hispanic Persons as Percent of All Employed Persons in the

	Civilian Labor Force, by Selected Occupation, 2004	130
Table 7.07	Employed Hispanic Persons, by Occupation, as Percent of All Employed Hispanic Persons, by Sex, by Type of Hispanic Origin, 2002	132
Table 7.08	Employed Hispanic Persons as Percent of All Employed Persons in the Civilian Labor Force, by Industry Group, 2004	134
Table 7.09	Full-Time and Part-Time Status of the Labor Force, 2002	135
Table 7.10	Unemployment Rates for the Civilian Labor Force, by Age, 1990 - 2004	137
Table 7.11	Unemployment Rates for the Civilian Labor Force, by Sex and Age, 1990 - 2004	138
Table 7.12	Unemployment Rates for the Hispanic Civilian Labor Force, by Sex, by Type of Hispanic Origin, 1990 - 2002	139
Table 7.13	Unemployment, by Reason for Unemployment, by Region, 2000, 2002	140
Table 7.14	Duration of Unemployment, by Region of Residence, 2000, 2002	142
Table 7.15	Workers Paid Hourly Rates With Earnings at or Below the Minimum Wage, 2001 and 2003	144
Table 7.16	Union Membership, by Sex, 2004	145
Table 7.17	Educational Attainment of Persons 16 Years and Over, by Labor Force Status and Sex, 2000 and 2004	146
Table 7.18	Unemployment Rates of the Civilian Labor Force 25 - 64 Years of Age, by Educational Attainment, 2000 - 2003	147
Table 7.19	Work at Home, 2001	148
Table 7.20	Unemployment, by Reason for Unemployment, 1994 - 2004	149
Table 7.21	Self Employed Workers, 1994 - 2004	150
Table 7.22	Employment Status of Families, 2001 - 2003	151

Chapter 8 - Earnings, Income, Poverty, & Wealth — 153

Table 8.01	Money Income of Households, 1980 - 2003	155
Table 8.02	Money Income of Households, by Selected Household Characteristic, 2001	156
Table 8.03	Money Income of Households, by Type of Hispanic Origin, 2000, 2002	158
Table 8.04	Money Income of Families, 1980 - 2003	159
Table 8.05	Money Income of Families, by Selected Family Characteristic, 1985	160
Table 8.06	Money Income of Families, by Selected Family Characteristic, 1990	162
Table 8.07	Money Income of Families, by Selected Family Characteristic, 2003	164
Table 8.08	Money Income of Families, by Type of Hispanic Origin, 2000, 2002	166
Table 8.09	Median Weekly Earnings of Families, by Type of Family and Number of Earners, 1985, 1990, 1993	167
Table 8.10	Median Income of Year-Round, Full-Time Workers, by Sex, 1980 - 2003	168
Table 8.11	Money Income of Persons 15 Years Old and Older, by Selected Characteristic, 1985	169
Table 8.12	Money Income of Persons 15 Years Old and Older, by Selected Characteristic, 1990	171
Table 8.13	Money Income of Persons 15 Years Old and Older, by Selected	

	Characteristic, 2003	173
Table 8.14	Earnings of Persons, by Sex, by Type of Hispanic Origin, 2002	175
Table 8.15	Per Capita Money Income, 1985 - 1997	176
Table 8.16	Families Below the Poverty Level, 1980 - 2003	177
Table 8.17	Families Below the Poverty Level, by Type of Family and Presence of Related Children, 2000 and 2003	178
Table 8.18	Poverty Status of Families, by Type of Hispanic Origin, 2002	179
Table 8.19	Persons Below the Poverty Level, 1980 - 2003	180
Table 8.20	Children Below the Poverty Level, 1980 - 2003	181
Table 8.21	Persons 65 Years Old and Over Below the Poverty Level, 1970 - 2003	182
Table 8.22	Income of Persons from Specified Sources, 2003	183
Table 8.23	Income of Households from Specified Sources, 1992	184
Table 8.24	Child Support Payments Agreed to or Awarded Custodial Parents, 2001	185

Chapter 9 - Crime & Corrections

187

Table 9.01	Victimization Rates for Personal Crimes, 2001 and 2002	189
Table 9.02	Victimization Rates for Personal Crimes, by Type of Crime, 2002	190
Table 9.03	Victimization Rates for Property Crimes, by Type of Crime, 2002	191
Table 9.04	Criminal History of Prisoners Under Sentence of Death, 2003	192
Table 9.05	Prisoners Under Jurisdiction of Federal and State Correctional Authorities, 1994 – 1997, 2000 - 2002	193
Table 9.06	Jail Inmates, 1990 - 2004	194
Table 9.07	Prisoners Under Sentence of Death, by State, 2004	195
Table 9.08	Chances of Going to State or Federal Prison, 1997	196
Table 9.09	Attitudes Toward the Police, 2002	197
Table 9.10	Attitudes Toward the Death Penalty, 2003	198
Table 9.11	Inmates Ever Tested for HIV and Results, 1996, 1997 and 2002	199
Table 9.12	Persons Stalked During Their Lifetime, 1996	200

Chapter 10 – Vital Statistics & Health

201

Table 10.01	AIDS (Acquired Immunodeficiency Syndrome) Cases, by Sex and Age, 1985 - 2003	203
Table 10.02	Death Rates for HIV Infection by Sex, 1987 - 2002	205
Table 10.03	AIDS (Acquired Immunodeficiency Syndrome) Cases, by Transmission Category, 1990 - 2001	206
Table 10.04	Vaccinations of Children 19 - 35 Months of Age for Selected Diseases, 2000 and 2003	208
Table 10.05	Health Insurance Coverage, 1990 - 2003	209
Table 10.06	Health Care Coverage for Persons Under 65 Years of Age, by Type of Coverage, 1984 - 2002	210
Table 10.07	Health Care Coverage for Persons Over 65 Years of Age, by Type of Coverage, 1995 - 2002	211

Table 10.08	Selected Characteristics of Live Births, 1990 - 2002	212
Table 10.09	Projected Fertility Rates, Women 10-49 Years Old, 2000 and 2010	214
Table 10.10	Births and Birth Rates, by Age of Mother, 2002 and 2003	215
Table 10.11	Birth Rates for Women 15 - 44 Years of Age, by Live Birth Order, 2000 and 2003	216
Table 10.12	Use of Selected Substances by Persons 12 Years and Older, 2000, 2003	217
Table 10.13	Death Rates for Malignant Neoplasms of the Breast, for Females, by Age, 1990 and 2002	218
Table 10.14	Death Rates for Motor Vehicle Accidents, by Sex and Age, 2000, 2002	219
Table 10.15	Death Rates for Assault (Homicide) by Sex and Age, 2000 and 2002	220
Table 10.16	Death Rates for Suicide, by Sex and Age, 2000 and 2002	221
Table 10.17	Dental Visits in the Past Year by Poverty Status, 2000 and 2002	222
Table 10.18	Abortions, 1992 - 2001	223
Table 10.19	Maternal Mortality Rates, by Age of the Mother, 1995 - 2002	224
Table 10.20	Work-Loss Days, 1998 and 2002	225
Table 10.21	Limitation of Activity, 1998 and 2002	226
Table 10.22	Medical Injury or Poisoning Episodes, 1998 and 2003	227
Table 10.23	Injuries, by Selected Characteristics, 2003	228
Table 10.24	Selected Characteristics of Persons With a Work Disability, 2002	229
Table 10.25	Adults Engaging in Leisure-Time Physical Activity, 1997 - 2003	230
Table 10.26	Health Status of Children, 2003	231

Chapter 11 - Special Topics — 233

Table 11.01	Selected Characteristics of Farms and Farm Operators, 2002	235
Table 11.02	Summary of Results of the 2000 Consumer Expenditure Survey	238
Table 11.03	Summary of Results of the 2002 Consumer Expenditure Survey	240
Table 11.04	Occupied Housing Units, by Tenure, 1980, 1999, 2001	242
Table 11.05	Housing Affordability: Families, 1995	243
Table 11.06	General Mobility, 1999 – 2000, and 2002 - 2003	245
Table 11.07	Hispanic Owned Firms, by Major Industry Group, 1992, 1997	246

Glossary — 247

Index — 267

Introduction

Hispanic Americans: A Statistical Sourcebook 2005 Edition is the fifteenth annual publication as part of the American Profiles Series – a series of statistical sourcebooks covering significant topics in American life. Hispanic Americans resulted from the view that, despite the fact that there is coverage of Hispanic Americans in an assortment of reference sources, there is a need for a single volume statistical reference devoted entirely to this important segment of the population.

Hispanic Americans provides an extensive collection of tables which display information on a wide variety of topics. With a few exceptions, each table presents information about the Hispanic population, the White population, and a total for Americans of all races and ethnic groups. The purpose in doing so is not to advance a specific perspective about Hispanic Americans but to provide a context within which the tabular data can be more fully understood and evaluated.

It is essential to understand before using this book that Hispanics (as viewed by most federal data collection agencies) are **not** a racial group. They are the only ethnic or cultural group on which the federal government gathers data. Persons of Hispanic origin may be Hispanic and white, or Hispanic and black, or Hispanic and Asian, etc. As a general guideline, the overwhelming majority of persons who identify themselves as Hispanic also identify themselves as white for federal data collection purposes.

Presenting data by race and ethnicity always puts one at risk of being labeled racist. Although undoubtedly there will be persons on both sides - those who see Hispanic Americans as a propagandistic derogation of the Hispanic community and those who feel that the book eloquently proves the inherent prejudice of our culture - the intent here is to serve neither cause. In fact, Hispanic Americans is not intended to serve any cause or advance any point of view but to serve as a reportorial resource, providing access to federal government information. By researching and presenting this sometimes difficult to find, hard to understand information, Hispanic Americans can serve students, business persons, social scientists, researchers, and others who need basic data about Hispanic Americans.

The use of the term 'Hispanic' itself can also be a cause for controversy. A number of terms have been used by Hispanic Americans to name themselves, such as Latino and Spanish. Hispanic is used here solely because it is the word currently used by the federal government in gathering data. In some surveys, data is further analyzed into subgroups of the Hispanic population (e.g., Mexican Americans, Cuban-Americans, etc.). Where such data is available in this detail, it is presented here.

Another sensitive question is, who is Hispanic? For federal data collection purposes, Hispanic persons are those who say they are Hispanic (or, Spanish, Latino, etc.). For statistical reporting purposes, being Hispanic is based solely on the self-identification of the respondent.

As was stated, most agencies of the federal government consider Hispanic to be a supplement to racial categories. However, some agencies collect data as if Hispanic origin was a racial category. For example, the Centers for Disease Control collects data about AIDS using the classifications of White non-Hispanic, Black non-Hispanic, and Hispanic. The Department of Education also collects data in this manner. These agencies are the exception to the rule, and such exceptions are noted in the table notes at the end of each table.

Organization

The main portion of this book has been divided into ten chapters of tables:

Chapter 1:	Demographics
Chapter 2:	Social Characteristics
Chapter 3:	Household & Family Characteristics
Chapter 4:	Education: Preprimary through High School
Chapter 5:	Education: Postsecondary & Educational Attainment
Chapter 6:	Government & Elections
Chapter 7:	The Labor Force, Employment & Unemployment
Chapter 8:	Earnings, Income, Poverty, & Wealth
Chapter 9:	Crime & Corrections
Chapter 10:	Vital Statistics & Health
Chapter 11:	Special Topics

The tables in each chapter represent results of a comprehensive review of all available federal government statistical information on the Hispanic population. This material was edited and organized into chapters and arranged in a sequence roughly following the pattern found in publications of the U.S. Bureau of the Census.

Each table presents pertinent information from the source or sources in a clear, comprehensible fashion. As users of this book will likely be a diverse group ranging from librarians to business planners, from social scientists to marketers, all with different uses for the same data, the information selected for presentation was chosen for its broad scope and general appeal.

The Sources

All of the information in <u>Hispanic Americans</u> comes from U.S. Government sources either originally or by way of republication by the federal government. In turn, most of the federal information is from the U.S. Bureau of the Census. Without question, the Bureau is the largest data gathering organization in the nation. It collects information on an exceptionally broad range of topics, not only for its own use and for the use of Congress and the Executive, but also for other federal agencies and departments. The reach of the Bureau is wider than most people realize. It encompasses the decennial Census of Population, the Current Population Survey, and the Annual Housing Survey. In cooperation with other agencies, the Bureau extends to the Consumer Expenditure Survey, the National Crime Survey, the National Family Growth Survey, and many others. The fact that the Bureau is responsible for so much of the federal government's data collection adds uniformity to the statistical information published by different agencies. Although the uniformity is not complete, there is enough to make the work of data users a lot easier. The influence of the Bureau of the Census extends beyond federal government data collection. Because of the sheer volume of data it collects, many private data collectors have adopted some of its procedures and terminology. This has the added value for researchers of making private and public data more compatible.

Observant readers will note that the source of many tables is a Census publication, <u>Statistical Abstract of the United States</u>. There are a number of reasons for this. First, due to federal budget cuts, a growing quantity of information used in <u>Statistical Abstract</u> has never been published elsewhere before or it has never been published in such a detailed way. Second, as the preeminent federal data publisher, the Census Bureau has access to a wealth of raw data in machine readable form. It is able to aggregate data geographically on regional lines and break out other detail such as age, sex, race, etc., using its own parameters for publication. Thus, even when information is published elsewhere, the manner of presentation in <u>Statistical Abstract</u> is likely to be unique. Data from this source is presented in a more general way so as to be useful to many different types of data users.

On all tables where <u>Statistical Abstract</u> is cited as the source, the original source also has been checked for additional information. To make more detailed research easier, <u>Statistical Abstract's</u> own source (if it is not the Bureau itself), is listed as well.

Types of Information

Regardless of its source, there are basically two types of data presented in the tables of this book.

The first is complete count data. For example, the five questions asked of all Americans by the Bureau of the Census in its decennial census was an attempt at a complete count of a given universe.

The second type of data is survey information. Here a fairly large, specifically chosen segment of a population is studied. This sample is drawn to be statistically representative of the entire population or universe. Information about housing units and money income are some of the items in this book based on this type of survey information. Of course, survey information is only as good as the survey itself; therefore, the reader should always be the judge of the significance and accuracy of the material presented as it applies to his or her own research. Although specific survey methodology is not discussed here, a full reference to each source is made on every table. Interested readers may consult the original source materials, which in most cases contain a detailed explanation of survey methodology.

The Tables

This section details how the tables have been prepared and presented. Table titles are the first source of valuable information:

Table 4.01   School Enrollment, by Age, 2000 and 2002

The table number contains the chapter number to the left of the decimal and the location of the table within the chapter to the right of the decimal. Thus Table 4.01 is the first table of Chapter 4. With a few exceptions, tables have been arranged within a chapter to present the oldest, most general information first, followed by newer, more specific information. This pattern is mirrored in the tables themselves, which present the oldest, most general information at the beginning.

In a table title, the word or words before the first comma identify the general topic of the table. Following the first comma is descriptive wording which identifies the detail presented about the general topic; i.e., the data is presented by age, sex, marital status, etc., in this case, by age. After the description of the presentation of the data, the years for which data is presented are shown.

It should be noted that both the table titles and the tables themselves retain the original terms of the source material. This has the advantage of making the book compatible with the original sources.

To further facilitate use, every table in the book presents data in two, three, five, or six columns. The left-most column or columns are for the Hispanic population; the center column or columns are for the White population; and the right-hand column or columns present data for all races and/or ethnic groups. For data which is available in subgroups of the Hispanic population, a separate six column table is provided, with columns for Hispanics of Mexican origin, Puerto Rican origin, Cuban origin, Central/South American origin, other Hispanic origin, and a total of all persons of Hispanic origin.

Along the left margin of each table appears a column of line descriptors. Here, after a general heading, subgroups of the heading (usually indented) are shown. Two principles cover arranging and presenting the line descriptors: the oldest, most general information appears first, progressing to the newer, more specific; and quantities appear first, followed by percentages, medians, means, and per capita amounts.

Wherever available and appropriate, a time span of data is presented, usually going back five to ten years. This provides readers with a historical context for the information. However, readers should be cautioned that the years selected have been chosen from no special knowledge of the subject, nor to make any specific point. Thus the fact that there has been a decrease or increase in a given indicator for the period displayed does not mean that the same trend will continue, or that it represents the continuation of a historical trend, or even that which appears to be a trend within this period actually is one. The time span and specific dates have been chosen largely to create a congruity of data, and a basis of comparison between different categories of information.

Table Notes

At the bottom of each table three key paragraphs appear: Source, Notes, and Units. The **Source** paragraph lists the source of the data presented in the table. When more than one source was used, the sources are listed in the same order in which the data itself appears in the table. As all sources are government publications, the issuing agency is listed as the author. All citations provide both the page and table number in the source from which the material was taken. This bibliographic detail on each table makes a separate bibliography at the end of the book unnecessary. A Superintendent of Documents Classification Number is also provided. This number is used as a locator number in most government depository libraries, and documents are shelved or filed according to it, just the way books in some public libraries are organized by the Dewey Decimal System.

An increasing number of sources are now available on the internet, and in many cases, only on the internet. For tables pulled exclusively from on-line sources, the Universal Resource Locator (URL) is listed as the source.

The paragraph of **Notes** includes pertinent facts about the data, the time of year covered by the survey, and the scope of the survey universe. In those cases where Hispanic origin is a separate race-like category (i.e., where the data is collected in such a way that one can be either Hispanic <u>or</u> white, but not both), this is stated. One general note can be made here at the outset about all tabular data: detail (subgroups) may not add to the total shown, due to either rounding or the fact that only selected subgroups are displayed.

The final paragraph of a table, **Units,** identifies the units used, specifically stating that the quantity is millions of persons, thousands of workers, dollars per capita, etc. Readers are urged to pay special attention to this especially when a median, mean, percent, rate, or a per capita amount is provided.

The Index

Every key term from the tables has been indexed. Readers should note that the index provides table numbers as opposed to page numbers.

The Glossary

It is important to be clear about terminology in a work such as this. Not only does the government have overtly specialized terms which clearly require a definition or explanation, but many government agencies use ordinary words in specialized ways. There are real differences between: a household and a family; a family and a married couple; the resident population and the civilian non-institutional population; a service industry and a service occupation; an urban area and a metropolitan area; to name just a few. All specialized terms are defined either in the table or in the glossary. Needless to say, it is absolutely vital to understand the meaning of all terms used in a table before drawing any conclusions from the data. When in doubt, consult the glossary.

For many tables, it is not possible to fully define a term or concept in the table notes, so the glossary serves as an important tool in using the tables. All terms that appear in either the title or text of a table which may be unclear or are used in a special way are defined in the glossary. Wherever possible, the definition is adapted (and in many cases taken verbatim) from the definition provided in the source publication. Not all source materials provide definitions, so sometimes a definition has been constructed by reviewing and summarizing explanatory and supplementary material from the source.

In compiling the glossary the intention was to provide short clear definitions, including only as much background material as necessary to make a term understandable. However, in practice this resulted in compromises. For certain terms (such as metropolitan area concepts), some methodological background is essential in order to achieve an understanding. Where such background is vital it has been included. Readers requiring additional technical or methodological detail are referred to the sources for more complete explanations.

A Suggestion on How to Use This Book

One way to use this book is by locating the subject of general interest in the Table of Contents, and turning to that chapter. While the Table of Contents is detailed enough to narrow a search and the index can speed access to specific items, sometimes paging through the dozen or so tables in a given field uncovers unanticipated information of genuine importance. It is just this type of serendipity that has lead to the inclusion of information in this book, and sometimes such an unexpected find can greatly enhance a research project.

A Final Word

As this book is updated on an annual basis, questions, comments, and criticisms from users are vital to making informed editorial choices about succeeding editions. If you have a suggestion or comment, be assured that it will be both appreciated and carefully considered. If you should find an error here, please let us know so that it may be corrected. Our goal is to provide accurate, easy to use, statistical compendiums that serve our readers' needs. Your help enables us to do our job better.

Chapter 1: Demographics

Table 1.01   Resident Population and Median Age, 1980 - 2002

	Hispanic		White		Total	
	total	median age	total	median age	total	median age
1980 (April 1)	14,609	23.2	194,713	30.9	226,546	30.0
1985 (July 1)	17,865	na	202,769	32.4	235,736	31.4
1986 (July 1)	18,523	na	204,326	32.7	241,096	31.7
1987 (July 1)	19,183	25.1	205,833	33.0	243,400	32.1
1988 (July 1)	19,847	25.8	207,357	33.1	245,807	32.3
1989 (July 1)	20,505	26.1	208,961	33.6	248,240	32.7
1990 (April 1)	22,354	na	199,686	na	248,710	32.8
1991 (July 1)	23,350	25.7	210,899	34.1	252,177	33.1
1992 (July 1)	24,238	25.8	212,912	34.4	255,082	33.4
1994 (July 1)	26,077	26.1	216,470	35.0	260,341	34.0
1995 (July 1)	26,994	26.2	218,085	35.3	262,755	34.3
1996 (July 1)	28,269	26.4	219,749	35.7	265,284	34.6
1997 (July 1)	29,348	26.4	221,334	36.0	267,636	34.9
1998 (July 1)	30,250	26.4	223,001	36.3	270,299	35.2
1999 (July 1)	31,337	26.5	224,611	36.6	272,691	35.5
2000 (April)	35,306	25.8	228,104	36.6	281,422	35.3
2001 (July)	36,972	26.2	230,290	36.9	284,797	35.6
2002 (July)	38,761	26.8	232,647	30.5	288,369	35.7

SOURCE: U.S. Bureau of the Census, <u>Statistical Abstract of the United States, 1989</u>; p. 17, table 21; <u>1990</u>; p. 17, table 19; <u>1991</u>; p. 17, table 19; <u>1993</u>; p. 14, table 12; p. 15, table 14; page 23, table 24; <u>1994</u>; pp. 22-23, table 22; <u>1995</u>; pp. 22-23, table 22; <u>1996</u>; pp. 22-23, table 22; <u>1997</u>; pp. 22-23, table 22; <u>1998</u>; pp. 22-23, table 22; <u>1999</u>; pp. 22-23, table 22; <u>2000</u>; pp. 20-21, table 19; <u>2002</u>; p. 18, table 15; <u>2003</u>; p. 15, table 13. C 3.134:(year)

NOTES: 'Total' includes other races and ethnic groups not shown separately.

UNITS: Population in thousands of persons; median age in years.

Table 1.02   Resident Population, by Age and Sex, 1998, 2000 - 2003

	Hispanic	White	Total
1998			
Both sexes			
total	30,250	223,001	270,299
under 5 years old	3,393	15,052	18,966
5-13 years old	5,219	27,907	35,389
14-17 years old	2,122	12,284	15,517
85 years old and older	177	3,666	4,054
2000			
Both sexes			
total	35,306	228,104	281,422
under 5 years old	3,718	14,656	19,176
5-13 years old	6,186	28,381	37,025
14-17 years old	2,438	12,522	16,093
85 years old and older	151	3,827	4,240
2001			
Both sexes			
total	36,972	230,290	284,797
under 5 years old	3,817	14,784	19,369
5-13 years old	6,428	28,316	37,002
14-17 years old	2,473	12,560	16,181
85 years old and older	160	3,974	4,404
2003			
Both sexes			
Total	39,899	234,196	290,810
under 5 years old	4,158	15,119	19,769
5-13 years old	6,807	28,057	36,752
14-17 years old	2,624	12,745	16,522
85 years old and older	193	4,244	4,713

SOURCE: U.S. Bureau of the Census, <u>Statistical Abstract of the United States, 1999</u>; p. 21, table 21; <u>2000</u>; p. 13, table 12; p. 15, table 14; p. 18, table 17; p. 19, table 18; <u>2002</u>; p. 18, table 15; <u>2004</u>; p. 15, table 14 (data from US. Bureau of the Census, *Current Population Reports*, Series P-25). C 3.134:(year)

NOTES: 'Total' includes other races and ethnic groups not shown separately.

UNITS: Resident population in thousands of persons.

Table 1.03   Hispanic Population, by Type of Origin, by Age, 2002

	Mexican	Puerto Rican	Cuban	Central/ South American	Other Hispanic	Total Hispanic
2002						
Total population	100.0%	100.0%	100.0%	100.0%	100.0%	100.0%
Under 5 years old	11.5	7.8	5.2	7.7	9.0	10.3
5-9 years old	10.9	9.7	6.0	7.4	9.6	10.1
10-14 years old	9.8	8.3	5.2	8.1	10.1	9.3
15-19 years old	8.5	8.9	5.1	8.6	7.7	8.3
20-24 years old	9.9	8.5	4.6	9.6	9.6	9.5
25-29 years old	9.8	8.6	6.3	9.8	8.0	9.4
30-34 years old	9.5	8.1	5.2	10.2	8.1	9.2
35-44 years old	13.6	14.5	15.6	18.5	14.5	14.5
45-54 years old	8.1	11.5	11.1	10.8	11.3	9.1
55-64 years old	4.4	7.5	12.9	5.0	5.9	5.2
65-74 years old	2.4	4.6	13.5	2.8	3.8	3.1
75-84 years old	1.3	1.4	6.2	1.2	2.2	1.5
85 years and over	0.3	0.6	3.0	0.2	0.3	0.4

SOURCE: U.S. Bureau of the Census, <u>Current Population Reports: The Hispanic Population of the United States, 2002</u>; Internet Release date: 18 June 2003;
"Table 1.1 Population by Sex, Age, Hispanic Origin, and Race: March 2002",
"Table 1.2 Population by Sex, Age, and Hispanic Origin Type: March 2002".

NOTES: Total population includes other races and ethnic groups not shown separately.
'Other Hispanic origin' includes persons from Spain and persons
identifying themselves generally as Hispanic, Spanish, Spanish-American,
Hispano, Latino, etc.

UNITS: Percent as a percent of total shown (100.0%).

Table 1.04 Hispanic Population, by Type of Origin, by Sex, 2000 and 2002

	male	female	both sexes
2000			
Total Hispanic population	16,435	16,369	32,804
by origin			
Mexican origin	11,120	10,582	21,701
Puerto Rican origin	1,463	1,496	2,959
Cuban origin	631	669	1,300
Central/South American origin	2,216	2,526	4,743
other Hispanic origin	1,005	1,095	2,101
2002			
Total Hispanic population	19,126	18,312	37,438
by origin			
Mexican origin	13,044	12,030	25,074
Puerto Rican origin	1,515	1,707	3,222
Cuban origin	688	688	1,376
Central/South American origin	2,698	2,651	5,349
other Hispanic origin	1,181	1,235	2,416

SOURCE: U.S. Bureau of the Census, <u>Current Population Reports: The Hispanic Population of the United States, 2000</u>, "Table 1. Selected Summary Measures of Age and Income by Hispanic Origin and Race: March 2000", published March 6, 2001.
U.S. Bureau of the Census, <u>Current Population Reports: The Hispanic Population of the United States, 2002</u>; Internet release date: 18 June 2003; "Table 1.1 Population by Sex, Age, Hispanic Origin, and Race: March 2002", "Table 1.2 Population by Sex, Age, and Hispanic Origin Type: March 2002".

NOTES: 'Other Hispanic origin' includes persons from Spain and persons identifying themselves generally as Hispanic, Spanish, Spanish-American, Hispano, Latino, etc.

UNITS: Resident population in percent, by sex, as a percent of all persons.

Table 1.05   Population Projections, by Age, 2005 and 2010

	Hispanic	White	Total
2005			
total	41,801	236,924	295,507
under 5 years	4,397	15,503	20,495
5 to 9 years	3,892	14,862	19,467
10 to 14 years	3,853	15,881	20,838
15 to 19 years	3,576	16,281	21,272
20 to 24 years	3,604	16,153	20,823
25 to 29 years	3,781	15,377	19,753
30 to 34 years	3,666	15,466	19,847
35 to 39 years	3,297	16,538	20,869
40 to 44 years	2,926	18,318	22,735
45 to 49 years	2,375	18,312	22,453
50 to 54 years	1,823	16,499	19,983
55 to 59 years	1,393	14,582	17,359
60 to 64 years	978	11,075	13,017
65 to 69 years	745	8,629	10,123
70 to 74 years	571	7,348	8,500
75 to 79 years	433	6,506	7,376
80 to 84 years	275	4,993	5,576
85 to 89 years	135	2,890	3,206
90 to 94 years	60	1,286	1,431
95 to 99 years	18	366	412
100 years old and over	3	60	71

continued on the next page

Table 1.05   continued

	Hispanic	White	Total
2010			
total	47,756	244,995	308,936
under 5 years	4,824	15,995	21,426
5 to 9 years	4,515	15,639	20,706
10 to 14 years	4,057	15,049	19,767
15 to 19 years	4,162	16,203	21,336
20 to 24 years	3,927	16,591	21,676
25 to 29 years	3,878	16,495	21,375
30 to 34 years	3,973	15,654	20,271
35 to 39 years	3,769	15,597	20,137
40 to 44 years	3,343	16,566	20,984
45 to 49 years	2,939	18,213	22,654
50 to 54 years	2,371	18,066	22,173
55 to 59 years	1,806	16,102	19,507
60 to 64 years	1,365	14,004	16,679
65 to 69 years	941	10,357	12,172
70 to 74 years	694	7,767	9,097
75 to 79 years	510	6,226	7,186
80 to 84 years	359	5,005	5,665
85 to 89 years	204	3,321	3,713
90 to 94 years	84	1,546	1,727
95 to 99 years	28	503	569
100 years old and over	6	98	114

SOURCE: U.S. Bureau of the Census, <u>Statistical Abstract of the United States, 2003;</u> p. 19, table 16; <u>2004;</u> p. 18, table 16 (data from US. Bureau of the Census, *Current Population Reports*, Series P-25). C 3.134: (year)

NOTES: 'Total' includes other races and ethnic groups not shown separately. Population projections as of July 1, of the year shown.

UNITS: Estimates of the total population in thousands of persons, includes armed forces overseas.

Table 1.06 Population Projections, by Sex, 2000 - 2050

	Hispanic	White	Total
2000			
both sexes	31,366	225,532	274,634
male	15,799	110,799	134,181
female	15,566	114,734	140,453
2005			
both sexes	36,057	232,463	285,981
male	18,082	114,350	139,785
female	17,975	118,113	146,196
2010			
both sexes	39,982	241,770	299,862
male	na	na	146,679
female	na	na	153,183
2025			
both sexes	47,089	265,306	337,815
male	na	na	165,009
female	na	na	172,806
2050			
both sexes	59,239	302,453	403,687
male	na	na	197,047
female	na	na	206,640

SOURCE: U.S. Bureau of the Census, Statistical Abstract of the United States, 1996; p. 25, table 24; p. 26, table 25; 2002; p. 13, table 10 (data from U.S. Bureau of the Census, *Current Population Reports*, Series P-25). C 3.134: (year)

NOTES: 'Total' includes other races and ethnic groups not shown separately. Population projections as of July 1, of the year shown.

UNITS: Estimates of the total population in thousands of persons, includes armed forces overseas.

Table 1.07   Population Projections, 2000 - 2100 (revised)

	Hispanic	White	Total
2000*	35,622	228,548	282,125
2005	38,188	234,221	287,715
2010*	47,756	244,995	308,936
2015	49,255	249,467	312,268
2020*	59,756	260,629	335,805
2025	61,433	265,305	337,814
2030*	73,055	275,731	363,584
2035	75,289	280,555	364,319
2040*	87,585	289,690	391,946
2045	90,343	295,019	390,397
2050*	102,560	302,626	419,854
2055	106,370	310,300	417,477
2060	114,796	318,752	432,010
2065	123,508	327,907	447,415
2070	132,492	337,719	463,639
2075	141,719	348,027	480,504
2080	151,154	358,664	497,829
2085	160,763	369,547	515,528
2090	170,514	380,674	533,605
2095	180,377	392,063	552,085
2100	190,330	403,696	570,954

SOURCE: U.S. Bureau of the Census, <u>Projections of the Resident Population by Race, Hispanic Origin, and Nativity: Middle Series, 1999 to 2100</u> Tables NP-T5-A - NP-T5-H <www.census.gov/population/www/projections/natproj.html> accessed 1 February 2000

*U.S. Bureau of the Census, "<u>Projected Population of the United States by Race, and Hispanic Origin: 2000 to 2050</u>", Table 1a (data from "U.S. Interim Projections by Age, Sex, Race, and Hispanic Origin," <http://www.census.gov/ipc/www/usinterimproj/>, Internet release date: 18 March, 2004).

NOTES: 'Total' includes other races and ethnic groups not shown separately. Population projections as of July 1, of the year shown.

UNITS: Estimates of the total population in thousands of persons, includes armed forces overseas.

Table 1.08   Resident Population, by State, 1980

	Hispanic	White	Total
Alabama	34	2,873	3,894
Alaska	9	310	402
Arizona	444	2,241	2,718
Arkansas	17	1,890	2,286
California	4,541	18,031	23,668
Colorado	341	2,571	2,890
Connecticut	125	2,799	3,108
Delaware	10	488	594
District of Columbia	18	172	638
Florida	585	8,185	9,746
Georgia	61	3,947	5,463
Hawaii	71	319	965
Idaho	37	902	944
Illinois	635	9,233	11,427
Indiana	87	5,004	5,490
Iowa	26	2,839	2,914
Kansas	63	2,168	2,364
Kentucky	27	3,379	3,661
Louisiana	100	2,912	4,206
Maine	5	1,110	1,125
Maryland	63	3,159	4,217
Massachusetts	141	5,363	5,737
Michigan	158	7,872	9,262
Minnesota	32	3,936	4,076
Mississippi	24	1,615	2,521
Missouri	52	4,345	4,917
Montana	10	740	787
Nebraska	28	1,490	1,570
Nevada	54	700	800
New Hampshire	5	910	921
New Jersey	494	6,127	7,365
New Mexico	477	978	1,303
New York	1,661	13,961	17,558

continued on the next page

Table 1.08   continued

	Hispanic	White	Total
North Carolina	56	4,458	5,882
North Dakota	3	626	653
Ohio	120	9,597	10,798
Oklahoma	58	2,598	3,025
Oregon	66	2,491	2,633
Pennsylvania	154	10,652	11,864
Rhode Island	19	897	947
South Carolina	34	2,147	3,122
South Dakota	4	640	691
Tennessee	34	3,835	4,591
Texas	2,983	11,198	14,229
Utah	60	1,383	1,461
Vermont	3	507	511
Virginia	80	4,230	5,347
Washington	121	3,779	4,132
West Virginia	13	1,875	1,950
Wisconsin	63	4,443	4,706
Wyoming	25	446	470

SOURCE: U.S. Bureau of the Census, <u>Census of Population: General Population Characteristics: United States Summary PC80-1-B1</u>; p. 1-125, table 62. C 3.223/6:980/B1
U.S. Bureau of the Census, <u>Census of Population: General Social and Economic Characteristics: United States Summary PC80-1-C1</u>; p. 1-280, table 233.   C 3.223/7:980/C1

NOTES: 'Total' includes other races and ethnic groups not shown separately.

UNITS: Population in thousands of persons.

Table 1.09   Resident Population, by State, 1990

	Hispanic	White	Total
Alabama	25	2,976	4,041
Alaska	18	415	550
Arizona	688	2,963	3,665
Arkansas	20	1,945	2,351
California	7,688	20,524	29,760
Colorado	424	2,905	3,294
Connecticut	213	2,859	3,287
Delaware	16	535	666
District of Columbia	33	180	607
Florida	1,574	10,749	12,938
Georgia	109	4,600	6,478
Hawaii	81	370	1,108
Idaho	53	950	1,007
Illinois	904	8,953	11,431
Indiana	99	5,021	5,544
Iowa	33	2,683	2,777
Kansas	94	2,232	2,478
Kentucky	22	3,392	3,685
Louisiana	93	2,839	4,220
Maine	7	1,208	1,228
Maryland	125	3,394	4,781
Massachusetts	288	5,405	6,016
Michigan	202	7,756	9,295
Minnesota	54	4,130	4,375
Mississippi	16	1,633	2,573
Missouri	62	4,486	5,117
Montana	12	741	799
Nebraska	37	1,481	1,578
Nevada	124	1,013	1,202
New Hampshire	11	1,087	1,109
New Jersey	740	6,130	7,730
New Mexico	579	1,146	1,515

continued on the next page

Table 1.09   continued

	Hispanic	White	Total
New York	2,214	13,385	17,990
North Carolina	77	5,008	6,629
North Dakota	5	604	639
Ohio	140	9,522	10,847
Oklahoma	86	2,584	3,146
Oregon	113	2,637	2,842
Pennsylvania	232	10,520	11,882
Rhode Island	46	917	1,003
South Carolina	31	2,407	3,487
South Dakota	5	638	696
Tennessee	33	4,048	4,877
Texas	4,340	12,775	16,987
Utah	85	1,616	1,723
Vermont	4	555	563
Virginia	160	4,792	6,187
Washington	215	4,309	4,867
West Virginia	8	1,792	1,856
Wisconsin	93	4,513	4,892
Wyoming	26	427	454

SOURCE: U.S. Bureau of the Census, <u>Statistical Abstract of the United States</u>, <u>1991</u>; p. 22, table 27 (data from U.S. Bureau of the Census, *Press Release CB91-100.* C 3.134:991

NOTES: 'Total' includes other races and ethnic groups not shown separately.

UNITS: Population in thousands of persons.

Table 1.10 Population of Cities with 250,000 or More Inhabitants, 2000

	Hispanic	White	Total
Albuquerque, NM	179.1	321.2	448.6
Anaheim, CA	153.4	179.6	328.0
Anchorage, AK	14.8	188.0	260.3
Arlington, TX	60.8	225.4	333.0
Atlanta, GA	18.7	138.4	416.5
Aurora, CO	54.8	190.3	276.4
Austin, TX	200.6	429.1	656.6
Baltimore, MD	11.1	206.0	651.2
Boston, MA	85.1	320.9	589.1
Buffalo, NY	22.1	159.3	292.6
Charlotte, NC	39.8	315.1	540.8
Chicago, IL	753.6	1,215.3	2,896.0
Cincinnati, OH	4.2	175.5	331.3
Cleveland, OH	34.7	198.5	478.4
Colorado Springs, CO	43.3	291.1	360.9
Columbus, OH	17.5	483.3	711.5
Corpus Christi, TX	150.7	198.7	277.5
Dallas, TX	422.6	604.2	1,188.6
Denver, CO	175.7	362.2	554.6
Detroit, MI	47.2	116.6	951.3
El Paso, TX	431.9	413.1	563.7
Fort Worth, TX	159.4	319.2	534.7
Fresno, CA	170.5	214.6	427.7
Honolulu, HI	16.2	73.1	371.7
Houston, TX	730.9	962.6	1,953.6
Indianapolis, IN	30.6	540.2	781.9
Jacksonville, FL	30.6	474.3	735.6
Kansas City, MO	30.6	267.9	441.5
Las Vegas, NV	113.0	334.2	478.4
Lexington-Fayette, KY	8.6	211.1	260.5
Long Beach, CA	165.1	208.4	461.5
Los Angeles, CA	1,719.1	1,734.0	3,694.8
Louisville, KY	4.8	161.3	256.2
Memphis, TN	19.3	223.7	650.1
Mesa, AZ	78.3	323.7	396.4
Miami, FL	238.4	241.5	362.5
Milwaukee, WI	71.6	298.4	597.0

Table 1.10   continued

	Hispanic	White	Total
Minneapolis, MN	29.2	249.2	382.6
Nashville-Davidson, TN	25.8	359.6	545.5
New Orleans, LA	14.8	136.0	484.7
New York, NY	2,160.6	3,576.4	8,008.3
Newark, NJ	80.6	72.5	273.5
Oakland, CA	87.5	125.0	399.5
Oklahoma City, OK	51.4	346.2	506.1
Omaha, NE	29.4	305.7	390.0
Philadelphia, PA	128.9	683.3	1,517.6
Phoenix, AZ	450.0	938.9	1,321.0
Pittsburgh, PA	4.4	226.3	334.6
Portland, OR	36.1	412.2	529.1
Raleigh, NC	19.3	174.8	276.1
Riverside, CA	97.3	151.4	255.2
Sacramento, CA	88.0	196.5	407.0
San Antonio, TX	671.4	774.7	1,144.6
San Diego, CA	310.8	736.2	1,223.4
San Francisco, CA	109.5	385.7	776.7
San Jose, CA	270.0	425.0	894.9
Santa Ana, CA	257.1	144.4	338.0
Seattle, WA	29.7	394.9	563.4
St. Louis, MO	7.0	152.7	348.2
St. Paul, MN	22.7	192.4	287.2
Tampa, FL	58.5	194.9	303.4
Toledo, OH	17.1	220.3	313.6
Tucson, AZ	173.9	341.4	486.7
Tulsa, OK	28.1	275.5	393.0
Virginia Beach, VA	17.8	303.7	425.3
Washington, DC	45.0	176.1	572.1
Wichita, KS	33.1	258.9	344.3

SOURCE: U.S. Bureau of the Census, <u>Statistical Abstract of the United States, 2003</u>; p. 38, table 32; p. 39, table 33. C 3.134:003

NOTES: As of April. Data refer to boundaries in effect on January 1, 2000.

UNITS: Population in thousands of persons.

Table 1.11   Resident Population, by State, Projections for 2020

	Hispanic	White	Total
Alabama	1.2%	72.0%	5,231
Alaska	4.8	65.2	866
Arizona	31.7	85.0	5,713
Arkansas	1.9	83.1	3,005
California	36.5	71.0	47,953
Colorado	20.0	90.1	4,871
Connecticut	12.9	85.2	3,617
Delaware	5.9	70.7	871
District of Columbia	6.1	33.0	636
Florida	21.5	78.9	19,449
Georgia	3.2	66.9	9,426
Hawaii	13.7	47.9	1,815
Idaho	11.7	95.3	1,600
Illinois	15.7	75.2	13,218
Indiana	4.0	87.7	6,488
Iowa	3.2	94.6	3,038
Kansas	7.9	87.4	3,130
Kentucky	1.0	89.7	4,313
Louisiana	3.6	63.9	5,193
Maine	1.4	97.7	1,400
Maryland	5.0	59.6	6,289
Massachusetts	9.9	86.5	6,363
Michigan	4.6	77.0	10,377
Minnesota	2.8	90.1	5,426
Mississippi	1.0	63.1	3,100
Missouri	2.2	85.5	6,123
Montana	2.6	90.4	1,071
Nebraska	6.5	92.5	1,885
Nevada	26.1	81.3	2,145
New Hampshire	2.2	95.6	1,399
New Jersey	17.0	73.5	9,058
New Mexico	55.4	82.7	2,338

continued on the next page

Table 1.11 continued

	Hispanic	White	Total
New York	15.9%	70.6%	19,111
North Carolina	2.4	72.3	9,014
North Dakota	1.4	90.8	719
Ohio	2.9	83.8	11,870
Oklahoma	5.0	80.0	4,020
Oregon	8.1	89.1	4,367
Pennsylvania	4.9	85.4	12,656
Rhode Island	11.3	88.6	1,090
South Carolina	1.8	66.5	4,685
South Dakota	1.6	83.7	863
Tennessee	1.3	80.6	6,434
Texas	40.3	82.9	25,592
Utah	8.0	90.9	2,749
Vermont	1.5	97.1	658
Virginia	4.7	72.5	8,388
Washington	8.9	84.8	7,960
West Virginia	1.1	95.6	1,852
Wisconsin	4.6	87.8	5,846
Wyoming	8.5	93.9	658

SOURCE: U.S. Bureau of the Census, <u>Statistical Abstract of the United States, 1991</u>; p. 22, table 27 (data from U.S. Bureau of the Census, *Current Population Reports*, Series P-25 and Census Press Release CB91-100). C 3.134:(year)
U.S. Bureau of the Census, <u>Population Projections for States, by Age, Sex, Race, and Hispanic Origin: 1993 to 2020</u>, tables 1 and 4. From *Current Population Reports*, P25-1111, downloaded from Census Bureau Bulletin Board. Telnet cenbbs.census.gov.

NOTES: 'Total' includes other races/ethnic groups not shown separately. 1990 data from the 1990 Census, 2000 data from projections by the US Bureau of the Census.

UNITS: Population in thousands of persons.

Chapter 2: Social Characteristics

Table 2.01 Marital Status, Persons 15 Years Old and Older, 1990 - 2003

	Hispanic		White		Total	
	number	percent	number	percent	number	percent
1990						
All marital statuses	14,576	100.0%	163,417	100.0%	191,793	100.0%
single, never married	4,691	32.2	39,516	24.2	50,223	26.2
married, spouse present	7,363	50.5	95,337	58.3	106,513	55.3
married, spouse absent	1,022	7.0	4,191	2.6	6,118	3.2
widowed	548	3.8	11,731	7.2	13,810	7.2
divorced	952	6.5	12,643	7.7	15,128	7.9
2000						
All marital statuses	22,793	100.0%	177,581	100.0%	213,773	100.0%
married, spouse present	11,221	49.2	99,258	55.9	113,002	52.9
married, spouse absent	666	2.9	1,971	1.1	2,730	1.3
widowed	881	3.9	11,532	6.5	13,665	6.4
divorced	1,623	7.1	16,547	9.3	19,881	9.3
separated	845	3.7	2,976	1.7	4,479	2.1
never married	7,558	33.2	45,297	25.5	60,016	28.1
2003						
All marital statuses	27,936	100.0%	184,361	100.0%	225,057	100.0%
married, spouse present	13,300	47.6	101,412	55.0	117,172	52.1
married, spouse absent	939	3.4	2,246	1.2	3,139	1.4
widowed	918	3.3	11,662	6.3	13,995	6.2
divorced	1,893	6.8	17,835	9.7	21,649	9.6
separated	1,024	3.7	3,158	1.7	4,723	2.1
never married	9,862	35.3	48,048	26.1	64,380	28.6

SOURCE: U.S. Bureau of the Census, <u>Current Population Reports: Marital Status and Living Arrangements, March, 1985</u>, Series P-20, #410; p. 17, table 1; <u>March, 1990</u>, #450; p. 17, table 1 C3.186/6:(year).
U.S. Bureau of the Census, <u>Current Population Reports: America's Families and Living Arrangements: 2000</u>; Series P-20, #537, table A1, issued June 2001; <u>2002</u>; #547, "Table A1. Marital Status of People 15 Years and Over, by Age, Sex, Personal Earnings, Race, and Hispanic Origin: 2002"; <u>2003</u>; Table A1. <www.census.gov>

NOTES: 'Total' includes other races and ethnic groups not shown separately.

UNITS: Number in thousands of persons 15 years old and older; percent as a percent of total (percents **not** standardized for age).

Table 2.02   Marital Status, Men 15 Years Old and Older, 1990 - 2003

	Hispanic		White		Total	
	Number	percent	number	percent	number	percent
Men:						
1990						
All marital statuses	7,254	100.0%	78,908	100.0%	91,033	100.0%
single, never married	2,674	36.9	22,078	28.0	27,422	30.1
married, spouse present	3,605	49.7	47,700	60.4	52,924	58.1
married, spouse absent	502	6.9	1,842	2.3	2,360	2.6
widowed	103	1.4	1,930	2.4	2,282	2.5
divorced	370	5.1	5,359	6.8	6,045	6.6
2000						
All marital statuses	11,327	100.0%	86,443	100.0%	103,114	100.0%
married, spouse present	5,550	49.0	49,672	57.5	56,501	54.8
married, spouse absent	402	3.5	979	1.1	1,365	1.3
widowed	170	1.5	2,196	2.5	2,604	2.5
divorced	669	5.9	7,246	8.4	8,572	8.3
separated	288	2.5	1,237	1.4	1,818	1.8
never married	4,249	37.5	25,113	29.1	32,253	31.3
2003						
All marital statuses	14,336	100.0%	89,998	100.%	108,696	100.0%
married, spouse present	6,599	46.0	50,822	56.5	58,586	53.9
married, spouse absent	642	4.5	1,228	1.4	1,651	1.5
widowed	183	1.3	2,257	2.5	2,697	2.5
divorced	803	5.6	7,587	8.4	8,976	8.3
separated	351	2.4	1,332	1.5	1,905	1.8
never married	5,758	40.2	26,772	29.7	34,881	32.1

SOURCE: U.S. Bureau of the Census, <u>Current Population Reports: Marital Status and Living Arrangements, March, 1985</u>, Series P-20, #410; p. 17, table 1; <u>March, 1990</u>, #450; p. 17, table 1 C3.186/6:(year).

U.S. Bureau of the Census, <u>Current Population Reports: America's Families and Living Arrangements: 2000</u>; Series P-20, #537, table A1, issued June 2001; <u>2002</u>; #547, "Table A1. Marital Status of People 15 Years and Over, by Age, Sex, Personal Earnings, Race, and Hispanic Origin: 2002"; <u>2003</u>; Table A1. <www.census.gov>

NOTES: 'Total' includes other races and ethnic groups not shown separately.

UNITS: Number in thousands of men 15 years old and older; percent as a percent of total (percents **not** standardized for age).

Table 2.03   Marital Status, Women 15 Years Old and Older, 1990 - 2003

	Hispanic		White		Total	
	Number	percent	number	percent	number	percent
Women:						
1990						
All marital statuses	7,323	100.0%	84,508	100.0%	99,838	100.0%
single, never married	2,017	27.5	17,438	20.6	22,718	22.8
married, spouse present	3,758	51.3	47,637	56.4	53,256	53.3
married, spouse absent	520	7.1	2,349	2.8	3,541	3.5
widowed	445	6.1	9,800	11.6	11,477	11.5
divorced	582	8.0	7,284	8.6	8,845	8.9
2000						
All marital statuses	11,466	100.0%	91,138	100.0%	110,660	100.0%
married, spouse present	5,671	49.5	49,586	54.4	56,501	51.1
married, spouse absent	264	2.3	992	1.1	1,365	1.2
widowed	711	6.2	9,336	10.2	11,061	10.0
divorced	954	8.3	9,301	10.2	11,309	10.2
separated	557	4.9	1,739	1.9	2,661	2.4
never married	3,309	28.9	20,184	22.1	27,763	25.1
2002						
All marital statuses	13,599	100.0%	94,363	100.0%	116,361	100.0%
married, spouse present	6,701	49.3	50,590	53.6	58,586	50.3
married, spouse absent	297	2.2	1,017	1.1	1,488	1.3
widowed	735	5.4	9,405	10.0	11,297	9.7
divorced	1,090	8.0	10,248	10.9	12,673	10.9
separated	673	4.9	1,826	1.9	2,817	2.4
never married	4,104	30.2	21,276	22.5	29,499	25.4

SOURCE: U.S. Bureau of the Census, <u>Current Population Reports: Marital Status and Living Arrangements, March, 1985</u>, Series P-20, #410; p. 17, table 1; <u>March, 1990</u>, #450; p. 17, table 1 C3.186/6:(year).
U.S. Bureau of the Census, <u>Current Population Reports: America's Families and Living Arrangements: 2000</u>; Series P-20, #537, table A1, issued June 2001; <u>2002</u>; #547, "Table A1. Marital Status of People 15 Years and Over, by Age, Sex, Personal Earnings, Race, and Hispanic Origin: 2002"; <u>2003</u>; Table A1. <www.census.gov>

NOTES: 'Total' includes other races and ethnic groups not shown separately.

UNITS: Number in thousands of women 15 years old and older; percent as a percent of total (percents **not** standardized for age).

Table 2.04 Marital Status of the Hispanic Population, by Type of Origin, 2000 and 2002

	Mexican	Puerto Rican	Cuban	Central/ South American	Other Hispanic	Total Hispanic
2000						
Total population 15 years old and over						
number	14,547	2,110	1,104	3,551	1,481	22,793
percent	100.0%	100.0%	100.0%	100.0%	100.0%	100.0%
married, spouse present	50.5	42.0	56.1	47.3	46.4	49.2
married, spouse absent	2.8	2.1	1.6	4.3	3.1	2.9
widowed	3.6	3.5	8.7	3.4	4.1	3.9
divorced	6.2	9.6	11.1	6.9	10.2	7.1
separated	3.4	5.0	2.2	4.4	4.5	3.7
never married	33.5	37.8	20.4	33.7	31.7	33.2
2002						
Total population 15 years old and over						
number	16,978	2,392	1,150	4,106	1,725	26,351
percent	100.0%	100.0%	100.0%	100.0%	100.0%	100.0%
married, spouse present	48.4	37.1	52.8	46.4	46.9	47.2
married, spouse absent	3.2	2.1	2.3	4.1	3.2	3.2
widowed	3.0	4.3	8.2	2.8	3.5	3.3
divorced	5.9	10.5	9.4	5.4	9.1	6.6
separated	2.9	6.2	2.9	3.5	4.9	3.4
never married	36.6	39.8	24.5	37.8	32.4	36.3

SOURCE: U.S. Bureau of the Census, Current Population Reports: The Hispanic Population of the United States, 2000; "Table 2.1. Population Age 15 Years and Over by Marital Status, Sex, Hispanic Origin and Race".
U.S. Bureau of the Census, Current Population Reports: The Hispanic Population of the United States, 2002; Internet Release date: 18 June 2003; "Table 2.1 Marital Status of the Population 15 Years and Over by Sex, Hispanic Origin, and Race: March 2002", "Table 2.2 Marital Status of the Population 15 Years and Over by Sex, and Hispanic Origin Type: March 2002".

NOTES: Total population includes other races and ethnic groups not shown separately. 'Other Hispanic origin' includes persons from Spain and persons identifying themselves generally as Hispanic, Spanish, Spanish-American, Hispano, Latino, etc.

UNITS: Total resident population in thousands of persons 15 years old and over; percent as a percent of total shown (100.0%).

Table 2.05 Characteristics of Unmarried and Married Male-Female Couples:
March 2000

	Unmarried couples	Married Couples
both Hispanic	332	4,739
neither Hispanic	3,268	50,015
one Hispanic and one non-Hispanic	222	1,743

SOURCE: U.S. Bureau of the Census, <u>Current Population Reports: America's Families and Living Arrangements, June, 2001</u> Series P20, #537; p. 15, table 8.
<www.census.gov>

UNITS: Thousands of couples.

Table 2.06 Hispanic Married Couple Households, by Type of Origin of the Husband and Wife, 1993

	Mexican	Puerto Rican	Cuban	Central/ South Amer	other Hispanic	total Hispanic
By origin of the wife:						
Total population	100.0%	100.0%	100.0%	100.0%	100.0%	100.0%
total Hispanic population	85.1	81.4	82.9	84.4	65.7	83.1
by origin						
Mexican origin	82.8	2.7	1.7	4.3	1.4	53.6
Puerto Rican origin	0.1	70.7	2.1	2.1	1.4	6.7
Cuban origin	0.1	1.2	77.1	2.8	0.7	5.5
Central/South American origin	1.6	3.7	1.3	74.8	2.1	12.1
other Hispanic origin	0.5	3.0	0.8	0.4	60.1	5.2
not of Hispanic origin	14.9	18.6	17.1	15.6	34.3	16.9
By origin of the husband:						
Total population	4.5%	0.6%	0.4%	1.0%	0.5%	7.1%
total Hispanic population	55.7	7.3	5.4	12.3	5.1	85.8
by origin						
Mexican origin	85.6	0.4	0.2	1.0	0.2	87.3
Puerto Rican origin	0.9	69.3	1.5	3.3	1.2	76.1
Cuban origin	1.3	1.7	79.7	6.5	0.9	90.1
Central/South American origin	7.4	2.3	0.6	77.4	1.2	88.9
other Hispanic origin	4.2	3.8	0.8	0.8	64.9	74.4
not of Hispanic origin	0.7	0.1	0.1	0.2	0.2	1.3

origin of the wife

SOURCE: U.S. Bureau of the Census, <u>The Hispanic Population in the United States: March, 1993</u>; p. 6, table A (data from U.S. Bureau of the Census, *Current Population Reports*). C 3.186/14-2:993

NOTES: Total population includes other races and ethnic groups not shown separately. 'Other Hispanic origin' includes persons from Spain and persons identifying themselves generally as Hispanic, Spanish, Spanish-American, Hispano, Latino, etc.

UNITS: Percent as a percent of total shown (100.0%).

Table 2.07   Age, Educational Attainment, and Residence, 1985

	Hispanic	White	Total
Age			
Persons of all ages	16,940	199,117	234,066
persons:			
under 5 years old	1,809	14,610	17,958
5-14 years old	3,355	27,417	33,792
15-44 years old	8,540	93,852	110,948
45-64 years old	2,407	39,033	44,549
65 years old and over	819	24,205	26,818
Years of school completed			
All persons 25 years old and over	8,455	124,905	143,524
persons completing:			
0-8 years of school	3,192	16,224	19,893
1-3 years high school	1,210	14,365	17,553
4 years high school	2,402	48,728	54,866
1-3 years college	932	20,652	23,405
4 or more years college	718	24,935	27,808
Residence			
Northeast	3,144	43,185	49,276
Midwest	1,389	52,280	58,587
South	5,288	63,155	79,165
West	6,964	40,394	46,489
nonfarm	na	na	na
farm	na	na	na
inside metro areas	na	na	na
outside metro areas	na	na	na

SOURCE: U.S. Bureau of the Census, <u>Statistical Abstract of the United States, 1987</u>, p. 35, table 39, (data from U.S. Bureau of the Census, *Current Population Reports*, Series P-25). C 3.134:987

U.S. Bureau of the Census, <u>Current Population Reports: Money Income of Households, Families and Persons in the United States, 1984</u>, Series P-60 (#151), pp. 10-17, table 4. C3.186/22:984

NOTES: 'Total' includes other races and ethnic groups not shown separately.

UNITS: Population in thousands of persons; percent distribution as a percent of total, 100.0%.

Table 2.08 Age, Educational Attainment, and Residence, 1990

	Hispanic	White	Total
Age			
Persons of all ages			
persons:	21,405	208,611	248,644
under 18 years old	7,457	51,929	65,049
18-24 years old	2,741	20,383	24,901
25-44 years old	7,139	68,807	81,570
45-64 years old	2,977	40,594	47,032
65 years old and over	1,091	26,898	30,093
Years of school completed			
All persons 25 years old			
and over	11,208	136,299	158,694
persons that:			
did not complete high school	5,455	27,409	34,228
completed high school,			
no college	3,285	53,250	61,272
completed some college, not			
a college graduate	1,379	25,358	29,169
completed college	1,088	30,283	34,025
Residence			
Northeast	3,531	43,727	50,799
Midwest	1,399	52,771	59,914
South	6,598	66,492	85,097
West	9,878	45,622	52,835
nonfarm	21,297	204,001	243,865
farm	108	4,610	4,779
inside metro areas	19,883	159,443	193,052
outside metro areas	1,522	49,168	55,592

SOURCE: U.S. Bureau of the Census, <u>Current Population Reports: Poverty in the United States: 1990</u>, Series P-60, #175; p. 24, table 5; pp. 84-87, table 11; p. 154, table 21. C3.186/11:990

NOTES: 'Total' includes other races and ethnic groups not shown separately.

UNITS: Population in thousands of persons; percent distribution as a percent of total, 100.0%.

Table 2.09   Age and Residence, 2003

	Hispanic	White	Total
Age			
Persons of all ages			
persons:	40,300	231,866	287,699
under 18 years old	13,730	55,779	72,999
18-24 years old	4,974	21,936	27,824
25-34 years old	7,423	30,799	39,201
35-44 years old	6,007	35,095	43,573
45-54 years old	3,925	33,873	41,068
55-59 years old	1,287	13,725	16,158
60-64 years old	875	10,354	12,217
65 years old and over	2,080	30,303	34,659
Residence			
Northeast	5,476	44,036	53,608
Midwest	3,500	55,322	64,655
South	14,388	79,023	103,347
West	16,936	53,485	66,089
inside metro areas	36,714	185,582	234,908
outside metro areas	3,586	46,284	52,791

SOURCE: U.S. Bureau of the Census, Current Population Reports: Poverty in the United States: 2003; "Table POV01: Age and Sex of All People, Family Members and Unrelated Individuals Iterated by Income-to-Poverty Ratio and Race: 2003, Below 100% of Poverty"; "Table POV41: Region, Division and Type of Residence – Poverty Status for All People, Family Members and Unrelated Individuals by Family Structure: 2003, Below 100% of Poverty".

NOTES: 'Total' includes other races not shown separately. 'White' as shown is equivalent to 'White Alone' that refers to people who reported 'White' did not report any other race category.

UNITS: Population in thousands of persons.

Chapter 3:
Household & Family Characteristics

Table 3.01   Selected Characteristics of Households, 1985

	Hispanic	White	Total
Marital status and sex of the householder			
All households, both sexes	4,883	75,328	86,789
male householder	3,357	53,868	60,025
married, wife present	2,638	43,444	47,683
married, wife absent	129	1,013	1,416
widowed	84	1,386	1,620
divorced	162	3,078	3,535
single, never married	344	4,947	5,772
female householder	1,526	21,461	26,763
married, husband present	186	2,199	2,667
married, husband absent	351	1,668	2,497
widowed	313	8,304	9,728
divorced	334	5,203	6,265
single, never married	342	4,087	5,606
Age of the householder			
All ages	4,883	75,328	86,789
15-24 years old	489	4,626	5,438
25-34 years old	1,363	17,010	20,013
35-44 years old	1,184	15,024	17,481
45-54 years old	743	10,792	12,628
55-64 years old	606	11,471	13,073
65 years old and over	497	16,406	18,155
Housing tenure			
All tenures	4,883	75,328	86,789
own housing unit	2,007	50,611	55,845
rent housing unit	2,876	24,667	30,943

continued on the next page

Table 3.01   continued

	Hispanic	White	Total
Size of the household			
All household sizes	4,883	75,328	86,789
one person	756	17,876	20,602
two persons	1,026	24,558	27,289
three persons	995	13,336	15,465
four persons	959	11,795	13,631
five persons	576	5,061	6,108
six persons	297	1,819	2,299
seven or more persons	275	882	1,296
persons per household	2.96	2.64	2.69
Residence			
All residences	4,883	75,328	86,789
Northeast	1,017	16,244	18,348
Midwest	376	19,599	21,697
South	1,553	24,283	29,581
West	1,937	15,202	17,163
inside metropolitan areas	na	na	na
outside metropolitan areas	na	na	na
nonfarm	na	na	na
farm	na	na	na

SOURCE: U.S. Bureau of the Census, <u>Current Population Reports: Money Income of Households Families and Persons in the United States; March 1984,</u> Series P-60, #151, pp. 10-14, table 4. C3.186/2:984

U.S. Bureau of the Census, <u>Current Population Reports: Household & Family Characteristics, March 1985</u>, Series P-20, #411, pp. 107-112, table 22. C3.186/17:985

NOTES: 'Total' includes other races and ethnic groups not shown separately.

UNITS: Number of households in thousands of households; persons per household, average.

Table 3.02 — Selected Characteristics of Households, 1990

	Hispanic	White	Total
Marital status and sex of the householder			
All households, both sexes	5,933	80,163	93,347
family households	4,840	56,590	66,090
married couple families	3,395	46,981	52,317
male householder, no wife present	329	2,303	2,884
female householder, no husband present	1,116	7,306	10,890
non-family households	1,093	23,573	27,257
male householder	587	9,951	11,606
-living alone	415	7,718	9,049
female householder	506	13,622	15,651
-living alone	442	12,161	13,950
Age of the householder			
All ages	5,933	80,163	93,347
15-24 years old	542	4,222	5,121
25-34 years old	1,721	17,137	20,472
35-44 years old	1,405	17,395	20,554
45-54 years old	930	12,404	14,514
55-64 years old	664	10,862	12,529
65 years old and over	671	18,144	20,156
Housing tenure			
All tenures	5,933	80,163	93,347
own housing unit	2,443	54,094	59,846
rent housing unit	3,383	24,685	31,895

continued on the next page

Table 3.02 continued

	Hispanic	White	Total
Size of the household			
All household sizes	5,933	80,163	93,347
one person	856	19,879	22,999
two persons	1,292	26,714	30,114
three persons	1,139	13,585	16,128
four persons	1,172	12,399	14,456
five persons	752	5,104	6,213
six persons	386	1,615	2,143
seven or more persons	336	877	1,295
persons per household	3.48	2.58	2.63
Residence			
All residences	5,933	80,163	93,347
Northeast	1,037	16,773	19,127
Midwest	398	20,339	22,760
South	1,953	26,155	32,262
West	2,544	16,896	19,197
inside metropolitan areas	5,479	61,155	72,331
outside metropolitan areas	454	19,009	21,016
nonfarm	8,897	78,556	91,710
farm	36	1,608	1,637

SOURCE: U.S. Bureau of the Census, <u>Current Population Reports: Money Income of Households Families and Persons in the United States: 1988 and 1989,</u> Series P-60, #172, pp. 9-12, table 1. C3.186/2:989

NOTES: 'Total' includes other races and ethnic groups not shown separately.

UNITS: Number of households in thousands of households; persons per household, average.

Table 3.03   Selected Characteristics of Households, 2003

	Hispanic	White	Total
Marital status and type of householder			
All households, both sexes	11,693	91,962	112,000
family households	9,273	62,609	76,217
married couple families	6,227	50,021	57,719
male householder, no spouse present	908	3,537	4,717
female householder, no spouse present	2,138	9,051	13,781
non-family households	2,420	29,353	35,783
male householder	1,343	13,283	16,136
-living alone	891	10,233	12,562
female householder	1,078	16,070	19,647
-living alone	863	13,860	17,024
Age of the householder			
All ages	11,693	91,962	112,000
15-24 years old	1,163	5,039	6,610
25-34 years old	3,181	14,919	19,159
35-44 years old	2,986	18,638	23,222
45-54 years old	2,022	18,974	23,137
55-64 years old	1,229	14,196	16,824
65 years old and over	1,113	20,196	23,048

continued on the next page

Table 3.03   continued

	Hispanic	White	Total
Size of the household			
All household sizes	11,693	91,962	112,000
one person	1,753	24,094	29,586
two persons	2,627	31,960	37,366
three persons	2,253	14,257	17,968
four persons	2,387	13,025	16,065
five persons	1,552	5,719	7,150
six persons	664	1,904	2,476
seven or more persons	456	1,002	1,388
Residence			
All residences	11,693	91,962	112,000
Northeast	1,697	17,613	21,017
Midwest	967	22,218	25,643
South	4,392	31,729	40,742
West	4,638	20,402	24,598
inside metropolitan areas	10,640	72,930	90,613
outside metropolitan areas	1,054	19,031	21,387

SOURCE: U.S. Bureau of the Census, <u>Current Population Reports: Income 2003</u>, "(Table) HINC-01. Selected Characteristics of Households, by Total Money Income in 2003".

NOTES: 'Total' includes other races not shown separately. 'White' as shown is equivalent to 'White alone' that refers to people who reported White and did not report any other race category.

UNITS: Number of households in thousands of households.

Table 3.04 Type and Tenure of Hispanic Households, by Type of Hispanic Origin, 2000 and 2002

	Mexican	Puerto Rican	Cuban	Central/ South American	Other Hispanic	Total Hispanic
2000						
Total households	5,733	1,004	523	1,372	687	9,319
Family households	4,794	770	385	1,109	504	7,561
Percent by tenure						
owner occupied	47.8%	35.0%	58.7%	37.6%	48.0%	45.5%
renter occupied	52.2	65.0	41.3	62.4	52.0	54.5
2002						
Total households	6,537	1,128	511	1,566	757	10,499
Family households	5,441	834	358	1,275	608	8,516
Percent by tenure						
owner occupied	50.0%	35.3%	56.9%	41.1%	50.8%	47.5%
renter occupied	50.0	64.7	43.1	58.9	49.2	52.5

SOURCE: U.S. Bureau of the Census, <u>Current Population Reports: The Hispanic Population of the United States, 2000</u>; published 6 March, 2001; "Table 3.1 Household Type by Hispanic Origin and Race of Householder: March 2000"; "Table 16.1 Household Tenure by Household Type, and by Hispanic Origin and Race of Householder: March 2000".

U.S. Bureau of the Census, <u>Current Population Reports: The Hispanic Population of the United States, 2002</u>; Internet Release date: 18 June 2003; "Table 16.1 Household Tenure by Household Type, and by Hispanic Origin and Race of Householder: March 2002"; "Table 16.2 Household Tenure by Household Type, and by Hispanic Origin Type of Householder: March 2002".

NOTES: Total population includes other races and ethnic groups not shown separately. 'Other Hispanic origin' includes persons from Spain and persons identifying themselves generally as Hispanic, Spanish, Spanish-American, Hispano, Latino, etc.

UNITS: Households in thousands of households; percent as a percent of all households by type (100.0%).

Table 3.05   Selected Characteristics of Family Households, 1985

	Hispanic	White	Total
Type of family			
All families	3,939	54,400	62,706
married couple families	2,824	45,643	50,350
male householder,			
no wife present	210	1,816	2,228
female householder,			
no husband present	905	6,941	10,129
Size of family			
All family sizes	3,939	54,400	62,706
two persons	962	22,711	25,349
three persons	948	12,743	14,804
four persons	936	11,517	13,259
five persons	552	4,894	5,894
six persons	276	1,704	2,175
seven or more persons	266	831	1,225
average per family	3.88	3.16	3.23
Number of related children			
under 18 years old			
All families	3,939	54,400	62,706
no children	1,337	28,169	31,594
one child	904	11,174	13,108
two children	865	9,937	11,645
three children	481	3,695	4,486
four children	215	1,049	1,329
five children	87	261	373
six or more children	50	115	171
average per family	1.44	0.88	0.92
average per family			
with children	2.18	1.83	1.85

continued on the next page

Table 3.05   continued

	Hispanic	White	Total
Number of earners			
All families	3,905	53,777	61,930
no earner	599	7,674	9,221
one earner	1,290	15,219	17,949
two earners	1,485	23,303	26,160
three earners	370	5,317	6,029
four earners or more	161	2,263	2,570
Housing tenure			
All tenures	3,939	54,400	62,706
own housing unit	1,772	40,865	45,015
rent housing unit	2,167	13,535	17,691
Residence			
All residences	3,939	54,400	62,706
Northeast	808	11,631	13,149
Midwest	313	14,309	15,839
South	1,273	17,953	21,781
West	1,545	10,507	11,938
nonfarm	na	na	na
farm	na	na	na
inside metropolitan areas	na	na	na
outside metropolitan areas	na	na	na

SOURCE: U.S. Bureau of the Census, <u>Current Population Reports: Money Income of Households, Families, and Persons in the United States, 1984</u>, Series P-60, #151, pp. 76-77, table 21. C3.186/2:984

U.S. Bureau of the Census, <u>Current Population Reports: Household & Family Characteristics, March 1985</u>, Series P-20, #437, pp. 13-45, table 1; pp. 107-111, table 22. C3.186/17:985

NOTES: 'Total' includes other races and ethnic groups not shown separately. 'Number of earners' excludes families with members in the armed forces.

UNITS: Number of households in thousands of family households.

Table 3.06 Selected Characteristics of Family Households, 1990

	Hispanic	White	Total
Type of family			
All families	4,840	56,590	66,090
married couple families	3,395	46,981	52,317
male householder, no			
wife present	329	2,303	2,884
female householder, no			
husband present	1,116	7,306	10,890
Size of family			
All family sizes	4,840	56,590	66,090
two persons	1,226	24,438	27,606
three persons	1,114	12,937	15,353
four persons	1,146	12,048	14,036
five persons	714	4,882	5,938
six persons	347	1,505	1,997
seven or more persons	293	781	1,170
average per family	3.83	3.11	3.17
Number of related children			
under 18 years old			
All families	4,840	56,590	66,090
no children	1,790	29,872	33,801
one child	1,095	11,186	13,530
two children	1,036	10,342	12,263
three children	579	3,853	4,650
four children	232	970	1,279
five children	73	247	379
six or more children	35	121	188
average per family	1.34	0.86	0.89
average per family			
with children	2.12	1.82	1.83

continued on the next page

Table 3.06   continued

	Hispanic	White	Total
Number of earners			
All families	4,840	56,590	66,090
no earner	615	7,816	9,439
one earner	1,554	14,970	18,146
two earners	1,860	25,737	29,235
three earners	541	5,832	6,724
four earners or more	271	2,236	2,546
Housing tenure			
All tenures	4,840	56,590	66,090
own housing unit	3,448	42,588	47,142
rent housing unit	2,678	14,003	18,948
Residence			
All residences	4,840	56,590	66,090
Northeast	815	11,837	13,494
Midwest	330	14,370	16,059
South	1,596	18,746	23,244
West	2,101	11,638	13,293
nonfarm	4,813	55,225	64,701
farm	28	1,365	1,390
inside metropolitan areas	6,256	42,592	50,619
outside metropolitan areas	1,215	13,999	15,471

SOURCE: U.S. Bureau of the Census, <u>Current Population Reports: Money Income of Households, Families, and Persons in the United States: 1988 and 1989</u>, Series P-60, #172, pp. 9-11, table 1; pp. 48-50, table 13; pp. 76-80, table 18. C3.186/2:989

U.S. Bureau of the Census, <u>Current Population Reports: Household & Family Characteristics: March 1990 and 1989</u>, Series P-20, #447, pp. 13-16, table 1; pp. 18-20, table 2. C3.186/17:989

NOTES: 'Total' includes other races and ethnic groups not shown separately. 'Number of earners' excludes families with members in the armed forces.

UNITS: Number of households in thousands of family households.

Table 3.07 Selected Characteristics of Family Households, 2003

	Hispanic	White	Total
Type of family			
All families	9,274	62,620	76,232
married couple families	6,228	50,025	57,725
male householder, no			
wife present	908	3,537	4,717
female householder, no			
husband present	2,138	9,058	13,791
Size of family			
All family sizes	9,274	62,620	76,232
two persons	2,512	29,092	34,096
three persons	2,056	13,166	16,749
four persons	2,276	12,409	15,245
five persons	1,421	5,345	6,662
six persons	620	1,761	2,305
seven or more persons	390	846	1,175

continued on the next page

Table 3.07   continued

	Hispanic	White	Total
Number of earners			
All families	9,274	62,620	76,232
no earner	917	9,005	10,929
one earner	3,595	18,861	24,168
two earners	3,634	27,846	32,981
three earners	796	5,137	6,102
four earners or more	332	1,770	2,053
Residence			
All residences	9,274	62,620	76,232
Northeast	1,304	11,695	13,994
Midwest	742	15,100	17,378
South	3,445	21,958	28,000
West	3,783	13,867	16,860
inside metropolitan areas	8,439	49,408	61,403
outside metropolitan areas	835	13,212	14,829

SOURCE: U.S. Bureau of the Census, <u>Current Population Reports: Income 2003</u>, "(Table) FINC-01. Selected Characteristics of Families by Total Money Income in 2003".

NOTES: Total' includes other races not shown separately. Number of families as of March of the <u>following</u> year. 'White' as shown is equivalent to 'White Alone' that refers to people who reported 'White' and did not report any other race category. 'Number of earners' excludes families with members in the armed forces.

UNITS: Number of households in thousands of family households.

Table 3.08 Type and Size of Hispanic Family Households, by Type of Hispanic Origin, 2002

	Mexican	Puerto Rican	Cuban	Central/ South American	Other Hispanic	Total Hispanic
All family households	100.0%	100.0%	100.0%	100.0%	100.0%	100.0%
married couple families	70.2	52.2	74.9	67.0	65.9	67.8
male householder	10.0	9.5	7.9	9.4	7.6	9.6
female householder	19.8	38.3	17.3	23.6	26.5	22.6
two persons	19.4	27.8	34.5	22.6	28.3	22.2
three persons	19.8	20.4	18.0	21.1	19.3	19.9
four persons	21.5	18.2	16.1	23.5	20.1	21.1
five persons	14.4	9.1	4.3	11.9	11.7	12.8
six persons	7.4	3.3	2.2	5.5	3.0	6.1
seven or more persons	6.3	1.5	1.0	3.2	2.0	4.8

Source: U.S. Bureau of the Census, <u>Current Population Reports: The Hispanic Population of the United States, 2002</u>; Internet Release date: 18 June 2003; "Table 4.1 Family and Nonfamily Household Type by Hispanic Origin and Race of Householder: March 2002"; "Table 4.2 Family and Nonfamily Household Type by Hispanic Origin Type of Householder: March 2002"; "Table 5.1 Household Type by Size, by Hispanic Origin and Race of Householder: March 2002"; "Table 5.2 Household Type by Size, and by Hispanic Origin Type of Householder: March 2002".

NOTES: Total population includes other races and ethnic groups not shown separately. 'Other Hispanic origin' includes persons from Spain and persons identifying themselves generally as Hispanic, Spanish, Spanish-American, Hispano, Latino, etc.

UNITS: Family households by type as a percent of all households as shown (100.0%).

Table 3.09 Single Parents Living With Own Children Under 18 Years Old, 2000 and 2003

	Hispanic	White	Total
2000			
Single Fathers			
with own children under 18	313	1,622	2,044
with own children under 12	260	1,145	1,441
with own children under 6	189	647	819
with own children under 3	129	393	511
with own children under 1	51	152	196
Single Mothers			
with own children under 18	1,565	6,216	9,681
with own children under 12	1,190	4,558	7,337
with own children under 6	720	2,519	4,115
with own children under 3	409	1,396	2,319
with own children under 1	141	499	824
2003			
Single Fathers			
with own children under 18	450	1,758	2,260
with own children under 12	360	1,187	1,547
with own children under 6	253	668	878
with own children under 3	152	404	530
with own children under 1	55	162	203
Single Mothers			
with own children under 18	1,807	6,471	10,142
with own children under 12	1,405	4,624	7,417
with own children under 6	872	2,575	4,234
with own children under 3	453	1,364	2,287
with own children under 1	155	446	734

SOURCE: U.S. Bureau of the Census, <u>Current Population Reports: America's Families and Living Arrangements: 2000</u>; Series P-20, #537, p. 8, table 4, issued June 2001; <u>2002</u>; #547, "Table FG5. One-Parent Family Groups with Own Children Under 18, by Labor Force Status, Race, and Hispanic Origin of the Reference Person: March 2002"; <u>2003</u>; Table FG5. <www.census.gov>

NOTES: 'Total' includes other races and ethnic groups not shown separately.

UNITS: Thousands of fathers or mothers.

Table 3.10 Living Arrangements of Children Under 18 Years of Age, 2000 and 2003

	Hispanic children	White children	All children
2000			
Living with both parents	7,561	42,497	49,795
Living with mother only	2,919	9,765	16,162
Living with father only	506	2,427	3,058
Living with neither parent	626	1,752	2,981
2003			
Living with both parents	8,584	41,805	49,903
Living with mother only	3,261	9,799	16,770
Living with father only	737	2,535	3,323
Living with neither parent	702	1,781	3,004

SOURCE: U.S. Bureau of the Census, Current Population Reports: America's Families and Living Arrangements: 2000; Series P-20, #537, pp. 1, 25, 37, and 60, table C2, issued June 2001; 2003; "Table C2. Household Relationship and Living Arrangements of Children Under 18 Years, by Age, Sex, Race, Hispanic Origin, and Metropolitan Residence: 2003". <www.census.gov>

NOTES: 'All children' includes children of other races and ethnic groups not shown separately.

UNITS: Thousands of children.

Table 3.11   Primary Child Care Arrangements Used for Preschoolers by Families With Employed Mothers, Spring 1997 and Spring 1999

	Hispanic children	White children	All children
Spring 1997			
All preschoolers with employed mothers	1,224	8,154	10,116
Mother while working	2.1%	6.0	5.1%
Father	24.6	32.8	30.6
Grandparent	30.8	28.8	29.6
Sibling	19.0	13.7	14.8
Other relative			
Daycare center	10.6	18.6	18.9
Nursery/preschool	4.1	7.2	7.0
Head start	7.0	3.4	4.2
Family day care	7.6	13.9	13.0
Other non-relative	13.1	10.1	9.8
Spring 1999			
All preschoolers with employed mothers	1,498	8,411	10,587
Designated parent	2.9	3.4%	3.2%
Other parent	20.6	20.4	19.3
Grandparent	23.7	19.4	21.7
Other relative or sibling	15.1	7.8	8.4
Daycare center	8.9	18.0	18.7
Nursery/preschool	2.7	4.1	4.0
Head start	0.3	0.2	0.4
Family day care	7.6	13.2	11.4
Other non-relative	12.4	10.2	9.7

SOURCE: U.S. Bureau of the Census, <u>Current Population Reports: Who's Minding the Kids? Child Care Arrangements: Spring 1997;</u> Series P70-86, table 2. C3.186/P70-86

U.S. Bureau of the Census, <u>Current Population Reports: Who's Minding the Kids? Child Care Arrangements: Spring 1999;</u> Series PPL-168, table 2B.

NOTES: 'All children' includes children of other races not shown separately. Because of multiple arrangements, numbers and percentages may exceed the total number of children. 'Designated parent' is selected in households where both parents are present to report child care arrangements for each child.

UNITS: Thousands of children living in family households.

Chapter 4: Education - Preprimary through High School

Table 4.01   School Enrollment by Age, 2000 and 2002

	enrollment			enrollment rate		
	Hispanic	White	Total	Hispanic	White	Total
2000						
all persons 3 years and over	10,163	46,660	72,214	32.6%	25.0%	27.5%
persons 3 and 4 years old	518	2,607	4,097	35.9	54.6	52.1
persons 5 and 6 years old	1,390	4,639	7,648	94.3	95.5	95.6
persons 7 to 9 years old	1,936	7,576	12,083	97.5	98.4	98.1
persons 10 and 13 years old	2,437	10,305	16,213	97.4	98.5	98.3
persons 14 and 15 years old	1,093	5,135	7,885	96.2	98.9	98.7
persons 16 and 17 years old	959	4,933	7,341	87.0	94.0	92.8
persons 18 and 19 years old	617	3,337	4,926	49.5	63.9	61.2
persons 20 and 21 years old	311	2,388	3,314	26.1	49.2	44.1
persons 22 to 24 years old	309	1,809	2,731	18.2	24.9	24.6
persons 25 to 29 years old	198	1,286	2,030	7.4	11.1	11.4
persons 30 to 34 years old	160	785	1,292	5.6	6.1	6.7
persons 35 to 44 years old	173	1,092	1,632	3.4	3.4	3.7
persons 45 to 54 years old	48	622	810	1.6	2.2	2.2
persons 55 years old and over	14	147	211	0.4	0.3	0.4
2002						
all persons 3 years and over	11,544	46,725	74,046	32.3%	24.9%	27.3%
persons 3 and 4 years old	609	2,652	4,187	41.0	57.8	54.5
persons 5 and 6 years old	1,446	4,330	7,353	94.4	95.3	95.2
persons 7 to 9 years old	2,174	7,144	11,858	97.9	98.1	98.0
persons 10 and 13 years old	2,849	10,302	16,667	98.1	98.6	98.5
persons 14 and 15 years old	1,267	5,104	8,022	98.1	98.6	98.4
persons 16 and 17 years old	1,092	4,985	7,669	90.9	95.3	94.3
persons 18 and 19 years old	662	3,366	5,007	50.6	67.1	63.3
persons 20 and 21 years old	333	2,605	3,696	24.6	53.1	47.8
persons 22 to 24 years old	344	1,966	3,003	15.3	27.3	25.6
persons 25 to 29 years old	294	1,367	2,196	8.4	12.2	12.1
persons 30 to 34 years old	153	821	1,345	4.4	6.3	6.6
persons 35 to 44 years old	193	1,202	1,772	3.3	4.0	4.1
persons 45 to 54 years old	108	684	979	3.1	2.3	2.4
persons 55 years old and over	19	197	292	0.5	0.4	0.5

SOURCE: U.S. Bureau of the Census, <u>Current Population Reports: School Enrollment, 2001;</u> "(Table) 1. Enrollment Status of the Population 3 Years Old and Over, by Age, Sex, Race, Hispanic 1 Origin, Nativity, and Selected Educational Characteristics: October 2000", published 1 June 2001; <u>2002;</u> Table 1; Internet release 9 January 2004.

NOTES: 'Total' includes other races and ethnic groups not shown separately. 'White' does not include 'Hispanic'.

UNITS: Enrollment in thousands of persons enrolled. All years: rate as a percent of the civilian non-institutionalized population, by age group.

Table 4.02   School Enrollment by Level and Control of School, 2002

	Hispanic	White	Total
Total enrolled	9,783	35,353	57,234
public	9,171	29,521	49,665
private	612	5,832	7,569
nursery school	637	2,881	4,471
public	476	1,172	2,246
private	161	1,709	2,225
kindergarten	727	2,065	3,571
public	688	1,585	2,976
private	39	480	594
elementary school	5,893	20,112	33,100
public	5,574	17,486	29,634
private	318	2,626	3,467
high school	2,526	10,295	16,091
public	2,433	9,279	14,808
private	93	1,016	1,283

SOURCE: U.S. Bureau of the Census, <u>Current Population Reports: School Enrollment</u>, "(Table) 5. Level of Enrollment Below College for People 3 to 24 Years Old, By Control of School, Sex, Metropolitan Status, Race and Hispanic Origin: October 2002", Internet release 9 January, 2004.

NOTES: 'Total' includes other races and ethnic groups not shown separately. 'White' does not include 'Hispanic'.

UNITS: Enrollment in thousands of persons enrolled; civilian non-institutionalized population.

Table 4.03 Estimates of the School Age Population, by Age and Sex, 2002

	Hispanic	White	Total
Both sexes			
3 years old and over	35,704	187,775	270,919
3 and 4 years old	1,485	4,592	7,679
5 and 6 years old	1,531	4,546	7,724
7 to 9 years old	2,219	7,284	12,101
10-13 years old	2,903	10,453	16,926
14 and 15 years old	1,292	5,177	8,149
16 and 17 years old	1,202	5,230	8,131
18 and 19 years old	1,309	5,016	7,907
20 and 21 years old	1,356	4,909	7,731
22 to 24 years old	2,253	7,207	11,730
25 to 29 years old	3,503	11,172	18,141
30 to 34 years old	3,452	12,985	20,343
35 to 44 years old	5,805	30,179	43,728
45 to 54 years old	3,504	29,895	40,013
55 years old and over	3,887	49,132	60,617
Male			
3 years old and over	18,252	91,514	131,858
3 and 4 years old	753	2,351	3,917
5 and 6 years old	805	2,310	3,980
7 to 9 years old	1,125	3,767	6,151
10-13 years old	1,497	5,385	8,680
14 and 15 years old	694	2,615	4,145
16 and 17 years old	574	2,729	4,149
18 and 19 years old	716	2,502	4,042
20 and 21 years old	725	2,449	3,893
22 to 24 years old	1,266	3,502	5,810
25 to 29 years old	1,842	5,579	8,989
30 to 34 years old	1,812	6,454	10,045
35 to 44 years old	2,963	14,951	21,422
45 to 54 years old	1,707	14,776	19,491
55 years old and over	1,773	22,143	27,144

continued on the next page

Table 4.03   continued

	Hispanic	White	Total
Female			
3 years old and over	17,451	96,261	139,061
3 and 4 years old	733	2,241	3,762
5 and 6 years old	726	2,235	3,744
7 to 9 years old	1,095	3,517	5,950
10-13 years old	1,407	5,068	8,246
14 and 15 years old	598	2,562	4,004
16 and 17 years old	627	2,500	3,982
18 and 19 years old	593	2,514	3,865
20 and 21 years old	631	2,459	3,838
22 to 24 years old	987	3,705	5,920
25 to 29 years old	1,661	5,592	9,152
30 to 34 years old	1,640	6,532	10,298
35 to 44 years old	2,842	15,228	22,306
45 to 54 years old	1,798	15,119	20,522
55 years old and over	2,114	26,989	33,472

SOURCE: U.S. Bureau of the Census, <u>Current Population Reports: School Enrollment</u>, "(Table) 1. Enrollment Status of the Population 3 Years Old and Over, by Age, Sex, Race, Hispanic 1 Origin, Nativity, and Selected Educational Characteristics: October 2002"; published 9 January, 2004.

NOTES: 'Total' includes other races and ethnic groups not shown separately. 'White' does not include 'Hispanic'.

UNITS: Estimates of the civilian non-institutionalized population, 3-years old and over as of October 1, in thousands of persons.

Table 4.04 Preprimary School Enrollment of Children 3 - 5 Years Old, by Selected Characteristic of the Mother, 2002

	Hispanic	White	Total
All children 3 and 4 years old enrolled in nursery school	522	2,521	3,858
mother employed part-time	91	551	742
mother employed full-time	201	946	1,569
mother unemployed	37	48	132
mother with 0-8 years of school	52	8	76
with mother high school graduate	164	534	920
with mother with bachelor's degree or more	72	1,099	1,394
All children 3 and 4 years old enrolled in kindergarten	87	131	148
mother employed part-time	12	20	23
mother employed full-time	29	47	43
mother unemployed	6	3	13
mother with 0-8 years of school	12	-	2
with mother high school graduate	32	31	37
with mother with bachelor's degree or more	6	66	53

continued on the next page

Table 4.04   continued

	Hispanic	White	Total
All children 5 years old enrolled in nursery school	106	336	565
mother employed part-time	15	66	86
mother employed full-time	34	140	226
mother unemployed	11	2	29
mother with 0-8 years of school	12	2	16
with mother high school graduate	17	90	132
with mother with bachelor's degree or more	7	120	149
All children 5 years old enrolled in kindergarten	548	1,625	2,752
mother employed part-time	69	375	491
mother employed full-time	198	560	1,025
mother unemployed	24	44	125
mother with 0-8 years of school	85	8	100
with mother high school graduate	168	407	725
with mother with bachelor's degree or more	27	570	697

SOURCE: U.S. Bureau of the Census, <u>Current Population Reports: School Enrollment</u>, "(Table) 4. Preprimary School Enrollment of People 3 to 6 Years Old, by Control of School, Mother's Labor Force Status and Education, Family Income, Race, and Hispanic Origin: October 2002"; Internet release 9 January 2004.

NOTES: 'Total' includes other races/ethnic groups not shown separately. Includes children enrolled in public and non-public nursery school and kindergarten programs. Excludes five year olds enrolled in elementary school. 'All children' includes children whose mothers' labor force status is unknown and children with no mother present in the household. 'White' does not include 'Hispanic'.

UNITS: Enrollment in thousands of children enrolled. – represents or rounds to zero.

Table 4.05 Enrollment in Public Elementary and Secondary Schools, by State, Fall, 2001

	Hispanic	White	Total
United States	17.1	60.3%	100.0%
Alabama	1.5	60.5%	100.0%
Alaska	3.6	60.4	"
Arizona	35.3	51.3	"
Arkansas	4.2	71.1	"
California	44.5	35.0	"
Colorado	23.3	66.8	"
Connecticut	13.7	69.2	"
Delaware	6.6	59.6	"
District of Columbia	9.4	4.6	"
Florida	20.4	52.5	"
Georgia	5.5	53.8	"
Hawaii	4.5	20.3	"
Idaho	11.2	85.4	"
Illinois	16.2	59.0	"
Indiana	3.9	83.0	"
Iowa	4.0	89.6	"
Kansas	9.8	77.8	"
Kentucky	1.1	87.7	"
Louisiana	1.6	48.7	"
Maine	0.6	96.2	"
Maryland	5.4	52.4	"
Massachusetts	10.8	75.7	"
Michigan	3.6	73.4	"
Minnesota	3.8	82.0	"
Mississippi	0.9	47.3	"
Missouri	2.0	79.0	"
Montana	1.9	85.9	"
Nebraska	8.2	81.8	"
Nevada	27.4	54.5	"
New Hampshire	2.1	95.0	"

continued on the next page

Table 4.05   continued

	Hispanic	White	Total
New Jersey	16.0	59.4	100.0%
New Mexico	51.0	34.3	"
New York	18.6	54.8	"
North Carolina	5.2	60.0	"
North Dakota	1.3	88.7	"
Ohio	1.9	80.1	"
Oklahoma	6.5	63.7	"
Oregon	11.5	79.1	"
Pennsylvania	4.8	77.7	"
Rhode Island	14.8	73.4	"
South Carolina	2.4	54.7	"
South Dakota	1.4	86.2	"
Tennessee	2.1	71.8	"
Texas	41.7	40.9	"
Utah	9.9	84.7	"
Vermont	1.0	95.8	"
Virginia	5.5	62.8	"
Washington	10.9	73.5	"
West Virginia	0.4	94.5	"
Wisconsin	5.0	80.1	"
Wyoming	7.2	87.3	"

SOURCE: U.S. Department of Education, National Center for Education Statistics, <u>Digest of Education Statistics, 2003</u>, p. 58, table 42. ED 1.113\(year)

NOTES: 'Total' includes other races and ethnic groups not shown separately. 'White' excludes persons of Hispanic origin.

UNITS: Enrollment as a percent of total enrollment, 100.0%.

Table 4.06 Public Elementary and Secondary School Teachers, by Selected Characteristic, 1999 - 2000

	Hispanic	White	Total
Total number of teachers	169,000	2,532,000	3,002,000
Percent of teachers, by highest degree earned			
bachelor's degree	65.8%	51.6%	na
master's degree	29.3	44.2	na
education specialist	3.0	3.0	na
doctorate	1.2	0.6	na
Percent of teachers, by years of full-time teaching experience			
less than 3 years	28.4%	17.1%	na
3-9 years	29.3	23.2	na
10-20 years	24.6	29.1	na
over 20 years	17.7	30.6	na

SOURCE: U.S. Bureau of Census, <u>Statistical Abstract of the United States, 2003;</u> p. 166, table 249. C 3.134:003

NOTES: 'Total' includes other races and ethnic groups not shown separately. 'White' excludes persons of Hispanic origin.

UNITS: Percent, as a percent of all public elementary and secondary school teachers, 100.0%.

Table 4.07 Private Elementary and Secondary School Teachers, by Selected Characteristic, 1999 - 2000

	Hispanic	White	Total
Total number of teachers	21,000	402,000	449,000
Percent of teachers, by highest degree earned			
bachelor's degree	55.4%	58.3%	na
master's degree	26.7	31.8	na
education specialist	2.8	1.7	na
doctorate	1.5	1.8	na
Percent of teachers, by years of full-time teaching experience			
less than 3 years	36.6%	29.1%	na
3-9 years	26.1	25.0	na
10-20 years	28.7	27.4	na
over 20 years	8.7	18.5	na

SOURCE: U.S. Bureau of Census, <u>Statistical Abstract of the United States, 2003</u>; p. 173, table 263.   C 3.134:003

NOTES: 'Total' includes other races and ethnic groups not shown separately. 'White' excludes persons of Hispanic origin.

UNITS: Percent, as a percent of all private elementary and secondary school teachers, 100.0%.

Table 4.08 Percent of Students At or Above Selected Reading Proficiency Levels by Age, 1999

	Hispanic	White	Total
9-year-olds			
level 150	87%	97%	93%
level 200	44	73	64
level 250	6	20	16
13-year-olds			
level 150	100%	100%	100%
level 200	89	96	93
level 250	43	69	61
level 300	6	18	15
17-year-olds			
level 150	100%	100%	100%
level 200	97	98	98
level 250	68	87	82
level 300	24	46	40

SOURCE: U.S. Department of Education, National Center for Education Statistics, <u>Digest of Education Statistics, 2002</u>, p. 138, table 114. ED 1.113:002

NOTES: 'Total' includes other races and ethnic groups not shown separately.

UNITS: Reading level shown as scale score on scale: 150=able to follow brief written directions and carry out simple discrete reading tasks; 200=able to understand, combine ideas, and make inferences based on short uncomplicated passages about specific or sequentially related information; 250=able to search for specific information, interrelate ideas, and make generalizations about literature, science, and social studies materials; 300=able to find, understand, summarize, and explain relatively complicated literary and informational material.

Table 4.09 Percent of Students At or Above Selected Science and Math Proficiency Levels by Age, 1999

	Hispanic	White	Total
Science Proficiency			
9-year-olds			
level 150	94.2%	99.3%	97.0%
level 200	56.3	86.7	77.4
level 250	11.6	39.2	31.4
level 300	0.3	4.1	3.0
13-year-olds			
level 200	78.3%	97.5%	92.7%
level 250	24.7	69.4	57.9
level 300	1.8	14.3	10.9
level 350	0.0	0.2	0.2
17-year-olds			
level 200	96.9%	99.4%	98.0%
level 250	73.3	92.6	85.0
level 300	27.2	57.2	47.4
level 350	4.7	12.4	9.7
Math Proficiency			
9-year-olds			
level 150	98.1%	99.6%	98.9%
level 200	67.5	88.6	82.5
level 250	10.5	37.1	30.9
level 300	0.1	2.2	1.7
13-year-olds			
level 200	97.2%	99.4%	98.7%
level 250	62.9	86.7	78.8
level 300	8.2	29.0	23.2
level 350	0.1	1.2	0.9
17-year-olds			
level 200	99.9%	100.0%	100.0%
level 250	93.6	98.7	96.8
level 300	37.7	69.9	60.7
level 350	3.1	10.4	8.4

SOURCE: U.S. Department of Education, National Center for Education Statistics, <u>Digest of Education Statistics, 2002</u>; p. 146, table 124; p 151, table 129. ED 1.113:002

NOTES: 'Total' includes other races and ethnic groups not shown separately.

UNITS: Math proficiency scale: 150=performs simple addition and subtraction, 200= use basic operations to solve simple problems, 250=uses intermediate level mathematics skills to solve two-step problems, 300=understands measurement and geometry and solves more complex problems, 350= understands and applies more advanced mathematical concepts.

Table 4.10   Student Use of Computers at School, 1993 - 2001

	<u>Hispanic</u>	<u>White</u>	<u>Total</u>
1993			
Total	52.3%	61.6%	59.0%
Elementary and secondary	52.3	63.8	60.1
College	52.1	54.0	54.7
1997			
Total	61.5%	71.1%	68.8%
Elementary and secondary	61.3	73.9	70.4
College	62.6	62.1	62.9
2001			
Total	78.8%	84.1%	82.9%
Elementary and secondary	78.9	85.9	84.2
under 6 years old	57.1	55.6	56.0
6 to 9 years old	77.3	88.2	85.4
10 to 14 years old	85.5	91.8	90.3
15 years old or over	83.8	89.2	88.0
College	78.0	78.6	78.5

SOURCE: U.S. Department of Education, National Center for Education Statistics, <u>Digest of Education Statistics, 2002</u>, p. 499, table 428. ED 1.113\002

NOTES: 'Total' includes other races and ethnic groups not shown separately. 'White' excludes persons of Hispanic origin.

UNITS: Percent of students using computers, as of October 1993, October 1997 and September 2001.

Table 4.11 Labor Force Status of 2004 High School Graduates and 2003-2004 High School Dropouts, October 2004

	Hispanic	White	Total
2004 high school graduates			
total	153	1,211	1,533
employed	129	1,037	1,282
unemployed	23	174	251
not in labor force	133	900	1,219
2003-2004 high school dropouts			
total	87	196	267
employed	61	140	160
unemployed	27	56	106
not in labor force	67	174	229

SOURCE: U.S. Department Labor, Bureau of Labor Statistics, "(Table) 1. Labor force status of 2004 high school graduates and 2003-2004 high school dropouts 16 to 24 years old by school enrollment, sex, race, and Hispanic origin, October 2004".

NOTES: 'High school dropouts' refers to persons who dropped out of school between October 2003 and October 2004

UNITS: Number of persons in thousands of persons.

Table 4.12 Percent of High School Dropout Among Persons 16 to 24 Years Old, by Sex, 1975 - 2001

	Hispanic			White			Total		
	Male	female	total	male	female	total	male	female	total
1975	26.7%	31.6%	29.2%	11.0%	11.8	11.4%	13.3%	14.5%	13.9%
1980	37.2	33.2	35.2	12.3	10.5	11.4	15.1	13.1	14.1
1985	29.9	25.2	27.6	11.1	9.8	10.4	13.4	11.8	12.6
1990	34.3	30.3	32.4	9.3	8.7	9.0	12.3	11.8	12.1
1995	30.0	30.0	30.0	9.0	8.2	8.6	12.2	11.7	12.0
1999	31.0	26.0	28.6	7.7	6.9	7.3	11.9	10.5	11.2
2000	31.8	23.5	27.8	7.0	6.9	6.9	12.0	9.9	10.9
2001	31.6	22.1	27.0	7.9	6.7	7.3	12.2	9.3	10.7

SOURCE: U.S. Department of Education, Center for Education Statistics, <u>Digest of Education Statistics 2002</u>, p. 132, table 108. ED 1.113:002

NOTES: 'Total' includes other races not shown separately. 'White' excludes persons of Hispanic origin. 'Dropouts' are 16- to 24-year-olds who are not enrolled in school and who have not completed a high school program regardless of when they left school.

UNITS: All data are based on October counts.

Table 4.13 SAT (Scholastic Aptitude Test) Scores, 1990 - 2003

	Hispanic	White	Total
1990-1991			
SAT-Scholastic Aptitude Test			
verbal score	458	518	499
math score	462	513	500
2000-2001			
SAT-Scholastic Aptitude Test			
verbal score	460	529	506
math score	465	531	514
2001-2002			
SAT-Scholastic Aptitude Test			
verbal score	458	527	504
math score	464	533	516
2002-2003			
SAT-Scholastic Aptitude Test			
verbal score	457	529	507
math score	464	534	519

SOURCE: U.S. Department of Education, Center for Education Statistics, <u>Digest of Education Statistics 2003</u>, p. 162, table 131. ED 1.113: (year)

NOTES: 'Total' includes other races and ethnic groups not shown separately.

UNITS: Average scores, (minimum score, 200; maximum score 800).

Chapter 5: Education - Postsecondary & Educational Attainment

Table 5.01 Enrollment in Institutions of Higher Education, by Type of Institution, 1980 - 2001

	Hispanic	White	Total
1980			
All institutions	471.7	9,883.0	12,086.8
4-year institutions	216.6	6,274.5	7,565.4
2-year institutions	255.1	3,558.5	4,521.4
1990			
All institutions	782.4	10,722.5	13,818.6
4-year institutions	358.2	6,768.1	8,578.6
2-year institutions	424.2	3,954.3	5,240.1
1995			
All institutions	1,093.8	10,311.2	14,261.8
4-year institutions	485.5	6,517.2	8,769.3
2-year institutions	608.4	3,794.0	5,492.5
2000			
All institutions	1,461.8	10,462.1	15,312.3
4-year institutions	617.9	6,658.0	9,363.9
2-year institutions	843.9	3,804.1	5,948.4
2001			
All institutions	1,560.6	10,774.5	15,928.0
4-year institutions	656.3	6,818.8	9,677.4
2-year institutions	904.3	3,955.7	6,250.6

SOURCE: U.S. Department of Education, Center for Education Statistics, <u>Digest of Education Statistics, 2003</u>, p. 260, table 210. ED 1.113: (year)

NOTES: 'Total' includes other races and ethnic groups not shown separately. 'White' excludes persons of Hispanic origin.

UNITS: Enrollment in thousands of students enrolled.

Table 5.02 Enrollment in Institutions of Higher Education, by State, Fall, 2001

	Hispanic	White	Total
UNITED STATES	1,560,587	10,774,519	15,927,987
Alabama	2,475	157,489	236,146
Alaska	884	20,356	27,756
Arizona	59,736	252,108	366,485
Arkansas	1,711	93,970	122,282
California	574,549	1,096,589	2,380,090
Colorado	27,699	209,578	269,292
Connecticut	11,330	123,921	165,027
Delaware	1,341	35,067	47,104
District of Columbia	3,834	41,516	87,252
Florida	122,615	448,234	735,554
Georgia	7,338	232,837	376,098
Hawaii	1,792	15,948	62,079
Idaho	2,595	62,741	69,674
Illinois	83,860	493,721	748,444
Indiana	8,511	283,793	338,715
Iowa	4,017	171,005	194,822
Kansas	6,915	154,191	184,943
Kentucky	1,926	187,946	214,839
Louisiana	5,352	144,650	228,871
Maine	739	56,393	61,127
Maryland	9,367	173,274	288,224
Massachusetts	23,118	312,647	425,071
Michigan	14,056	453,825	585,998
Minnesota	4,875	264,997	308,233
Mississippi	870	84,419	137,882
Missouri	7,456	269,035	331,580
Montana	719	38,584	44,932
Nebraska	2,892	99,716	113,817
Nevada	11,196	63,118	93,368
New Hampshire	1,415	58,969	65,031

continued on the next page

Table 5.02   continued

	Hispanic	White	Total
New Jersey	41,698	213,982	346,507
New Mexico	45,764	49,811	112,861
New York	11,302	661,498	1,057,794
North Carolina	8,302	298,827	427,784
North Dakota	314	37,982	42,843
Ohio	9,772	466,724	569,223
Oklahoma	5,933	137,130	189,785
Oregon	7,701	157,613	191,378
Pennsylvania	15,111	508,268	630,299
Rhode Island	4,394	61,984	77,235
South Carolina	2,517	130,386	191,590
South Dakota	374	40,378	45,534
Tennessee	3,507	197,569	258,534
Texas	254,848	598,471	1,076,678
Utah	6,166	158,038	177,045
Vermont	736	33,328	36,351
Virginia	11,844	272,762	389,853
Washington	14,911	250,677	325,132
West Virginia	711	82,780	91,319
Wisconsin	7,377	275,572	315,850
Wyoming	1,146	28,413	31,095

SOURCE: U.S. Department of Education, Center for Education Statistics, <u>Digest of Education Statistics, 2003</u>, p. 262, table 212. ED 1.113\(year)

NOTES: 'Total' includes other races and ethnic groups not shown separately. 'White' excludes Hispanic.

UNITS: Enrollment in number of students enrolled.

Table 5.03   Enrollment Rates of 18 - 24 Year Olds in Institutions of Higher Education, 1975 – 2001

	Hispanic	White	Total
Enrollment as a percent of 18-24 year olds			
1975	20.4%	27.4%	26.3%
1980	16.1	27.3	25.7
1985	16.9	30.0	27.8
1990	16.2	35.2	32.1
1991	17.8	36.8	33.3
1992	21.3	37.3	34.4
1993	21.7	36.8	34.0
1994	18.8	38.1	34.6
1995	20.7	37.9	34.3
1996	20.1	39.5	35.5
1997	22.4	40.6	36.2
1998	20.4	40.6	36.5
1999	18.7	39.4	35.6
2000	21.7	38.7	35.5
2001	21.7	39.3	36.2
Enrollment as a percent of high school graduates			
1975	33.0%	32.3%	32.5%
1980	27.6	32.1	31.8
1985	26.8	34.9	33.7
1990	26.8	39.2	37.7
1991	31.4	41.0	39.3
1992	37.5	42.8	42.0
1993	36.1	42.6	41.6
1994	33.1	43.7	42.3
1995	35.2	44.0	42.3
1996	34.5	45.1	43.4
1997	36.1	46.8	44.6
1998	33.9	46.9	45.2
1999	31.6	45.3	43.7
2000	36.2	44.1	43.2
2001	34.6	45.3	44.2

Source: U.S. Department of Education, National Center for Education Statistics, Digest of Education Statistics, 2002, p. 225, table 186. ED 1.113\002

NOTES: 'Total' includes other races and ethnic groups not shown separately. 'White' does not include Hispanic.

UNITS: Percent as a percent of 18-24 year olds, and high school graduates as shown, 100.0%.

Table 5.04 Enrollment of Persons 14 - 34 Years Old in Institutions of Higher Education, by Sex, 1975 - 1999

| | Enrollment | | | percent distribution | | |
	Hispanic	White	Total	Hispanic	White	Total
1975						
Total	927	8,141	9,697	9.6%	84.0%	100.0%
men	433	4,566	5,342	4.5	47.1	55.1
women	494	3,576	4,355	5.1	36.9	44.9
1980						
Total	996	8,453	10,181	9.8%	83.0%	100.0%
men	431	4,225	5,193	4.2	41.5	51.0
women	565	4,228	5,244	5.5	41.5	49.0
1985						
Total	1,036	8,781	10,863	9.5%	80.0%	100.0%
men	458	4,361	5,345	4.2	40.1	49.2
women	578	4,420	5,518	5.3	40.7	50.8
1990						
Total	1,167	8,892	11,303	10.3%	78.7%	100.0%
men	508	4,289	na	4.5	38.0	na
women	659	4,594	na	5.8	40.6	na
1993						
Total	1,227	8,592	11,409	10.8%	75.3%	100.0%
men	515	4,168	na	4.5	36.5	na
women	713	4,424	na	6.2	38.8	na
1999						
Total	1,081	8,853	12,506	8.6%	70.8%	100.0%
men	472	4,310	na	3.8	34.5	na
women	609	4,543	na	4.9	36.3	na

SOURCE: U.S. Department of Education, Center for Education Statistics, <u>Digest of Education Statistics, 2000</u>, p. 243, table 213. ED 1.113\000

NOTES: 'Total' includes other races and ethnic groups not shown separately. 'White' excludes Hispanic.

UNITS: Enrollment in thousands of students enrolled; percent as a percentage of 14-34 year olds, by sex as shown, 100.0%.

Table 5.05 School Enrollment by Attendance Status, Type and Control of School, Fall, 2002

	Hispanic	White	Total
Total enrolled			
two-year college			
full time	334	1,499	2,464
part time	351	1,153	1,914
four-year college			
full time	573	5,245	7,271
part time	188	1,185	1,776
graduate college			
full time	98	929	1,406
part time	113	1,226	1,666
Total public			
two-year college			
full time	302	1,304	2,179
part time	333	1,038	1,768
four-year college			
full time	454	3,878	5,497
part time	156	915	1,385
graduate college			
full time	58	569	916
part time	72	785	1,088
Total private			
two-year college			
full time	32	196	285
part time	18	116	146
four-year college			
full time	119	1,366	1,774
part time	33	270	391
graduate college			
full time	40	360	490
part time	41	441	579

SOURCE: U.S. Bureau of the Census, <u>Current Population Reports: School Enrollment</u>, "(Table) 9. School Enrollment of the Population 15 Years Old and Over, by Attendance Status, Type and Control of School, Age, Sex, Race and Hispanic Origin: October 2002", Internet release 9 January 2004.

NOTES: 'Total' includes other races and ethnic groups not shown separately. 'White' excludes 'Hispanic' persons.

UNITS: Enrollment in thousands of students.

Table 5.06 College Enrollment, October 2000 and 2002

	<u>Hispanic</u>	<u>White</u>	<u>Total</u>
2000			
total enrolled	1,426	10,636	15,314
year enrolled in college			
1st year	453	2,540	3,823
2nd year	348	2,487	3,609
3rd year	228	1,881	2,711
4th year	200	1,615	2,257
5th year	67	708	994
6th year or higher	131	1,406	1,919
2002			
total enrolled	1,656	11,236	16,497
year enrolled in college			
1st year	543	2,862	4,416
2nd year	407	2,258	3,486
3rd year	277	2,227	3,109
4th year	219	1,735	2,414
5th year	105	765	1,157
6th year or higher	106	1,390	1,915

SOURCE: U.S. Bureau of the Census, <u>Current Population Reports: School Enrollment, 2000</u>; "(Table) 10. Attendance Status of College Students 15 Years Old and Over, by Age, Sex, Year and Type of College, Race and Hispanic Origin: October 2000"; published 1 June 2001; <u>2002</u>; Table 10; Internet release 9 January 2004.

NOTES: 'Total' includes other races and ethnic groups not shown separately. College enrollment at the undergraduate level in two and four year institutions. 'White' excludes 'Hispanic' persons.

UNITS: College enrollment in thousands of students.

Table 5.07 Undergraduates Receiving Financial Aid: Average Amount Awarded per Student, by Type and Source of Aid, 1995-96, and 1999-2000

	Hispanic	White	Total
1995-96			
All full-time, full-year enrolled undergraduates	588	4,500	6,306
undergraduates receiving:			
any aid, total	$ 5,999	$ 6,836	$ 6,832
- from federal source	4,644	5,549	5,362
- from non-federal sources	3,328	3,848	3,883
grants, total	$ 3,486	$ 3,762	$ 3,864
- from federal source	2,113	1,894	2,001
- from non-federal sources	3,017	3,541	3,599
loans, total	$ 4,168	$ 4,437	$ 4,345
- from federal source	4,137	4,366	4,288
- from non-federal sources	2,235	2,912	2,747
work-study funds, total	$ 1,152	$ 1,367	$ 1,371
1999-2000			
All full-time, full-year enrolled undergraduates	NA	NA	6,364
undergraduates receiving:			
any aid, total	$ 7,084	$ 8,659	$ 8,474
- from federal source	5,335	6,261	6,158
- from non-federal sources	3,581	5,288	4,996
grants, total	$ 4,244	$ 5,053	$ 4,949
- from federal source	2,680	2,382	2,524
- from non-federal sources	3,130	4,658	4,425
loans, total	$ 5,400	$ 5,483	$5,437
- from federal source	4,926	4,781	4,825
- from non-federal sources	4,178	5,106	4,939
work-study funds, total	$ 1,650	$ 1,658	$ 1,672

SOURCE: U.S. Department of Education, Center for Education Statistics, <u>Digest of Education Statistics, 2001</u>, p. 364, table 321; <u>2002</u>; p. 358, table 316; p. 359, table 317. ED 1.113\(year).

NOTES: 'Total' includes other races and ethnic groups not shown separately. 'White' excludes Hispanic persons.

UNITS: Average 1995-96 award in dollars per student, for students enrolled in Fall, 1995. Number of undergraduates, in thousands.

Table 5.08 Employment Status of Students 15 - 17 Years of Age, Enrolled in School, 1998-99

	Hispanic	White	Total
Age 15			
students with an employer job	45.4%	67.4%	59.4%
students who worked during			
the school year	35.8	50.9	44.1
students who worked Summer only	9.7	16.5	15.3
Age 16			
students with an employer job	67.6%	82.5%	77.4%
students who worked during			
the school year	57.9	73.1	67.0
students who worked Summer only	9.7	9.4	10.4
Age 17			
students with an employer job	77.4%	90.1%	86.6%
students who worked during			
the school year	69.2	82.6	77.7
students who worked Summer only	8.2	7.5	8.9

SOURCE: U.S. Bureau of Census, <u>Statistical Abstract of the United States, 2002</u>; p. 150, table 227, (data from U.S. Bureau of Labor Statistics, *Employment Experience of Youths: Results from a Longitudinal Survey*, December 20, 2001). C 3.134:002

NOTES: 'Total' includes other races not shown separately. Excludes freelance work, such as babysitting or mowing lawns.

UNITS: Percent of students 15 to 17 years old at the beginning of the 1998-99 school year.

Table 5.09   Enrollment in Schools of Medicine, Dentistry and Related Fields, 1980-81 and 2001-2002

	Hispanic	White	Total
1980-81			
allopathic medicine	4.2%	85.0%	100.0%
osteopathic medicine	1.1	94.9	"
podiatry	1.5	91.3	"
dentistry	2.3	88.5	"
optometry	1.8	91.4	"
pharmacy	2.1	88.6	"
veterinary medicine	1.1	95.2	"
registered nursing	na	na	"
2001-2002			
dentistry	5.9%	65.3%	100.0%
allopathic medicine	6.4	63.2	"
osteopathic medicine	3.5	75.9	"
registered nursing	4.9	78.4	"
optometry	5.6	60.3	"
pharmacy	3.7	58.8	"
podiatry	6.5	62.1	"

SOURCE: U.S. Department of Health and Human Services, <u>Health United States, 2004</u>; pp. 314-315, table 107.   HE 20.6223: (year)

NOTES: 'Total' includes other races and ethnic groups not shown separately. 'White' excludes Hispanic persons.

UNITS: Enrollment as a percentage of all students enrolled, 100.0%.

Table 5.10   Earned Degrees Conferred, by Type of Degree, 1991 - 2002

	Hispanic	White	Total
1991-92			
Bachelor's degrees	40,761	936,771	1,129,833
Master's degrees	9,358	268,371	348,682
Doctor's degrees	811	25,813	40,090
First Professional degrees	2,766	59,800	72,129
1997-98			
Bachelor's degrees	65,937	900,317	1,183,033
Master's degrees	16,215	307,587	429,296
Doctor's degrees	1,270	28,747	45,925
First Professional degrees	3,547	59,273	78,353
1999-2000			
Bachelor's degrees	74,963	928,013	1,237,875
Master's degrees	19,093	317,999	457,056
Doctor's degrees	1,291	27,520	44,808
First Professional degrees	3,865	59,601	80,057
2000-2001			
Bachelor's degrees	77,745	927,357	1,244,171
Master's degrees	21,543	320,480	468,476
Doctor's degrees	1,516	27,454	44,904
First Professional degrees	3,806	58,598	79,707
2001-2002			
Bachelor's degrees	82,969	958,585	1,291,900
Master's degrees	22,387	327,635	482,118
Doctor's degrees	1,432	26,905	44,160
First Professional degrees	3,965	58,874	80,698

SOURCE: U.S. Department of Education, Center for Education Statistics, <u>1998 Education Indicators</u>, pp. 228-229, table 2:5-1. ED 1.109:989
U.S. Department of Education, Center for Education Statistics, <u>Digest of Education Statistics, 1994</u>, pp. 276-288, tables 252-264. <u>2000</u>; p. 313, table 266; p. 316, table 269; p. 319, table 272; p. 322, table 275; <u>2001</u>; p. 328, table 269; p. 331, table 272; p. 334, table 275; p. 337, table 278; <u>2002</u>; p. 323, table 265; p. 326, table 268; p. 329, table 271; p. 332, table 274; <u>2003</u>; p. 335, table 265; p. 338, table 268; p. 341, table 271; p. 344, table 274. ED 1.113\9(year)

NOTES: 'Total' includes other races and ethnic groups not shown separately. 'White' excludes Hispanic persons. 'First professional Degrees' include degrees awarded in chiropractic, dentistry, law, medicine, optometry, osteopathy, pharmacy, podiatry, theology, and veterinary medicine.

UNITS: Earned degrees conferred in number of degrees.

Table 5.11 Associate Degrees Conferred, by Major Field of Study, 2001 - 2002

	Hispanic	White	Total
All Fields, Total	60,003	417,739	595,133
agriculture and natural resources	120	6,118	6,494
architecture and related programs	28	331	443
area, ethnic and cultural studies	17	240	319
biological sciences/life sciences	137	1,074	1,517
business	9,823	73,361	108,911
communications	167	2,252	2,819
communications technologies	185	1,518	2,021
computer and information sciences	3,024	19,943	30,965
construction trades	117	2,216	2,639
education	1,050	6,318	9,267
engineering	124	1,284	1,724
engineering related technologies	3,468	22,920	32,895
English language and literature/letters	101	625	864
foreign languages and literatures	143	298	517
health professions and related sciences	5,903	60,300	79,888
home economics	1,252	5,652	9,480
law and legal studies	626	4,785	6,825
liberal arts/general studies/humanities	23,275	144,594	207,163
library science	5	85	96
mathematics	112	407	685
mechanics and repairers	1,343	9,012	12,086
multi/interdisciplinary studies	1,476	8,826	13,204
parks, recreation, and fitness studies	68	629	830
philosophy and religion	27	67	134
physical sciences	200	1,707	2,308
precision production trades	1,033	8,470	10,818
protective services	1,832	12,276	16,689
psychology	270	1,166	1,705
public administration and services	460	1,862	3,323
military technologies and R.O.T.C.	3	32	62
social sciences and history	946	3,326	5,593
theological studies/religious vocations	16	314	414
transportation	96	901	1,159
visual and performing arts	2,545	14,546	20,911

SOURCE: U.S. Department of Education, National Center for Education Statistics, <u>Digest of Education Statistics, 2003</u>, p. 320, table 262. ED 1.113\(year)

NOTES: 'Total' includes other races and ethnic groups not shown separately. 'White' excludes Hispanic persons.

UNITS: Earned Associate degrees conferred in number of degrees.

Table 5.12 Bachelor's Degrees Conferred, by Major Field of Study, 2001 - 2002

	Hispanic	White	Total
All Fields, Total	82,969	958,585	1,291,900
agriculture and natural resources	744	20,659	23,353
architecture and related programs	640	6,518	8,808
area, ethnic and cultural studies	775	3,841	6,557
biological sciences/life sciences	3,256	42,831	60,256
business	17,557	199,906	281,330
communications	3,510	49,483	62,791
communications technologies	94	781	1,110
computer and information sciences	2,442	28,311	47,299
construction trades	10	182	202
education	4,893	90,475	106,383
engineering	3,208	41,192	59,481
engineering related technologies	875	10,567	14,117
English language and literature/letters	2,908	43,129	53,162
foreign languages and literatures	2,558	10,885	15,318
health professions and related sciences	3,700	53,533	70,517
home economics	724	14,722	18,153
law and legal studies	146	1,359	1,971
liberal arts/general studies/humanities	4,106	27,786	39,333
library science	1	67	74
mathematics	695	9,190	12,395
mechanics and repairers	21	104	164
multi/interdisciplinary studies	2,793	19,866	27,629
parks, recreation, and fitness studies	1,068	16,795	20,554
philosophy and religion	472	7,661	9,306
physical sciences	709	13,900	17,851
precision production trades	24	391	468
protective services	2,659	17,262	25,536
psychology	6,381	55,824	76,671
public administration and services	1,847	12,529	19,392
military technologies and R.O.T.C.	0	3	3
social sciences and history	9,917	96,346	132,874
theological studies/religious vocations	258	6,699	7,785
transportation	181	3,339	4,020
visual and performing arts	3,787	52,224	66,773

SOURCE: U.S. Department of Education, National Center for Education Statistics, <u>Digest of Education Statistics, 2003</u>, p. 335, table 265. ED 1.113\(year)

NOTES: 'Total' includes other races and ethnic groups not shown separately. 'White' excludes Hispanic persons.

UNITS: Earned Bachelor's degrees conferred in number of degrees.

Table 5.13   Master's Degrees Conferred, by Major Field of Study,
2001 - 2002

	Hispanic	White	Total
All Fields, Total	22,387	327,635	482,118
agriculture and natural resources	117	3,454	4,519
architecture and related programs	220	2,797	4,566
area, ethnic and cultural studies	125	959	1,578
biological sciences/life sciences	261	4,265	6,205
business	5,024	76,435	120,785
communications	189	3,512	5,510
communications technologies	11	312	549
computer and information sciences	307	5,144	16,113
construction trades	2	2	9
education	7,751	107,793	136,579
engineering	775	11,215	26,015
engineering related technologies	21	583	869
English language and literature/letters	243	5,897	7,268
foreign languages and literatures	351	1,598	2,861
health professions and related sciences	1,740	33,012	43,644
home economics	130	1,911	2,616
law and legal studies	167	1,304	4,053
liberal arts/general studies/humanities	119	2,156	2,754
library science	212	4,280	5,113
mathematics	85	1,727	3,487
multi/interdisciplinary studies	156	2,236	3,211
parks, recreation, and fitness studies	71	2,231	2,754
philosophy and religion	36	1,063	1,334
physical sciences	148	3,056	5,034
precision production trades	1	0	2
protective services	159	2,119	2,935
psychology	921	10,931	14,888
public administration and services	1,743	16,889	25,448
social sciences and history	670	8,660	14,112
theological studies/religious vocations	164	3,570	4,952
transportation	31	604	709
visual and performing arts	437	7,906	11,595

SOURCE: U.S. Department of Education, National Center for Education Statistics,
<u>Digest of Education Statistics, 2003</u>, p. 338, table 268. ED 1.113\(year)

NOTES: 'Total' includes other races and ethnic groups not shown separately. 'White'
excludes Hispanic persons.

UNITS: Earned Master's degrees conferred in number of degrees.

Table 5.14 Doctor's Degrees Conferred, by Major Field of Study, 2001 - 2002

	Hispanic	White	Total
All Fields, Total	1,432	26,905	44,160
agriculture and natural resources	25	562	1,166
architecture and related programs	8	71	183
area, ethnic and cultural studies	11	125	216
biological sciences/life sciences	127	2,691	4,489
business	22	612	1,158
communications	8	243	374
communications technologies	0	6	9
computer and information sciences	21	288	750
education	312	4,938	6,967
engineering	93	1,696	5,195
engineering related technologies	0	5	15
English language and literature/letters	49	1,101	1446
foreign languages and literatures	96	463	843
health professions and related sciences	82	2,461	3,523
home economics	10	227	355
law and legal studies	1	18	79
liberal arts/general studies/humanities	2	94	113
library science	1	25	45
mathematics	9	396	958
multi/interdisciplinary studies	14	259	384
parks, recreation, and fitness studies	4	107	151
philosophy and religion	13	466	606
physical sciences	68	2,054	3,803
protective services	1	43	49
psychology	263	3,454	4,341
public administration and services	13	386	571
social sciences and history	120	2,485	3,902
theological studies/religious vocations	22	862	1,355
visual and performing arts	37	767	1,114

SOURCE: U.S. Department of Education, National Center for Education Statistics, <u>Digest of Education Statistics, 2003</u>, p. 341, table 271. ED 1.113\(year)

NOTES: 'Total' includes other races and ethnic groups not shown separately. 'White' excludes Hispanic persons.

UNITS: Earned Doctor's degrees conferred in number of degrees.

Table 5.15 First Professional Degrees Conferred, by Field of Study,
2001 - 2002

	<u>Hispanic</u>	<u>White</u>	<u>Total</u>
All Fields, Total	3,965	58,874	80,698
Dentistry	173	2,630	4,239
Medicine	757	10,148	15,237
Optometry	40	800	1,280
Osteopathic medicine	67	1,825	2,416
Pharmacy	229	4,551	7,076
Podiatry	15	332	474
Veterinary medicine	61	2,055	2,289
Chiropractic medicine	121	2,426	3,284
Law	2,368	30,125	38,981
Theological professions	132	3,782	5,195

SOURCE: U.S. Department of Education, National Center for Education Statistics, <u>Digest of Education Statistics, 2003</u>, p. 332, table 274. ED 1.113\(year)

NOTES: 'Total' includes other races and ethnic groups not shown separately. 'White' excludes Hispanic persons.

UNITS: Earned first professional degrees conferred, in number of degrees.

Table 5.16 Educational Attainment: Years of School Completed by Persons 25 Years Old and Older, 2000 and 2003

	Hispanic	White	Total
2000			
All persons 25 years old and over	17,150	147,067	175,230
percent of the population:			
not a high school graduate	43.0%	15.1%	15.8%
high school graduate	27.9	33.4	33.1
with some college, no degree	13.5	17.4	17.6
with associate's degree	5.0	8.0	7.8
with bachelor's degree	7.3	17.3	17.0
with advanced degree	3.3	8.8	8.6
2003			
All persons 25 years old and over	21,189	153,188	185,183
percent of the population:			
not a high school graduate	43.0%	14.9%	15.4%
high school graduate	27.4	32.2	32.0
with some college, no degree	13.0	17.0	17.2
with associate's degree	5.2	8.3	8.2
with bachelor's degree	8.3	18.2	17.9
with advanced degree	3.1	9.5	9.3

SOURCE: U.S. Bureau of the Census, Statistical Abstract of the United States, 2001; p. 140, table 217; 2004; p. 142, table 214. C 3.134:(year)

NOTES: 'Total' includes other races and ethnic groups not shown separately. Data as of March.

UNITS: Percent as a percent of the population 25 years old and older; number in thousands of persons 25 years old and older.

Table 5.17 College Completion, Persons 25 Years Old and Older, by Sex, 1970 - 2003

	Hispanic	White	Total
1970			
total	na%	11.6%	11.0%
men	na	15.0	14.1
women	na	8.6	8.2
1980			
total	7.9	17.8	17.0
men	9.7	22.1	20.9
women	6.2	14.0	13.6
1990			
total	9.2	22.0	21.3
men	9.8	25.3	24.4
women	8.7	19.0	18.4
2000			
total	10.6	28.1	25.6
men	10.7	30.8	27.8
women	10.6	25.5	23.6
2002			
total	11.1	27.2	26.7
men	11.0	29.1	28.5
women	11.2	25.4	25.1
2003*			
total	12.1	28.2	27.7
men	11.8	30.0	29.4
women	12.3	26.4	26.1

SOURCE: U.S. Bureau of the Census, Current Population Reports: Educational Attainment in the United States: March 1998 (Update); Series P-20, #513, table 1, pp. 1-5; 2000; #536, pp. 1-8, table 1a; 2002; PPL-169, pp. 1-21, table 1a; 2003; #550, table 1a; 2004; table 1a.   C3.186/23:(year)

NOTES: 'Total' includes other races not shown separately. '*' indicates year in which 'White' as shown is equivalent to 'White Alone' that refers to people who reported 'White' and did not report any other race category.

UNITS: Percent as a percent of all persons 25 years old and older completing four or more years of college (1970-1991) or Bachelor's degree or more (1992 and later).

Table 5.18 Educational Attainment of the Hispanic Population, 25 Years Old and Over, by Type of Origin, 2000 and 2002

	Mexican	Puerto Rican	Cuban	Central/ South American	Other Hispanic	Total Hispanic
2000						
less than 9th grade	32.3%	17.5%	18.1%	22.3%	15.1%	27.3%
9th to 12th grade (no diploma)	16.8	18.1	8.9	13.4	13.3	15.7
high school graduate	26.4	29.5	33.0	29.5	32.3	27.9
some college or associate degree	17.7	21.9	17.0	17.5	24.8	18.5
bachelor's degree	5.1	8.6	13.9	11.8	8.9	7.3
Advanced degree	1.8	4.4	9.2	5.6	5.6	3.3
2002						
less than 9th grade	32.1%	15.4%	19.2%	22.3%	12.8%	27.0%
9th to 12th grade (no diploma)	17.3	17.8	10.0	13.0	13.2	16.0
high school graduate	26.7	29.5	34.8	28.9	29.9	27.9
some college or associate degree	16.4	23.2	17.4	18.5	24.4	18.0
bachelor's degree	5.6	10.4	12.4	12.5	14.0	8.1
Advanced degree	1.9	3.6	6.2	4.8	5.7	3.0

SOURCE: U.S. Bureau of the Census, Current Population Reports: The Hispanic Population of the United States, 2000; "Table 7.1. Educational Attainment of the Population 25 Years and Over by Sex, Hispanic Origin and Race: March 2000," published March 6, 2001; 2002; Internet Release date: 18 June 2003; "Table 7.1 Educational Attainment of the Population 25 Years and Over by Sex, Hispanic Origin and Race: March 2002"; "Table 7.2 Educational Attainment of the Population 25 Years and Over by Sex, and Hispanic Origin Type: March 2002".

NOTES: Total population includes other races and ethnic groups not shown separately. 'Other Hispanic origin' includes persons from Spain and persons identifying themselves generally as Hispanic, Spanish, Spanish-American, Hispano, Latino, etc.

UNITS: Persons completing educational levels in percent as a percent of all persons, by origin, 100.0%.

Table 5.19   Highest Educational Level and Degree Earned, Persons 18 Years Old and Older, 2000 and 2002

	Hispanic	White	Total
2000			
Total civilian non-institutional population	21,109	148,091	201,762
less than 7 years of elementary school	3,873	1,690	6,684
7 or 8 years of elementary school	1,310	4,024	6,249
1 to 3 years of high school	3,303	11,136	18,394
4 years of high school	597	1,428	2,760
high school graduate	5,966	49,806	66,141
some college	3,196	30,037	39,940
Associate degree	959	11,675	14,715
Bachelor's degree	1,332	25,797	31,708
Master's degree	372	8,640	10,527
First professional degree	117	2,200	2,613
Doctorate degree	84	1,659	2,032
2002			
Total civilian non-institutional population	24,550	150,443	209,454
less than 7 years of elementary school	4,490	1,573	7,157
7 or 8 years of elementary school	1,430	3,880	6,222
1 to 3 years of high school	3,729	11,075	18,644
4 years of high school	846	1,701	3,400
high school graduate	6,977	49,114	66,682
some college	3,584	29,677	40,282
Associate degree	1,189	12,529	16,183
Bachelor's degree	1,710	27,364	34,368
Master's degree	384	9,514	11,574
First professional degree	143	2,249	2,752
Doctorate degree	68	1,767	2,190

SOURCE: U.S. Department of Education, National Center for Education Statistics, Digest of Education Statistics, 2001; p. 18, table 9; 2003; p. 18, table 9 (data from U.S. Bureau of the Census, *Current Population Reports*, unpublished data.) ED 1.113\(year)

NOTES: 'Total' includes other races and ethnic groups not shown separately. 'White' excludes persons of Hispanic origin.

UNITS: Persons in thousands, by highest educational level attained.

Table 5.20 Employment of 12th Graders, 1992

	Hispanic	White	Total
Most recent type of work for employed students, total	100.0%	100.0%	100.0%
lawn work or odd jobs	0.9	2.5	2.2
food service	24.8	22.8	24.0
delivery person	1.1	1.5	1.6
baby-sitter or child care	2.2	4.8	4.3
camp counselor/life guard	0.5	0.9	0.7
farm worker	1.1	2.7	2.2
mechanic	1.5	1.5	1.4
grocery clerk or cashier	11.6	14.8	14.5
beautician	0.3	0.1	0.2
house cleaning	2.0	0.8	0.9
construction	1.9	2.1	2.0
office or clerical	8.7	6.3	6.9
health services	1.1	1.6	1.6
salesperson	11.9	12.0	11.8
warehouse worker	1.7	2.2	2.1
other	28.8	23.5	23.5

SOURCE: U.S. Department of Education, Center for Education Statistics, <u>Digest of Education Statistics, 2001</u>; p. 454, table 386 (Data from U.S. Department of Education, National Center for Education Statistics, "National Education Longitudinal Study of 1988,"Second Follow-up); <u>2003</u>; p. 459, table 381. ED 1.113\(year)

NOTES: 'Total' includes other races/ethnic groups not shown separately.

UNITS: Percent as a percent of all high school seniors of a given race/ethnicity who were employed in 1992.

Chapter 6: Government & Elections

Table 6.01   Hispanic Elected Public Officials, by Type of Office Held, 1985 - 2003

	State executives & legislators	County & municipal officials	Judicial & law enforcement	Education & school boards	Total
1985	129	1,316	517	1,185	3,147
1986	122	1,352	530	1,188	3,202
1987	127	1,412	568	1,199	3,317
1988	124	1,425	574	1,226	3,360
1989	133	1,724	575	1,341	3,783
1990	144	1,819	583	1,458	4,004
1991	151	1,867	596	1,588	4,202
1992	150	1,908	628	2,308	4,994
1993	182	2,023	633	2,332	5,170
1994	199	2,197	651	2,412	5,459
2000	223	1,846	454	2,682	5,205
2001	223	1,846	454	2,682	5,205
2002	208	1,960	532	1,603	4,303
2003	231	1,958	549	1,694	4,432

SOURCE: U.S. Bureau of the Census, Statistical Abstract of the United States, 2002; p. 252, table 392; 2003; p. 268, table 418; 2004; p. 255, table 406 (data from National Association of Latino Elected and Appointed Officials, *National Roster of Hispanic Elected Officials*).
C 3.134:(year)

NOTES: Data as of September. Total includes US Representatives not shown separately.

UNITS: Number of Hispanic elected public officials.

Table 6.02 Members of Congress, 1981 - 2005

	Hispanic	White	Total
House of Representatives			
97th Congress, 1981	6	415	434
98th Congress, 1983	8	411	"
99th Congress, 1985	10	412	435
100th Congress, 1987	11	408	433
101st Congress, 1989	10	406	435
102nd Congress, 1991	11	407	"
103rd Congress, 1993	17	393	"
104th Congress, 1995	17	391	"
106th Congress, 1999	19	na	"
107th Congress, 2001	19	na	443
108th Congress, 2003	22	na	435
109th Congress, 2001	na	na	435
Senate			
97th Congress, 1981	0	97	100
98th Congress, 1983	0	98	"
99th Congress, 1985	0	98	"
100th Congress, 1987	0	98	"
101st Congress, 1989	0	98	"
102nd Congress, 1991	0	98	"
103rd Congress, 1993	0	97	"
104th Congress, 1995	0	97	"
106th Congress, 1999	0	na	"
107th Congress, 2001	0	na	"
108th Congress, 2003	0	na	"
109th Congress, 2001	2	96	"

SOURCE: U.S. Bureau of the Census, Statistical Abstract of the United States, 1995; p. 281, table 444; 2002; p. 247, table 382; 2003; p. 263, table 408; 2004; p. 250, table 396 (data from Congressional Quarterly, Inc.). C 3.134:(year)
U.S. Senate HTTP://WWW.SENATE.GOV/

NOTES: 'Total' includes other races and ethnic groups not shown separately.

UNITS: Number of members of the House and Senate respectively, as shown.

Table 6.03 Voting Age Population, Registration, and Voting, 1972 - 2002

	Hispanic	White	Total
Voting age population			
1972	5.6	121.2	136.2
1974	6.1	125.1	141.3
1976	6.6	129.3	146.5
1978	6.8	133.4	151.6
1980	8.8	137.7	157.1
1982	8.8	143.6	165.5
1984	9.5	146.8	170.0
1986	11.8	149.9	173.9
1988	12.9	152.8	178.1
1990	13.8	155.6	182.1
1992	14.7	157.8	185.7
1994	17.5	160.3	190.3
1996	18.4	162.8	193.7
1998	20.3	165.8	198.2
2000	21.6	168.8	202.6
2002	25.1	174.1	210.4
Presidential election years			
percent reporting registration			
1972	44.4%	73.4%	72.3%
1976	37.8	68.3	66.7
1980	36.3	68.4	66.9
1984	40.1	69.6	68.3
1988	35.5	67.9	66.6
1992	35.0	70.1	68.2
1996	35.7	67.7	65.9
2000	57.3	70.4	69.5
percent reporting voting			
1972	37.4%	64.5	63.0%
1976	31.8	60.9	59.2
1980	29.9	60.9	59.2
1984	32.6	61.4	59.9
1988	28.8	59.1	57.4
1992	28.9	63.6	61.3
1996	26.7	56.0	54.2
2000	45.1	60.5	59.5

continued on the next page

Table 6.03   continued

	Hispanic	White	Total
Congressional election years			
percent reporting registration			
1974	34.9%	63.5%	62.6%
1978	32.9	63.8	62.6
1982	35.3	65.6	64.1
1986	35.9	65.3	64.3
1990	32.3	63.8	62.2
1994	31.3	64.6	62.5
1998	33.7	63.9	62.1
2002	32.6	63.1	60.9
percent reporting voting			
1974	22.9%	46.3%	44.7%
1978	23.5	47.3	45.9
1982	25.3	49.9	48.5
1986	24.2	47.0	46.0
1990	21.0	46.7	45.0
1994	20.2	47.3	45.0
1998	20.0	43.3	41.9
2002	18.9	44.1	42.3

SOURCE: U.S. Bureau of the Census, <u>Statistical Abstract of the United States, 1989</u>; p. 257, table 432 , <u>1999</u>; p. 300, table 487 (data from U.S. Bureau of the Census, *Current Population Reports*, Series P-20). C 3.134:9(year)

U.S. Bureau of the Census, <u>Current Population Reports: Voting and Registration in the Election of November, 1988</u>, Series P-20, #440; pp. 48-49, table 8; <u>1990</u>, Series P-20, #453; pp. 16-17, table 2; <u>1992</u>, Series P-20, #466; pp. 4-5, table 2; <u>1994</u>; Table 1, Table VI; <u>1996</u>, Series P-20, #504; table 23; <u>2000</u>, Series P-20, #542; p. 5, Table A; <u>2002</u>, Series P-20, #552; Table 2.

NOTES: 'Total' includes other races and ethnic groups not shown separately.

UNITS: Voting age population in millions of persons; percent reporting registration and percent reporting voting as a percent of the voting age population.

Table 6.04   Voting Age Population, Selected Characteristics, 1990

	Hispanic	White	Total
Voting age population, 1990			
by age			
total 18 years and over	13,756	155,587	182,118
18-20 years old	1,139	8,722	10,800
21-24 years old	1,572	11,635	14,031
25-34 years old	4,180	35,682	45,652
35-44 years old	2,886	32,281	37,889
45-54 years old	1,707	21,983	25,648
55-64 years old	1,200	18,477	21,223
65-74 years old	728	16,180	18,126
75 years and over	344	10,627	11,748
by sex			
male	6,787	74,625	86,621
female	6,968	80,962	95,496
by years of school completed			
elementary			
0-4 years of school	1,417	2,617	3,669
5-7 years of school	1,903	5,096	6,445
8 years of school	910	6,564	7,617
high school			
1-3 years high school	2,353	16,733	20,956
4 years high school	4,160	61,342	71,492
college			
1-3 years college	1,881	31,481	36,300
4 years college	679	18,900	21,350
5 or more years college	452	12,855	14,288
by family income			
under $5,000	801	4,503	6,799
$5,000-$9,999	1,425	6,978	9,808
$10,000-$14,999	1,877	11,049	13,759
$15,000-$19,999	1,185	8,677	10,496
$20,000-$24,999	1,162	10,619	12,304
$25,000-$34,999	1,832	20,827	23,627
$35,000-$49,999	1,384	22,698	25,367
$50,000 and over	1,231	30,330	32,818
income not reported	768	9,555	11,576

SOURCE: U.S. Bureau of the Census, <u>Current Population Reports: Voting and Registration in the Election of November, 1990</u>, Series P-20, #453, pp. 16-17, table 2; pp. 47-48, table 8; p. 64, table 13.
C 3.186/3-2:990

NOTES: 'Total' includes other races and ethnic groups not shown separately.

UNITS: Voting age population in thousands of persons.

Table 6.05 Selected Characteristics of Persons Registered to Vote, 1990

	Hispanic	White	Total
Persons registered to vote, 1990			
by age			
total 18 years and over	32.3%	63.8%	62.2%
18-20 years old	17.2	37.0	35.4
21-24 years old	20.9	43.1	43.3
25-34 years old	27.4	53.2	52.0
35-44 years old	34.8	67.2	65.5
45-54 years old	38.3	71.3	69.8
55-64 years old	45.5	74.9	73.5
65-74 years old	56.6	79.7	78.3
75 years and over	46.0	74.8	73.7
by sex			
male	30.0%	63.0%	61.2%
female	34.5	64.6	63.1
by years of school completed			
0-4 years of elementary school	15.3%	26.4%	29.5%
5-7 years of elementary school	15.8	38.7	41.1
8 years of elementary school	28.1	54.3	53.3
1-3 years of high school	24.6	48.2	47.9
4 years of high school	36.6	61.2	60.0
1-3 years of college	50.6	70.2	68.7
4 years of college	51.1	77.1	74.5
5 or more years of college	59.3	83.5	81.5
by households income			
under $5,000	28.2%	53.1%	50.7%
$5,000-$9,999	22.7	47.6	48.3
$10,000-$14,999	23.9	55.4	54.8
$15,000-$19,999	29.0	57.5	56.8
$20,000-$24,999	21.7	59.0	58.0
$25,000-$34,999	37.7	65.0	63.9
$35,000-$49,999	46.5	69.4	68.3
$50,000 and over	51.7	77.8	76.4
income not reported	29.6	59.7	57.6

SOURCE: U.S. Bureau of the Census, Current Population Reports: Voting and Registration in the Election of November, 1990, Series P-20, #453, pp. 16-17, table 2; pp. 47-48, table 8; p. 64, table 13. C 3.186/3-2:990

NOTES: 'Total' includes other races and ethnic groups not shown separately.

UNITS: Person reporting registration to vote as a percent of the voting age population, 100.0%.

Table 6.06   Selected Characteristics of Persons Voting, 1990

	Hispanic	White	Total
Persons voting, 1990			
by age			
total 18 years and over	21.0%	46.7%	45.0%
18-20 years old	10.1	19.4	18.4
21-24 years old	7.8	21.8	22.0
25-34 years old	16.5	34.9	33.8
35-44 years old	24.2	50.0	48.4
45-54 years old	25.4	54.9	53.2
55-64 years old	33.5	60.4	58.9
65-74 years old	43.8	65.7	64.1
75 years and over	33.4	55.8	54.5
by sex			
male	19.4%	46.4%	44.6%
female	22.6	46.9	45.4
by years of school completed			
elementary			
0-4 years of school	9.4%	14.8%	16.5%
5-7 years of school	11.3	23.7	25.7
8 years of school	15.6	35.7	34.8
high school			
1-3 years high school	13.5	31.3	30.9
4 years high school	22.5	43.6	42.2
college			
1-3 years college	36.0	51.4	50.0
4 years college	38.8	61.6	59.0
5 or more years college	45.8	69.6	67.8
by households income			
under $5,000	14.9%	35.1%	32.2%
$5,000-$9,999	14.6	31.3	30.9
$10,000-$14,999	14.5	38.5	37.7
$15,000-$19,999	16.6	39.9	38.8
$20,000-$24,999	14.9	42.5	41.3
$25,000-$34,999	26.3	47.5	46.4
$35,000-$49,999	29.8	51.8	51.0
$50,000 and over	37.8	60.5	59.2
income not reported	19.3	45.1	43.3

SOURCE: U.S. Bureau of the Census, <u>Current Population Reports: Voting and Registration in the Election of November, 1990</u>, Series P-20, #453, pp. 16-17, table 2; pp. 47-48, table 8; p. 64, table 13.
C 3.186/3-2:990

NOTES: 'Total' includes other races and ethnic groups not shown separately.

UNITS: Persons reporting voting as a percent of the voting age population, 100.0%.

Table 6.07   Voting Age Population, Selected Characteristics, 2000

	Hispanic	White	Total
Voting age population, 2000			
Total, 18 years and over	21,598	168,733	202,609
by sex			
male	10,653	69,290	97,087
female	10,945	74,361	105,523
by age			
18-24 years old	4,169	21,295	26,712
25-44 years old	10,640	66,378	81,780
45-64 years old	4,962	52,038	61,352
65-74 years old	1,110	15,493	17,819
75 years and over	718	13,529	14,945
by educational attainment			
less than 9th grade	5,272	10,626	12,894
9th to 12th grade, no diploma	3,931	15,822	20,108
high school graduate or GED	6,295	55,530	66,339
some college or associate degree	4,036	45,923	55,308
bachelor's degree	1,438	27,382	32,254
advanced degree	627	13,450	15,706
by employment status			
in civilian labor force	15,280	115,103	138,378
unemployed	826	3,544	4,944

continued on the next page

Table 6.07   continued

	Hispanic	White	Total
by family income			
less than $5,000	532	1,405	2,230
$5,000-$9,999	998	2,732	4,242
$10,000-$14,999	1,073	5,390	7,286
$15,000-$24,999	3,249	11,568	14,600
$25,000-$34,999	2,934	14,578	17,692
$35,000-$49,999	2,518	18,907	22,349
$50,000-$74.999	2,182	24,250	28,144
$75,000 and over	1,695	31,021	35,030
income not reported	1,304	17,518	20,721

SOURCE: U.S. Bureau of the Census, <u>Current Population Reports: Voting and Registration in the Election of November, 2000</u>, "(Table 2). Reported Voting and Registration, by Race, Hispanic Origin, Sex, and Age, for the United States: November 2000"; "(Table 6). Reported Voting and Registration, by Race, Hispanic Origin, Sex, and Educational Attainment: November 2000"; "(Table 7). Reported Voting and Registration, by Race, Hispanic Origin, Sex, Employment Status and Class of Worker: November 2000"; " (Table 9). Reported Voting and Registration of Family Members, by Race, Hispanic Origin, and Family Income: November 2000;" published 27 February 2002.

NOTES: 'Total' includes other races and ethnic groups not shown separately.

UNITS: Voting age population in thousands of persons.

Table 6.08   Selected Characteristics of Persons Registered to Vote, 2000

	Hispanic	White	Total
Voting age population, 2000			
Total, 18 years and over	34.9%	65.6%	63.9%
by sex			
male	31.7	64.0	62.2
female	38.1	67.2	65.6
by age			
18-24 years old	23.2	46.3	45.4
25-44 years old	31.1	61.2	59.6
45-64 years old	45.1	72.7	71.2
65-74 years old	57.2	77.3	76.2
75 years and over	55.9	77.2	76.1
by educational attainment			
less than 9th grade	17.4	34.8	36.1
9th to 12th grade, no diploma	25.4	44.8	45.9
high school graduate or GED	38.0	61.3	60.1
some college or associate degree	51.1	71.8	70.0
bachelor's degree	53.5	79.6	76.3
advanced degree	64.7	83.1	79.4
by employment status			
in civilian labor force	34.2	65.5	64.0
unemployed	22.6	44.9	46.1

continued on the next page

Table 6.08   continued

	Hispanic	White	Total
by family income			
less than $5,000	25.6%	40.7%	44.0
$5,000-$9,999	28.2	45.3	48.8
$10,000-$14,999	26.4	47.5	49.8
$15,000-$24,999	26.3	55.1	54.9
$25,000-$34,999	30.0	61.9	61.0
$35,000-$49,999	41.1	68.8	67.1
$50,000-$74.999	49.3	75.9	73.8
$75,000 and over	63.5	80.7	78.4
income not reported	32.1	55.5	54.2

SOURCE: U.S. Bureau of the Census, <u>Current Population Reports: Voting and Registration in the Election of November, 2000</u>; "(Table 2). Reported Voting and Registration, by Race, Hispanic Origin, Sex, and Age, for the United States: November 2000"; "(Table 6). Reported Voting and Registration, by Race, Hispanic Origin, Sex, and Educational Attainment: November 2000"; "(Table 7). Reported Voting and Registration, by Race, Hispanic Origin, Sex, Employment Status and Class of Worker: November 2000"; " (Table 9). Reported Voting and Registration of Family Members, by Race, Hispanic Origin, and Family Income: November 2000"; published 27 February 2002.

NOTES: 'Total' includes other races and ethnic groups not shown separately.

UNITS: Persons registered to vote as a percent of the voting age population, 100.0%..

Table 6.09   Selected Characteristics of Persons Voting, 2000

	Hispanic	White	Total
Voting age population, 2000			
Total, 18 years and over	27.5%	47.4%	41.9%
by sex			
male	25.1	47.3	41.4
female	29.8	47.4	42.4
by age			
18-24 years old	15.4	33.0	32.3
25-44 years old	23.2	51.2	49.8
45-64 years old	38.3	65.6	64.1
65-74 years old	50.9	71.1	69.9
75 years and over	48.7	66.2	64.9
by educational attainment			
less than 9th grade	14.0	25.8	26.8
9th to 12th grade, no diploma	17.4	32.7	33.6
high school graduate or GED	28.7	50.4	49.4
some college or associate degree	41.1	62.0	60.3
bachelor's degree	47.0	73.4	70.3
advanced degree	59.8	79.3	75.5
by employment status			
in civilian labor force	26.7	56.2	54.8
unemployed	15.5	34.6	35.1

continued on the next page

Table 6.09   continued

	Hispanic	White	Total
by family income			
less than $5,000	16.2%	27.3%	28.2%
$5,000-$9,999	20.8	32.5	34.7
$10,000-$14,999	19.7	35.6	37.7
$15,000-$24,999	19.4	43.3	43.4
$25,000-$34,999	23.6	51.8	51.0
$35,000-$49,999	31.5	58.8	57.5
$50,000-$74.999	39.5	67.1	65.2
$75,000 and over	57.0	73.8	71.5
income not reported	27.1	49.6	48.2

SOURCE: U.S. Bureau of the Census, <u>Current Population Reports: Voting and Registration in the Election of November, 2000</u>; "(Table 2). Reported Voting and Registration, by Race, Hispanic Origin, Sex, and Age, for the United States: November 2000"; "(Table 6). Reported Voting and Registration, by Race, Hispanic Origin, Sex, and Educational Attainment: November 2000"; "(Table 7). Reported Voting and Registration, by Race, Hispanic Origin, Sex, Employment Status and Class of Worker: November 2000"; " (Table 9). Reported Voting and Registration of Family Members, by Race, Hispanic Origin, and Family Income: November 2000"; published 27 February 2002.

NOTES: 'Total' includes other races and ethnic groups not shown separately.

UNITS: Persons reporting voting as a percent of the voting age population, 100.0%.

Table 6.10   Voting Age Population, Selected Characteristics, 2002

	Hispanic	White	Total
Voting age population, 2002			
Total, 18 years and over	25,162	174,099	210,421
by sex			
male	12,855	84,466	100,939
Female	12,307	89,633	109,481
by age			
18-24 years old	4,825	21,728	27,377
25-44 years old	12,860	66,238	82,228
45-64 years old	5,586	56,204	66,924
65-74 years old	1,131	15,653	17,967
75 years and over	760	14,276	15,925
by educational attainment			
less than 9th grade	5,689	10,195	12,333
9th to 12th grade, no diploma	4,561	16,161	20,908
high school graduate or GED	7,341	57,210	68,866
some college or associate degree	4,983	47,538	57,343
bachelor's degree	1,848	28,693	34,095
advanced degree	740	14,302	16,877
by employment status			
in civilian labor force	17,922	118,094	142,635
unemployed	1,307	5,488	7,735

continued on the next page

Table 6.10   continued

	Hispanic	White	Total
by family income			
less than $5,000	529	1,280	2,159
$5,000-$9,999	1,042	2,707	4,051
$10,000-$14,999	1,697	4,960	6,696
$15,000-$24,999	3,556	11,696	14,665
$25,000-$34,999	2,988	13,412	16,868
$35,000-$49,999	3,370	18,200	21,945
$50,000-$74.999	2,640	24,932	28,921
$75,000 and over	2,320	35,540	40,309
income not reported	1,577	18,188	22,278

SOURCE: U.S. Bureau of the Census, <u>Current Population Reports: Voting and Registration in the Election of November, 2002</u>; published July 2004; "(Table 2). Reported Voting and Registration, by Race, Hispanic Origin, Sex, and Age, for the United States: November 2002"; "(Table 6). Reported Voting and Registration, by Race, Hispanic Origin, Sex, and Educational Attainment: November 2002"; "(Table 7). Reported Voting and Registration, by Race, Hispanic Origin, Sex, Employment Status and Class of Worker: November 2002"; "(Table 9). Reported Voting and Registration of Family Members, by Race, Hispanic Origin, and Family Income: November 2002".

NOTES: 'Total' includes other races not shown separately.

UNITS: Voting age population in thousands of persons.

Table 6.11   Selected Characteristics of Persons Registered to Vote, 2002

	Hispanic	White	Total
Voting age population, 2002			
Total, 18 years and over	32.6%	63.1%	60.9%
by sex			
Male	29.4	61.3	58.9
Female	35.9	64.8	62.8
by age			
18-24 years old	20.8	39.2	38.2
25-44 years old	28.9	57.4	55.4
45-64 years old	43.6	71.3	69.4
65-74 years old	56.1	77.9	76.1
75 years and over	53.0	76.7	75.5
by educational attainment			
less than 9th grade	17.0	31.6	32.4
9th to 12th grade, no diploma	21.9	41.1	41.6
high school graduate or GED	34.1	58.7	57.1
some college or associate degree	49.4	68.8	66.7
bachelor's degree	46.6	76.7	73.3
advanced degree	54.7	81.3	76.6
by employment status			
in civilian labor force	32.6	62.8	60.9
Unemployed	25.6	48.6	48.1

continued on the next page

Table 6.11   continued

	Hispanic	White	Total
by family income			
less than $5,000	20.4%	39.5%	45.2%
$5,000-$9,999	25.6	40.1	41.5
$10,000-$14,999	31.0	50.3	49.7
$15,000-$24,999	23.7	51.0	51.3
$25,000-$34,999	28.8	58.5	56.2
$35,000-$49,999	32.6	64.1	62.0
$50,000-$74.999	44.9	72.0	69.8
$75,000 and over	56.9	77.8	75.5
income not reported	29.9	54.4	52.0

SOURCE: U.S. Bureau of the Census, <u>Current Population Reports: Voting and Registration in the Election of November, 2002</u>; published July 2004; "(Table 2). Reported Voting and Registration, by Race, Hispanic Origin, Sex, and Age, for the United States: November 2002"; "(Table 6). Reported Voting and Registration, by Race, Hispanic Origin, Sex, and Educational Attainment: November 2002"; "(Table 7). Reported Voting and Registration, by Race, Hispanic Origin, Sex, Employment Status and Class of Worker: November 2002"; "(Table 9). Reported Voting and Registration of Family Members, by Race, Hispanic Origin, and Family Income: November 2002".

NOTES: 'Total' includes other races not shown separately.

UNITS: Persons registered to vote as a percent of the voting age population, 100.0%.

Table 6.12   Selected Characteristics of Persons Voting, 2002

	Hispanic	White	Total
Voting age population, 2002			
Total, 18 years and over	18.9%	44.1%	42.3%
by sex			
male	17.3	43.5	41.4
female	20.5	44.6	43.0
by age			
18-24 years old	8.1	17.4	17.2
25-44 years old	15.3	35.3	34.1
45-64 years old	28.7	54.8	53.1
65-74 years old	43.3	65.1	63.1
75 years and over	38.8	60.1	58.6
by educational attainment			
less than 9th grade	10.1	19.0	19.4
9th to 12th grade, no diploma	10.5	23.1	23.3
high school graduate or GED	18.8	38.3	37.1
some college or associate degree	28.1	47.3	45.8
bachelor's degree	32.4	59.1	56.2
advanced degree	42.4	67.7	63.2
by employment status			
in civilian labor force	18.3	42.7	41.3
unemployed	12.4	28.2	27.2

continued on the next page

Table 6.12   continued

	Hispanic	White	Total
by family income			
less than $5,000	7.6%	19.6%	22.0%
$5,000-$9,999	11.5	19.8	20.7
$10,000-$14,999	17.1	31.1	30.5
$15,000-$24,999	12.5	31.9	32.0
$25,000-$34,999	16.3	40.2	38.3
$35,000-$49,999	18.1	44.2	42.7
$50,000-$74.999	28.2	51.7	50.1
$75,000 and over	36.5	58.3	56.6
income not reported	20.7	40.5	38.6

SOURCE: U.S. Bureau of the Census, Current Population Reports: Voting and Registration in the Election of November, 2002; published July 2004; "(Table 2). Reported Voting and Registration, by Race, Hispanic Origin, Sex, and Age, for the United States: November 2002"; "(Table 6). Reported Voting and Registration, by Race, Hispanic Origin, Sex, and Educational Attainment: November 2002"; "(Table 7). Reported Voting and Registration, by Race, Hispanic Origin, Sex, Employment Status and Class of Worker: November 2002"; "(Table 9). Reported Voting and Registration of Family Members, by Race, Hispanic Origin, and Family Income: November 2002".

NOTES: 'Total' includes other races not shown separately.

UNITS: Persons reporting voting as a percent of the voting age population, 100.0%.

Chapter 7: The Labor Force, Employment & Unemployment

Table 7.01 Labor Force Participation of the Civilian Noninstitutional
Population 16 Years Old & Over, by Age, 1985 - 2004

	Hispanic	White	Total
1985			
civilian noninstitutional population			
all persons 16 years old and over	11,915	153,679	178,206
- persons 16-19 years old	1,298	11,900	14,506
- persons 20 years old and over	10,617	141,780	163,700
- persons 65 years old and over	843	24,352	26,977
civilian labor force			
all persons 16 years old and over	7,698	99,926	115,461
- persons 16-19 years old	579	6,841	7,901
- persons 20 years old and over	7,119	93,085	107,560
- persons 65 years old and over	82	2,605	2,907
labor force participation rate			
all persons 16 years old and over	64.6%	65.0%	64.8%
- persons 16-19 years old	44.6	57.5	54.5
- persons 20 years old and over	67.1	65.7	65.7
- persons 65 years old and over	9.7	10.7	10.8

continued on the next page

Table 7.01   continued

	Hispanic	White	Total
1990			
civilian noninstitutional population			
all persons 16 years old and over	14,297	160,415	188,049
- persons 16-19 years old	1,424	11,095	13,794
- persons 20 years old and over	12,873	149,320	174,255
- persons 65 years old and over	na	26,643	29,730
civilian labor force			
all persons 16 years old and over	9576	107,177	124,787
- persons 16-19 years old	672	6,374	7,410
- persons 20 years old and over	8,904	100,803	117,377
- persons 65 years old and over	na	3,189	3,535
labor force participation rate			
all persons 16 years old and over	67.0%	66.8%	66.4%
- persons 16-19 years old	47.2	57.5	53.7
- persons 20 years old and over	69.2	62.8	62.4
- persons 65 years old and over	na	12.0	11.9

continued on the next page

Table 7.01 continued

	Hispanic	White	Total
2000			
civilian noninstitutional population all persons 16 years old and over	22,393	174,428	209,699
- persons 16-19 years old	2,341	12,707	16,042
- persons 65 years old and over	1,791	28,947	32,705
civilian labor force all persons 16 years old and over	15,368	117,574	140,863
- persons 16-19 years old	1,083	7,075	8,369
- persons 65 years old and over	218	3,749	4,200
labor force participation rate all persons 16 years old and over	68.6%	67.4%	67.2%
- persons 16-19 years old	46.3	55.7	52.2
- persons 65 years old and over	12.2	13.0	12.8

continued on the next page

Table 7.01   continued

	Hispanic	White	Total
2004			
civilian noninstitutional			
population			
all persons 16 years old			
and over	28,109	182,643	223,357
- persons 16-19 years old	2,608	12,599	16,222
- persons 65 years old			
and over	2,115	30,245	34,609
civilian labor force			
all persons 16 years old			
and over	19,272	121,086	147,401
- persons 16-19 years old	995	5,929	7,114
- persons 65 years old			
and over	306	4,408	4,998
labor force participation rate			
all persons 16 years old			
and over	68.6%	66.3%	66.0%
- persons 16-19 years old	38.2	47.1	43.9
- persons 65 years old			
and over	14.5	14.6	14.4

SOURCE: U.S. Department of Labor, Bureau of Labor Statistics, <u>Handbook of Labor Statistics, 1989</u>, pp. 13-30, tables 3-5. L 2.3/5:989
U.S. Department of Labor, Bureau of Labor Statistics, *Employment and Earnings*, <u>January, 1991</u>; pp. 164-166, table 3; <u>January, 2001</u>; pp. 168-170, table 3; <u>January, 2002</u>; pp. 166-168, table 3, p. 169, table 5; <u>January, 2004</u>; pp. 196-199, table 3, p. 200, table 4 (data from the Current Population Survey). L2.41/2:(vol)/1:(year)

NOTES: 'Total' includes other races and ethnic groups not shown separately.

UNITS: Civilian noninstitutional population and civilian labor force in thousands of persons; participation rate as a percent (the civilian noninstitutional population divided by the civilian labor force).

Table 7.02 Labor Force Participation of the Civilian Noninstitutional Population 16 Years Old and Over, by Sex and Age, 1985 - 2004

	Hispanic		White		Total	
	male	female	male	female	male	female
1985						
civilian noninstitutional population						
all persons 16 years old and over	5,885	6,029	73,373	80,306	84,469	93,736
- persons 16-19 years old	654	644	5,987	5,912	7,275	7,231
- persons 20 years old and over	5,232	5,385	67,386	74,394	77,195	86,506
- persons 65 years old and over	354	489	10,010	14,342	11,084	15,913
civilian labor force						
all persons 16 years old and over	4,729	2,970	56,472	43,455	64,411	51,050
- persons 16-19 years old	334	245	3,576	3,265	4,134	3,767
- persons 20 years old and over	4,395	2,725	52,895	40,190	60,277	47,283
- persons 65 years old and over	53	29	1,595	1,010	1,750	1,156
labor force participation rate						
all persons 16 years old and over	80.3%	49.3%	77.0%	54.1%	76.3%	54.5%
- persons 16-19 years old	51.0	38.1	59.7	55.2	56.8	52.1
- persons 20 years old and over	84.0	50.6	78.5	54.0	78.1	54.7
- persons 65 years old and over	14.9	5.9	15.9	7.0	15.8	7.3

continued on the next page

Table 7.02   continued

	Hispanic		White		Total	
	male	female	male	female	male	female
1990						
civilian noninstitutional population						
all persons 16 years old and over	7,087	7,210	77,082	83,332	89,650	98,399
- persons 16-19 years old	721	703	5,600	5,495	6,947	6,847
- persons 20 years old and over	6,366	6,507	71,482	77,837	82,703	91,552
- persons 65 years old and over	na	na	11,129	15,514	12,392	17,337
civilian labor force						
all persons 16 years old and over	5,755	3,821	58,298	47,879	68,234	56,554
- persons 16-19 years old	401	271	3,329	3,046	3,866	3,544
- persons 20 years old and over	5,354	3,550	54,969	44,833	64,368	53,010
- persons 65 years old and over	na	na	1,865	1,325	2,033	1,502
labor force participation rate						
all persons 16 years old and over	81.2%	53.0%	76.9%	57.5%	76.1%	57.5%
- persons 16-19 years old	55.6	38.5	59.4	55.4	55.7	51.8
- persons 20 years old and over	84.1	54.6	78.3	57.6	77.8	57.9
- persons 65 years old and over	na	na	16.8	8.5	16.4	8.7

continued on the next page

Table 7.02   continued

	Hispanic		White		Total	
	male	female	male	female	male	female
2000						
civilian noninstitutional population all persons 16 years old						
and over	11,064	11,329	84,647	89,781	100,731	108,968
- persons 16-19 years old	1,205	1,136	6,496	6,211	8,151	7,890
- persons 65 years old						
and over	759	1,032	12,390	16,557	13,925	18,780
civilian labor force all persons 16 years old						
and over	8,919	6,449	63,861	53,714	75,247	65,616
- persons 16-19 years old	613	470	3,679	3,396	4,317	4,051
- persons 65 years old						
and over	138	80	2,198	1,550	2,439	1,762
labor force participation rate all persons 16 years old						
and over	80.6%	56.9%	75.4%	59.8%	74.7%	60.2%
- persons 16-19 years old	50.9	41.4	56.6	54.7	53.0	51.3
- persons 65 years old						
and over	18.2	7.7	17.7	9.4	17.5	9.4

continued on the next page

Table 7.02   continued

	Hispanic		White		Total	
	male	female	male	female	male	female
2004						
civilian noninstitutional population						
all persons 16 years old						
and over	14,417	13,692	89,044	93,599	107,710	115,647
- persons 16-19 years old	1,336	1,272	6,429	6,169	8,234	7,989
- persons 65 years old						
and over	894	1,221	12,946	17,299	14,684	19,925
civilian labor force						
all persons 16 years old						
and over	11,587	7,685	65,994	55,092	78,980	68,421
- persons 16-19 years old	567	429	3,050	2,879	3,616	3,498
- persons 65 years old						
and over	186	119	2,478	1,930	2,787	2,211
labor force participation rate						
all persons 16 years old						
and over	80.4%	56.1%	74.1%	58.9%	73.3%	59.2%
- persons 16-19 years old	42.4	33.7	47.4	46.7	43.9	43.8
- persons 65 years old						
and over	20.8	9.8	19.1	11.2	19.0	11.1

SOURCE: U.S. Department of Labor, Bureau of Labor Statistics, <u>Handbook of Labor Statistics, 1989</u>, pp. 13-30, tables 3-5. L 2.3/5:989

U.S. Department of Labor, Bureau of Labor Statistics, *Employment and Earnings*, <u>January, 1991</u>; pp. 164-166, table 3; <u>January, 2001</u>; pp. 168-170, table 3; <u>January, 2002</u>; pp. 166-168, table 3, p. 169, table 4; <u>January, 2005</u>; pp. 196-199, table 3, p. 200, table 4 (data from the Current Population Survey). L2.41/2:(vol)/1:(year)

NOTES: 'Total' includes other races and ethnic groups not shown separately.

UNITS: Civilian noninstitutional population and civilian labor force in thousands of persons; participation rate as a percent (the civilian noninstitutional population divided by the civilian labor force).

Table 7.03 Labor Force Participation of the Hispanic Civilian Noninstitutional Population 16 Years Old and Over, by Type of Hispanic Origin, 1990, 2000 and 2002

	Mexican	Puerto Rican	Cuban	Central/ South American	Other Hispanic	Total Hispanic
1990						
Total population 16 years and over						
number	8,696	1,492	839	2,106	1,079	114,212
percent	100.0%	100.0%	100.0%	100.0%	100.0%	100.0%
In the labor force						
number	5,871	805	554	1,509	709	9,449
percent	67.5%	54.0%	66.0%	71.7%	65.7%	66.5%
Male population 16 years and over						
number	4,493	673	402	991	511	7,069
percent	100.0%	100.0%	100.0%	100.0%	100.0%	100.0%
In the labor force						
number	3,647	466	301	829	385	5,629
percent	81.2%	69.2%	74.9%	83.7%	75.3%	79.6%
Female population 16 years and over						
number	4,203	819	438	1,114	568	7,143
percent	100.0%	100.0%	100.0%	100.0%	100.0%	100.0%
In the labor force						
number	2,224	339	253	680	324	3,821
percent	52.9%	41.4%	57.8%	61.0%	57.0%	53.5%

continued on the next page

Table 7.03   continued

	Mexican	Puerto Rican	Cuban	Central/ South American	Other Hispanic	Total Hispanic
2000						
Total population 16 years and over						
Number	14,144	2,040	1,073	3,472	1,440	22,170
Percent	100.0%	100.0%	100.0%	100.0%	100.0%	100.0%
In the labor force						
Number	9,720	1,309	658	2,492	984	15,163
Percent	68.7%	64.2%	61.3%	71.8%	68.4%	68.4%
Male population 16 years and over						
Number	7,197	959	518	1,618	669	10,961
Percent	100.0%	100.0%	100.0%	100.0%	100.0%	100.0%
In the labor force						
Number	5,903	667	383	1,361	502	8,817
Percent	82.0%	69.6%	74.0%	84.1%	75.1%	80.4%
Female population 16 years and over						
Number	6,947	1,081	555	1,854	771	11,209
Percent	100.0%	100.0%	100.0%	100.0%	100.0%	100.0%
In the labor force						
Number	3,816	642	275	1,131	482	6,346
Percent	54.9%	59.3%	49.5%	61.0%	62.5%	56.6%

continued on the next page

Table 7.03   continued

	Mexican	Puerto Rican	Cuban	Central/ South American	Other Hispanic	Total Hispanic
2002						
Total population 16 years and over						
number	16,516	2,312	1,134	4,009	1,672	25,642
percent	100.0%	100.0%	100.0%	100.0%	100.0%	100.0%
In the labor force						
number	11,490	1,406	651	2,934	1,108	17,588
percent	69.6%	60.8%	57.4%	73.2%	66.3%	68.6%
Male population 16 years and over						
number	8,620	1,075	559	2,014	783	13,051
percent	100.0%	100.0%	100.0%	100.0%	100.0%	100.0%
In the labor force						
number	6,987	721	365	1,672	569	10,313
percent	81.1%	67.0%	65.2%	83.0%	72.7%	79.0%
Female population 16 years and over						
number	7,896	1,237	574	1,995	889	12,591
percent	100.0%	100.0%	100.0%	100.0%	100.0%	100.0%
In the labor force						
number	4,504	685	286	1,262	539	7,275
percent	57.0%	55.4%	49.8%	63.3%	60.6%	57.8%

SOURCE: U.S. Bureau of the Census, <u>The Hispanic Population in the United States: March, 1990</u>, pp. 8-9, table 2 (data from U.S. Bureau of the Census, *Current Population Reports*). C 3.186/14-2:990

U.S. Bureau of the Census, <u>Current Population Reports: The Hispanic Population of the United States, 2000</u>; "Table 9.1. Labor Force Status of the Civilian Population 16 Years and Over by Sex, Hispanic Origin and Race: March 2000," published March 6, 2001; <u>2002</u>; Internet Release date: 18 June 2003; "Table 9.1 Labor Force Status of the Civilian Population 16 Years and Over by Sex, Hispanic Origin, and Race: March 2002"; "Table 9.2 Labor Force Status of the Civilian Population 16 Years and Over by Sex, and Hispanic Origin Type: March 2002".

NOTES: 'Other Hispanic origin' includes persons from Spain and persons identifying themselves generally as Hispanic, Spanish, Spanish-American, Hispano, Latino, etc.

UNITS: Total population in thousands of persons 16 years old and over; percent as a percent of total shown (100.0%).

Table 7.04 Civilian Labor Force and Civilian Labor Force Participation Rates: Projections for 2008 and 2012

	Hispanic	White	Total
2008			
civilian labor force			
total	19.6	126.7	154.6
men	11.0	67.7	81.1
women	8.6	59.0	73.4
labor force participation rate			
total	67.7%	67.9%	67.6%
men	77.9	74.5	73.7
women	57.9	61.5	61.9
2012			
civilian labor force			
total	23.8	130.4	162.3
men	13.7	70.6	85.3
women	10.1	59.8	77.0
labor force participation rate			
total	68.8%	66.2%	67.2%
men	79.0	73.5	73.1
women	58.6	59.2	61.6

SOURCE: U.S. Bureau of the Census, <u>Statistical Abstract of the United States, 2000</u>; p. 403, table 644; <u>2002</u>; p. 367, table 561; <u>2004</u>; p. 371, table 570 (data from U.S. Department of Labor, Bureau of Labor Statistics) C 3.134:(year)

NOTES: 'Total' includes other races and ethnic groups not shown separately.

UNITS: Civilian labor force population 16 years old and over in millions of persons; labor force participation rate as a percent (the civilian noninstitutional population divided by the civilian labor force).

Table 7.05 Employed Members of the Civilian Labor Force, by Sex and Age, 1990 - 2004

	Hispanic		White		Total	
	male	female	male	female	male	female
1990						
all employed persons 16 years old and over	5,304	3,504	56,432	45,654	64,435	53,479
- persons 16-19 years old	323	218	2,856	2,662	3,237	3,024
- persons 20 years old and over	4,981	3,286	53,576	42,992	61,198	50,455
- persons 65 years old and over	na	na	1,812	1,288	1,972	1,455
2000						
all employed persons 16 years old and over	8,478	6,014	61,696	51,780	72,293	62,915
- persons 16-19 years old	517	385	3,227	3,043	3,713	3,563
- persons 65 years old and over	130	152	2,130	1,512	2,357	1,713
2004						
all employed persons 16 years old and over	10,832	7,098	62,712	52,527	74,524	64,728
- persons 16-19 years old	446	346	2,553	2,486	2,952	2,955
- persons 65 years old and over	174	114	2,390	1,870	2,683	2,135

SOURCE: U.S. Department of Labor, Bureau of Labor Statistics, *Employment and Earnings*, January, 1991; pp. 164-166, table 3; January, 2001; pp. 168-170, table 3; January, 2002; pp. 166-169, table 3 and table 4; January, 2005; pp. 196-199, table 3, p. 200, table 4 (data from the Current Population Survey). L2.41/2:(vol)/1:(year)

NOTES: 'Total' includes other races and ethnic groups not shown separately. Data covers members of the civilian labor force.

UNITS: Employed members of the civilian labor force in thousands of persons, by age group as shown.

Table 7.06   Employed Hispanic Persons as Percent of All Employed Persons in the Civilian Labor Force, by Selected Occupation, 2004

	Hispanic	Total
2004		
All occupations	12.9%	139,252
Management occupations	6.3	14,555
chief executive	3.7	1,680
general and operations managers	7.1	795
computer and information systems managers	5.2	337
financial managers	6.9	1,045
education administrators	5.3	757
medical and health services managers	4.7	508
Business and financial operations occupations	6.5	5,680
accountants and auditors	6.7	1,723
insurance underwriters	4.9	98
wholesale and retail buyers, except farm products	8.0	212
Computer and mathematical occupations	5.5	3,140
computer scientists and systems analysts	6.6	700
database administrators	3.3	94
operations research analysts	5.9	90
Architecture and engineering occupations	5.7	2,760
architects, except naval	7.1	207
aerospace engineers	4.2	113
chemical engineers	3.4	63
civil engineers	4.6	293
engineering technicians, except drafters	8.8	416
Life, physical, and social science occupations	5.1	1,365
medical scientists	3.1	93
environmental scientists and geoscientists	2.3	86
psychologists	4.6	185
Legal occupations	5.7	1,554
lawyers	3.4	954
judges, magistrate, and other judicial workers	7.4	64
Education, training and library occupations	6.9	7,900
Healthcare practitioner and technical occupations	5.5	6,721
dentists	4.1	167
physicians and surgeons	5.3	830
registered nurses	4.4	2,464

continued on the next page

Table 7.06   continued

	Hispanic	Total
Arts, design, entertainment, sports and media occupations	7.5	2,687
Healthcare support occupations	13.1	2,921
Protective service occupations	11.1	2,847
fire fighters	8.6	268
police and sheriff's patrol officers	12.7	664
Food preparation and serving related occupations	19.3	7,279
Building and grounds cleaning and maintenance	32.0	5,185
Personal care and service occupations	12.7	4,488
Sales and related occupations	10.3	15,983
cashiers	15.9	2,971
retail salespersons	10.9	3,130
real estate brokers and sales agents	6.7	912
Office and administrative occupations	11.1	19,481
Farming, fishing and forestry occupations	39.0	991
Construction and extraction occupations	25.0	8,522
carpenters	21.8	1,764
construction laborers	38.1	1,234
electricians	13.6	781
Installation, maintenance and repair	14.1	5,069
Production occupations	20.0	9,462
electrical and electronic assemblers	21.1	226
machinist	10.9	445
printing machine operators	15.2	195
medical, dental, ophthalmic laboratory technicians	15.4	92
Transportation and material moving	18.3	8,491
aircraft pilots and flight engineers	3.2	118
bus drivers	12.8	602
industrial truck and tractor operators	25.0	530
refuse and recyclable material collectors	14.4	81

SOURCE: U.S. Department of Labor, Bureau of Labor Statistics, *Employment and Earnings*, January, 2005, pp. 209-214, table 11 (data from the Current Population Survey). L 2.41/2:408/1: (year)

NOTES: Only selected subcategories of occupational groups displayed.

UNITS: Employed Hispanic persons as a percent of all employed persons, by occupation. Employed persons in thousands.

Table 7.07 Employed Hispanic Persons, by Occupation, as Percent of All Employed Hispanic Persons, by Sex, by Type of Hispanic Origin, 2002

	Mexican	Puerto Rican	Cuban	Central/ South American	Other Hispanic	Total Hispanic
Total employed						
number	10,529	1,271	611	2,735	1,013	16,160
percent	100.0%	100.0%	100.0%	100.0%	100.0%	100.0%
All employed males						
number	6,392	638	346	1,562	520	9,457
percent	100.0%	100.0%	100.0%	100.0%	100.0%	100.0%
by occupation						
managerial and professional	563	103	75	204	128	1,073
percent	8.8%	16.1%	21.6%	13.0%	24.6%	11.3%
technical, sales, and administrative support	781	137	91	226	104	1,338
percent	12.2%	21.4%	26.2%	14.5%	20.0%	14.1%
service occupations	1,130	138	48	324	68	1,708
percent	17.7%	21.7%	13.8%	20.7%	13.0%	18.1%
precision production, craft, and repair	1,569	119	67	321	100	2,175
percent	24.5%	18.7%	19.3%	20.5%	19.1%	23.0%
operators, fabricators, and laborers	1,816	131	64	425	104	2,539
percent	28.4%	20.6%	18.4%	27.2%	19.9%	26.8%
farming, forestry, and fishing	533	9	3	63	17	625
percent	8.3%	1.5%	0.7%	4.0%	3.3%	6.6%

continued on the next page

Table 7.07   continued

	Mexican	Puerto Rican	Cuban	Central/ South American	Other Hispanic	Total Hispanic
All employed females						
number	4,138	633	265	1,174	493	6,703
percent	100.0%	100.0%	100.0%	100.0%	100.0%	100.0%
by occupation						
managerial and professional	690	145	66	197	118	1,216
percent	16.7%	22.8%	24.8%	16.8%	24.0%	18.1%
technical, sales, and administrative support	1,528	277	114	363	197	2,479
percent	36.9%	43.8%	42.9%	31.0%	39.9%	37.0%
service occupations	1,110	142	62	423	126	1,862
percent	26.8%	22.4%	23.2%	36%	25.5%	27.8%
precision production, craft, and repair	136	11	7	35	15	204
percent	3.3%	1.7%	2.8%	3.0%	3.0%	3.0%
operators, fabricators, and laborers	574	55	17	148	35	829
percent	13.9%	8.8%	6.3%	12.6%	7.1%	12.4%
farming, forestry, and fishing	100	3	-	7	3	113
percent	2.4%	0.4%	0.1%	0.6%	0.6%	1.7%

SOURCE: U.S. Bureau of the Census, <u>Current Population Reports: The Hispanic Population of the United States, 2002</u>; Internet Release date: 18 June 2003; "Table 10.1 Occupation of the Employed Civilian Population 16 Years and Over by Sex, Hispanic Origin, and Race: March 2002"; "Table 10.2 Occupation of the Employed Civilian Population 16 Years and Over by Sex, and Hispanic Origin Type: March 2002".

NOTES: Total population includes other races and ethnic groups not shown separately. 'Other Hispanic origin' includes persons from Spain and persons identifying themselves generally as Hispanic, Spanish, Spanish-American, Hispano, Latino, etc. '-' represents or rounds to zero.

UNITS: Employed persons in thousands of persons 16 years old and over; percent as a percent of total shown (100.0%).

Table 7.08   Employed Hispanic Persons as Percent of All Employed Persons in the Civilian Labor Force, by Industry Group, 2004

2004	Hispanic	Total
All industries	12.9%	139,252
agriculture, forestry, fishing, and hunting	19.6	2,232
mining	11.3	539
construction	21.4	10,768
manufacturing	14.3	16,484
durable goods	11.8	10,329
nondurable goods	18.6	6,155
wholesale and retail trade	12.3	20,869
wholesale trade	13.3	4,600
retail trade	12.0	16,269
transportation and warehousing	13.4	5,844
utilities	7.0	1,168
information	9.2	3,463
finance and insurance	7.8	6,940
real estate and rental and leasing	12.3	3,029
legal services	7.6	1,591
architectural, engineering and related services	5.1	1,361
scientific research and development services	5.1	509
management, administrative and waste services	23.3	5,722
educational services	8.2	12,058
hospitals	8.3	5,700
health services, except hospitals	9.4	8,118
social assistance	13.6	2,844
arts, entertainment, and recreation	10.8	2,690
accommodation and food services	19.6	9,131
services	15.0	6,903
public administration	8.3	6,365

SOURCE: U.S. Department of Labor, Bureau of Labor Statistics, *Employment and Earnings*, January, 2005, pp. 226-230, table 18 (data from the Current Population Survey).   L 2.41/2:40/1: (year)

NOTES: Only selected subcategories of industry groups are displayed.

UNITS: Employed Black persons as a percent of all employed persons, by industry group. Employ persons are 16 years and older and in thousands.

Table 7.09 Full-Time and Part-Time Status of the Labor Force, by Region, 2002

	Hispanic	White	Total
2002			
Northeast			
Employed persons			
Full-time workers, total	1,887	17,818	21,240
35 hours of more	1,704	15,605	18,650
at work 1 to 34 hours			
for economic reasons	31	197	231
not at work	52	705	821
Part-time workers, total	314	4,228	4,786
at work for economic reasons	71	400	503
not at work	12	268	298
Unemployed persons			
Looking for full-time work	184	976	1,308
Looking for part-time work	-	198	242
Midwest			
Employed persons			
Full-time workers, total	1,266	23,108	26,061
35 hours of more	1,129	20,240	22,858
at work 1 to 34 hours			
for economic reasons	29	329	374
not at work	37	848	940
Part-time workers, total	210	5,638	6,186
at work for economic reasons	52	466	571
not at work	-	367	398
Unemployed persons			
Looking for full-time work	112	1,194	1,550
Looking for part-time work	-	272	329

continued on the next page

Table 7.09 continued

	Hispanic	White	Total
South			
Employed persons			
Full-time workers, total	5,195	31,949	40,689
35 hours of more	4,614	28,150	35,828
at work 1 to 34 hours			
for economic reasons	118	451	579
not at work	141	1,037	1,330
Part-time workers, total	842	5,808	7,172
at work for economic reasons	201	628	897
not at work	34	370	436
Unemployed persons			
Looking for full-time work	382	1,561	2,456
Looking for part-time work	56	281	393
West			
Employed persons			
Full-time workers, total	5,987	20,924	25,116
35 hours of more	5,318	18,332	22,066
at work 1 to 34 hours			
for economic reasons	166	396	451
not at work	155	691	831
Part-time workers, total	1,092	4,848	5,695
at work for economic reasons	263	647	798
not at work	42	302	352
Unemployed persons			
Looking for full-time work	517	1,387	1,780
Looking for part-time work	83	289	355

SOURCE: U.S. Department of Labor, Bureau of Labor Statistics, <u>Geographic Profile of Employment and Unemployment, 2002</u>, table 2. L 2.3/12:002

NOTES: 'Total' includes other races and ethnic groups not shown separately. The full-time labor force includes persons working part time for economic reasons (slack work; material shortages; repairs to plant or equipment; start or termination of a job during the week; and inability to find full time work). '-' represents data not shown for not meeting Bureau of Labor Statistics' publication standards for reliability.

UNITS: Members of the civilian labor force in thousands of persons, by status, as shown.

Table 7.10   Unemployment Rates for the Civilian Labor Force, by Age,
1990 - 2004

	Hispanic	White	Total
1990			
unemployment rate			
all ages	8.0%	4.7%	5.5%
- persons 16-19 years old	19.5	13.4	15.5
- persons 25 years old and over	6.8	3.8	4.4
- persons 55 years old and over	6.4	3.4	3.6
2000			
unemployment rate			
all ages	5.7%	3.5%	4.0%
- persons 16-19 years old	16.7	11.4	13.1
- persons 20-24 years old	7.5	5.8	7.1
- persons 25-54 years old	4.4	2.7	3.1
- persons 55-64 years old	4.5	2.4	2.5
- persons 65 years old and over	5.7	2.8	3.1
2004			
unemployment rate			
all ages	7.0%	4.8%	5.5%
- persons 16-19 years old	20.4	15.0	17.0
- persons 20-24 years old	9.3	7.9	9.4
- persons 25-54 years old	5.7	4.0	4.6
- persons 55-64 years old	5.8	3.6	3.8
- persons 65 years old and over	6.0	3.3	3.6

SOURCE: U.S. Department of Labor, Bureau of Labor Statistics, <u>Handbook of Labor Statistics, 1989</u>, pp. 136-141, table 28, (data from the Current Population Survey). L 2.3/5:989

U.S. Department of Labor, Bureau of Labor Statistics, *Employment and Earnings*, <u>January, 1991</u>; p. 208, table 39; p. 212, table 44; <u>January, 2001</u>; p. 168-169, table 3; p. 171, table 4; <u>January, 2002;</u> pp. 166-169, table 3; <u>January, 2005;</u> pp. 196-199, table 3; p. 200, table 4 (data from the Current Population Survey). L 2.41/2:(vol.)/1:(year)

NOTES: 'Total' includes other races and ethnic groups not shown separately. Data covers members of the civilian labor force.

UNITS: Unemployment rate, by age group as shown.

Table 7.11 Unemployment Rates for the Civilian Labor Force, by Sex and Age, 1990 - 2004

	Hispanic		White		Total	
	male	female	male	female	male	female
1990						
unemployment rate						
all ages	7.8%	8.3%	4.8%	4.6%	5.5%	5.6%
- persons 16-19 years old	19.4	19.6	14.2	12.6	16.3	14.7
- persons 20 years old and over	7.0	7.4	4.3	4.1	4.9	4.8
- persons 65 years old and over	na	na	2.8	2.8	3.0	3.1
2000						
unemployment rate						
all ages	4.9%	6.7%	3.4%	3.6%	3.9%	4.1%
- persons 16-19 years old	15.7	18.1	12.3	10.4	14.0	12.1
- persons 20-24 years old	6.5	8.9	5.9	5.8	7.3	7.0
- persons 25-54 years old	3.7	5.3	2.5	2.9	2.9	3.3
- persons 55-64 years old	4.1	5.1	2.4	2.4	2.4	2.5
- persons 65 years old and over	6.3	4.8	3.1	2.4	3.4	2.8
2004						
unemployment rate						
all ages	6.5%	7.6%	5.0%	4.7%	5.6%	5.4%
- persons 16-19 years old	21.2	19.3	16.3	13.6	18.4	15.5
- persons 20-24 years old	9.4	9.1	8.5	7.1	10.1	8.7
- persons 25-54 years old	5.0	6.7	4.0	3.9	4.6	4.6
- persons 55-64 years old	5.7	5.8	3.7	3.5	3.9	3.6
- persons 65 years old and over	6.9	4.6	3.5	3.1	3.7	3.4

SOURCE: U.S. Department of Labor, Bureau of Labor Statistics, *Employment and Earnings*, January, 1991; p. 208, table 39; p. 212, table 44; January, 2001; p. 168-169, table 3, p. 171, table 4; January, 2002, pp. 166-169, table 3; January, 2005; pp. 196-199, table 3; p. 200, table 4 (data from the Current Population Survey). L 2.41/2:(vol.)/1:(year)

NOTES: 'Total' includes other races and ethnic groups not shown separately. Data covers members of the civilian labor force.

UNITS: Unemployment rate, by age group as shown.

Table 7.12 Unemployment Rates for the Hispanic Civilian Labor Force, by Sex, and Type of Hispanic Origin, 1990, 2000 and 2002

	Mexican	Puerto Rican	Cuban	Central/ South American	Other Hispanic	Total Hispanic
1990						
Unemployment rate						
both sexes	9.0%	8.6%	5.8%	6.6%	6.2%	8.2%
males	8.6	8.2	6.3	6.9	6.2	8.0
females	9.8	9.1	5.1	6.3	5.9	8.5
2000						
Unemployment rate						
both sexes	7.0%	8.1%	5.8%	5.1%	7.8%	6.8%
males	6.1	8.0	6.7	4.5	8.8	6.2
females	8.5	8.3	4.6	5.9	6.7	7.7
2002						
Unemployment rate						
both sexes	8.4%	9.6%	6.1%	6.8%	8.6%	8.1%
males	8.5	11.5	5.2	6.6	8.6	8.3
females	8.1	7.6	7.2	7.0	8.5	7.9

SOURCE: U.S. Bureau of the Census, <u>The Hispanic Population in the United States:</u>, March, 1990, pp. 8-9, table 2; March, 1992, pp. 14-15, table 2 (data from U.S. Bureau of the Census, *Current Population Reports*). C 3.186/14-2:(year)

U.S. Bureau of the Census, <u>Current Population Reports: The Hispanic Population of the United States, 2000;</u> "Table 9.2. Employment Status of the Population 16 Years and Over in the Civilian Labor Force by Sex, Hispanic Origin and Race: March 2000," published March 6, 2001; <u>2002;</u> Internet Release date: 18 June 2003; "Table 9.3 Employment Status of the Population 16 Years and Over in the Civilian Labor Force by Sex, Hispanic Origin, and Race: March 2002"; "Table 9.4 Employment Status of the Population 16 Years and Over in the Civilian Labor Force by Sex and Hispanic Origin Type: March 2002".

NOTES: Total population includes other races and ethnic groups not shown separately. 'Other Hispanic origin' includes persons from Spain and persons identifying themselves generally as Hispanic, Spanish, Spanish-American, Hispano, Latino, etc.

UNITS: Total population in thousands of persons 16 years old and over; percent as a percent of total shown (100.0%).

Table 7.13   Unemployment by Reason for Unemployment, by Region, 2000 and 2002

	Hispanic	White	Total
2000			
Northeast			
job losers	45.7%	50.3%	48.2%
job leavers	8.7	13.0	12.6
re-entrants to the labor force	34.6	30.5	32.1
new entrants to the labor force	11.0	6.2	7.2
Midwest			
job losers	46.3%	47.8%	45.8%
job leavers	10.4	14.6	13.8
re-entrants to the labor force	35.8	32.6	35.4
new entrants to the labor force	na	na	5.0
South			
job losers	40.0%	41.6%	40.6%
job leavers	16.1	17.0	15.2
re-entrants to the labor force	32.9	33.8	35.1
new entrants to the labor force	11.0	7.7	9.1
West			
job losers	46.6%	44.9%	44.3%
job leavers	9.4	12.7	12.4
re-entrants to the labor force	32.1	34.4	35.0
new entrants to the labor force	12.2	8.0	8.2

continued on the next page

Table 7.13   continued

	Hispanic	White	Total
2002			
Northeast			
job losers	56.0%	62.2%	59.7%
job leavers	7.2	9.0	8.8
re-entrants to the labor force	28.0	24.0	25.7
new entrants to the labor force	8.7	4.8	5.8
Midwest			
job losers	57.6%	57.9%	55.5%
job leavers	8.8	11.0	10.2
re-entrants to the labor force	26.4	26.1	28.7
new entrants to the labor force	7.2	5.0	5.6
South			
job losers	49.9%	53.3%	52.1%
job leavers	12.1	13.2	11.8
re-entrants to the labor force	29.5	27.9	29.4
new entrants to the labor force	8.7	5.6	6.7
West			
job losers	56.3%	56.1%	54.8%
job leavers	6.7	10.6	9.7
re-entrants to the labor force	28.0	26.7	28.3
new entrants to the labor force	9.0	6.6	7.2

SOURCE: U.S. Department of Labor, Bureau of Labor Statistics, <u>Geographic Profile of Employment and Unemployment, 2000</u>; table 10; <u>2002</u>; table 10. L 2.3/12:(year)

NOTES: 'Total' includes other races and ethnic groups not shown separately. Data covers members of the civilian labor force.

UNITS: Unemployed members of the civilian labor force in thousands of persons, by reason for unemployment as shown.

Table 7.14 Duration of Unemployment, by Region of Residence, 2000 and 2002

	Hispanic	White	Total
2000			
Northeast			
less than 5 weeks	34.6%	42.0%	40.1%
5-14 weeks	30.7	31.9	32.1
15 weeks and over	34.6	26.1	27.9
27 weeks and over	22.8	13.0	14.3
52 weeks and over	15.7	7.4	8.5
Midwest			
less than 5 weeks	50.7%	50.1%	47.4%
5-14 weeks	31.3	31.1	32.0
15 weeks and over	16.4	18.8	20.6
27 weeks and over	9.0	8.4	9.8
52 weeks and over	na	na	4.5
South			
less than 5 weeks	46.3%	49.1%	45.2%
5-14 weeks	32.2	31.6	32.4
15 weeks and over	21.6	19.4	22.5
27 weeks and over	10.6	8.8	10.8
52 weeks and over	5.9	4.8	5.9
West			
less than 5 weeks	47.1%	47.1%	46.0%
5-14 weeks	31.9	31.3	31.2
15 weeks and over	21.1	21.6	22.9
27 weeks and over	11.2	10.5	11.5
52 weeks and over	5.4	5.1	5.7

continued on the next page

Table 7.14   continued

	Hispanic	White	Total
2002			
Northeast			
less than 5 weeks	31.4%	31.9%	30.3%
5-14 weeks	30.9	30.2	30.4
15 weeks and over	38.2	37.9	39.4
27 weeks and over	19.3	20.7	21.6
52 weeks and over	9.7	8.9	9.7
Midwest			
less than 5 weeks	37.6%	36.4%	34.9%
5-14 weeks	33.6	31.9	31.5
15 weeks and over	28.8	31.8	33.6
27 weeks and over	12.0	15.5	16.5
52 weeks and over	4.0	6.6	7.5
South			
less than 5 weeks	41.6%	39.0%	35.3%
5-14 weeks	33.4	31.2	31.1
15 weeks and over	24.9	29.8	33.6
27 weeks and over	10.8	15.4	17.8
52 weeks and over	5.9	7.2	8.4
West			
less than 5 weeks	39.5%	37.6%	36.4%
5-14 weeks	29.3	30.1	30.0
15 weeks and over	31.2	32.3	33.6
27 weeks and over	15.3	17.3	18.4
52 weeks and over	8.3	8.1	8.7

SOURCE: U.S. Department of Labor, Bureau of Labor Statistics, <u>Geographic Profile of Employment and Unemployment, 2000</u>; table 11; <u>2002</u>; table 11.
L 2.3/12:(year)

NOTES: 'Total' includes other races and ethnic groups not shown separately.

UNITS: Duration of unemployment by region as a percent of total unemployment in each region, 100.0%.

Table 7.15 Workers Paid Hourly Rates With Earnings at or Below the Minimum Wage, 2001 and 2003

	Hispanic	White	Total
2001			
Number of workers			
All workers paid hourly rates	10,030	59,152	72,486
at or below $5.15 per hour	302	1,861	2,238
at $5.15 per hour	114	502	636
below $5.15 per hour	187	1,359	1,602
Percent of all workers paid hourly rates			
All at or below $5.15 per hour	3.0%	3.1%	3.1%
at $5.15 per hour	1.1	0.8	0.9
below $5.15 per hour	1.9	2.3	2.2
Median hourly earnings	$8.98	$10.25	$10.17
2003			
Number of workers			
All workers paid hourly rates	11,462	59,109	72,946
at or below $5.15 per hour	308	1,746	2,100
at $5.15 per hour	94	421	545
below $5.15 per hour	214	1,325	1,555
Percent of all workers paid hourly rates			
All at or below $5.15 per hour	2.7%	3.0%	2.9%
at $5.15 per hour	0.8	0.7	0.7
below $5.15 per hour	1.9	2.2	2.1
Median hourly earnings	$9.76	$10.97	$10.85

SOURCE: U.S. Bureau of the Census, <u>Statistical Abstract of the United States, 2003</u>; p. 405, table 617; <u>2004</u>; p. 413, table 627 (data from the U.S. Bureau of Labor Statistics).   C3.134:(year)

NOTES: 'Total' includes other races/ethnic groups not shown separately. Workers 16 years and over.

UNITS: Number of workers in thousands; 'percent of all workers paid hourly rates' in percent, as a percent of total, 100.0%; median hourly earnings of workers paid hourly rates in dollars per hour.

Table 7.16   Union Membership, by Sex, 2004

	Hispanic	White	Total
Men			
total employed	9,857	53,432	64,145
members of unions			
number	1,016	7,260	8,878
as a percent of total			
employed	10.3%	13.6%	13.8%
represented by unions			
total	1,130	7,854	9,638
as a percent of total			
employed	11.5%	14.7%	15.0%
Women			
total employed	6,676	47,908	59,408
members of unions			
number	661	5,121	6,593
as a percent of total			
employed	9.9%	10.7%	11.1%
represented by unions			
total	758	5,803	7,450
as a percent of total			
employed	11.4%	12.1%	12.5%

SOURCE: U.S. Department of Labor, Bureau of Labor Statistics, *Employment and Earnings*, January 2004, p. 255, table 40, (data from the Current Population Survey). L 2.41/2:40/1: (year)

NOTES: 'Total' includes other races/ethnic groups not shown separately. 'Members of unions' includes members of a labor union or an employee association similar to a union. 'Represented by unions' includes members of a labor union or an employee association similar to a union as well as workers who report no union affiliation but whose jobs are covered by a union or an employee association contract.

UNITS: Total employed, members of unions and represented by unions in thousands of persons 16 years old and older; percent as shown.

Table 7.17 Educational Attainment of Persons 16 Years and Over, by Labor Force Status and Sex, 2000 and 2004

	Hispanic		White		Total	
	male	female	male	female	male	female
2000						
High school graduate						
Employed	2,446	1,739	16,710	14,588	22,377	19,681
Unemployed	140	110	697	535	1,136	951
Not in labor force	415	1,106	5,577	11,677	7,173	14,757
Bachelor's degree						
Employed	551	510	10,789	9,363	13,028	11,786
Unemployed	19	20	171	172	250	225
Not in labor force	66	161	1,896	3,292	2,248	4,032
2004*						
High school graduate						
Employed	3,002	2,099	18,351	15,198	21,950	18,800
Unemployed	252	157	1,370	855	1,853	1,231
Not in labor force	594	1,383	6,917	13,288	8,482	15,749
Bachelor's degree						
Employed	820	758	11,993	10,627	14,064	12,954
Unemployed	36	32	410	315	490	422
Not in labor force	118	235	2,434	4,232	2,810	5,087

SOURCE: U.S. Bureau of the Census, <u>Current Population Reports: Educational Attainment in the United States: March 2000 (Update)</u>; Series P-20, #536, pp. 1-7, 11, 12, table 5a; <u>2003</u>; #550, table 5a; 2004; table 5a. <www.census.gov>

NOTES: 'Total' includes other races and ethnic groups not shown separately. '*' indicates year in which 'White' as shown is equivalent to 'White Alone' that refers to people who reported 'White' and did not report any other race category.

UNITS: Number of persons in thousands.

Table 7.18 Unemployment Rates of the Civilian Labor Force 25 - 64 Years of Age, by Educational Attainment, 2000 - 2003

	Hispanic	White	Total
2000			
Total	5.5%	3.0%	3.3%
number	569	2,644	3,589
less than a high school diploma	8.3	7.5	7.9
high school graduate, no college	4.6	3.3	3.8
less than a bachelor's degree	3.1	2.7	3.0
college graduate	3.2	1.4	1.5
2001			
Total	5.5%	3.1%	3.5%
number	665	2,995	4,072
less than a high school diploma	8.9	7.2	8.1
high school graduate, no college	4.0	3.6	4.2
less than a bachelor's degree	3.1	2.7	2.9
college graduate	2.9	1.8	2.0
2003			
Total	6.4%	4.3%	4.8%
number	975	4,389	6,028
less than a high school diploma	8.2	7.8	8.8
high school graduate, no college	5.9	4.8	5.5
less than a bachelor's degree	5.7	4.2	4.8
college graduate	4.1	2.8	3.1

SOURCE: U.S. Bureau of the Census, Statistical Abstract of the United States, 1999; p. 432, table 684; 2001; p. 389, table 604; 2002; p. 390, table 598; 2004; p. 396, table 608 (data from U.S. Department of Labor, Bureau of Labor Statistics). C.134:(year)

NOTES: 'Total' includes other races/ethnic groups not shown separately. Data is for persons 25 years old and over.

UNITS: Unemployment rates (percent of the civilian labor force that is unemployed) as a percent of the total civilian labor force. Number in thousands.

Table 7.19 Work at Home, 2001

	Hispanic	White	Total
2001			
worked at home	191	3,138	3,436
percent who worked less than 8 hours	15.9%	24.4%	24.5%
8 hours or more			
total	51.8	48.0	47.6
35 hours or more	27.6	15.0	15.7
mean hours:			
worked at home	23.2	17.7	18.0

SOURCE: U.S. Department of Labor, Bureau of Labor Statistics, "Table 3: Hours of paid job-related work at home on primary job among wage and salary workers, May 2001"; pp. 1-2, table 3. <http://stats.bls.gov/news.release/homey.t03.htm> accessed 5 March, 2003.

NOTES: Data refer to employed persons in nonagricultural industries who reported that they usually work at home at least once per week as part of their primary job excluding self-employed. Detail for the above race and Hispanic-origin groups will not sum to totals because data for the "other races" group are not presented and Hispanics are included in both the white and black population groups.

UNITS: Numbers in thousands of persons. Percent as a percent of persons working at home.

Table 7.20   Unemployment, by Reason for Unemployment, 1994 - 2004

	Hispanic	White	Total
1994			
Total	1,187	5,892	7,996
job losers	573	2,972	3,815
job leavers	89	638	791
re-entrants to the labor force	402	1,898	2,786
new entrants to the labor force	124	385	604
2000			
Total	876	4,099	5,655
job losers	390	1,866	2,492
job leavers	98	593	775
re-entrants to the labor force	289	1,356	1,957
new entrants to the labor force	99	284	431
new entrants to the labor force	115	284	431
2001			
Total	1,037	4,923	6,742
job losers	532	2,576	3,428
job leavers	105	635	832
re-entrants to the labor force	297	1,412	2,029
new entrants to the labor force	104	301	453
2004			
Total	1,342	5,847	8,149
job losers	693	3,105	4,197
job leavers	121	654	858
re-entrants to the labor force	377	1,638	2,408
new entrants to the labor force	152	450	686

SOURCE: U.S. Department of Labor, Bureau of Labor Statistics, *Employment and Earnings*, January, 1996, p. 196, table 28; January, 2002, p. 201, table 28); January, 2005; p. 239, table 27; p.240, table 28   (data from the Current Population Survey). L2.41/2:(vol.)/1:(year)

NOTES: 'Total' includes other races and ethnic groups not shown separately. Data covers members of the civilian labor force.

UNITS: Unemployed members of the civilian labor force in thousands of persons, by reason for unemployment as shown.

Table 7.21 Self-Employed Workers, 1994 - 2004

	Hispanic	White	Total
1994	533	8,179	9,003
1995	507	8,105	8,902
1996	561	8,106	8,971
1997	598	8,153	9,056
1998	590	8,030	8,962
1999	651	7,846	8,790
2000	616	7,692	8,674
2001	659	7,639	8,594
2002	845	7,914	8,923
2003	935	8,160	9,344
2004	1,008	8,252	9,467

SOURCE: U.S. Department of Labor, Bureau of Labor Statistics, *Employment and Earnings*, January, 1994, p. 230, table 41; January, 1999, p. 184, table 12; January, 2000, p. 184, table 12; January, 2001, p. 184, table 12; January, 2002, p. 182, table 12; January, 2004; p. 215, table 12; p. 216, table 13; January, 2005; p. 216, table 12; p. 217, table 13 (data from the Current Population Survey). L2.41/2:(vol.)/1:(year)

NOTES: 'Total' includes other races and ethnic groups not shown separately.

UNITS: Self-employed workers in thousands of persons.

Table 7.22 Employment Status of Families, 2001 - 2003

	Hispanic	White	Total
2001			
Total families	7,766	59,943	71,980
With employed member(s)	6,746	49,804	59,699
some usually work full time	6,355	46,429	55,599
With no employed member	1,020	10,140	12,281
With unemployed member(s)	771	3,506	4,775
some member(s) employed	567	2,629	3,441
some usually work full time	514	2,351	3,076
2002			
Total families	8,650	61,494	74,169
With employed member(s)	7,485	50,785	61,121
some usually work full time	6,989	47,193	56,742
With no employed member	1,165	10,709	13,048
With unemployed member(s)	965	4,275	5,809
some member(s) employed	686	3,164	4,126
some usually work full time	615	2,808	3,668
2003			
Total families	9,185	61,995	75,301
With employed member(s)	7,907	51,002	61,761
some usually work full time	7,383	47,356	57,229
With no employed member	1,277	10,993	13,540
With unemployed member(s)	1,020	4,411	6,079
some member(s) employed	715	3,245	4,285
some usually work full time	640	2,873	3,790

SOURCE: U.S. Department Labor, Bureau Labor Statistics, <u>Employment Characteristics of Families, 2001</u>, "(Table) 1. Employment and unemployment in families, by race and Hispanic origin, 2000-2001 annual averages".
U.S. Department of Labor, Bureau Labor Statistics, "Employment and unemployment in families by race and Hispanic or Latino ethnicity, 2002-2003 annual averages".

NOTES: 'Total' includes other races and ethnic groups not shown separately.

UNITS: Number of families in thousands of families.

Chapter 8: Earnings, Income, Poverty & Wealth

Table 8.01 Money Income of Households, 1980 – 2003

	Hispanic	White	Total
Median income			
1980	$28,864	$39,506	$37,447
1985	28,478	40,614	38,510
1990	30,475	42,622	40,865
1995	27,401	42,871	40,845
2000	35,429	46,910	44,853
2001	34,880	46,261	43,882
2002*	33,861	46,119	43,381
2003*	32,997	45,631	43,318
Mean income			
1980	$35,256	$46,334	$44,537
1985	35,584	49,339	47,394
1990	38,175	53,105	51,046
1995	37,399	56,012	53,865
2000	46,977	63,294	61,031
2001	46,122	62,883	60,488
2002*	45,915	61,544	59,177
2003*	44,468	61,587	59,067

SOURCE: U.S. Bureau of the Census, Current Population Reports: Income 2003; "Table H-5: Households by Total Money Income, Race, and Hispanic Origin of Householder: 1967 to 2003.

NOTES: 'Total' includes other races not shown separately. '*' indicates a change in race classification: 'White' or 'White alone' refers to people who reported White and not any other race category.

UNITS: Median and mean money income in 2001 CPI-U-RS 28/ adjusted dollars as shown.

Table 8.02 Money Income of Households, by Selected Household Characteristic, 2001

	Hispanic	White	Total
2001			
Number of households	10,499	90,682	109,297
percent of households with			
current dollar incomes of:			
under $5,000	3.9%	2.4%	3.1%
$5,000-$9,999	6.7	5.2	5.9
10,000-$14,999	8.3	6.7	6.9
$15,000-$24,999	17.5	13.0	13.3
$25,000-$34,999	15.4	12.2	12.4
$35,000-$49,999	17.3	15.5	15.4
$50,000-$74,999	16.5	18.8	18.4
$75,000-$99,999	7.5	11.4	10.8
$100,000 and over	7.0	14.8	13.8
median income	$33,565	$44,517	$42,228
mean income	$44,383	$60,512	$58,208
Median income by:			
type of residence			
inside metropolitan area	$34,256	$47,759	$45,219
outside metropolitan area	28,527	34,971	33,601
type of household			
family households	$36,018	$55,051	$52,275
married couple families	40,942	61,137	60,471
non-family households	22,141	26,114	25,631
male householder living alone	20,720	29,049	28,283
female householder living alone	12,677	18,199	17,868
age of householder			
15-24 years old	$29,530	$30,860	$28,196
25-34 years old	34,447	47,412	45,080
35-44 years old	36,585	56,642	53,320
45-54 years old	41,652	61,643	58,045
55-64 years old	35,734	47,907	45,864
65 years old and over	16,870	23,769	23,118

continued on the next page

Table 8.02 continued

	Hispanic	White	Total
2001 - continued			
size of household			
one person	$16,511	$22,079	$21,761
two persons	30,045	47,109	45,245
three persons	34,199	58,007	54,481
four persons	38,077	65,815	62,595
five persons	39,832	62,931	59,898
six persons	42,004	59,573	57,548
seven or more persons	47,080	57,488	54,560
number of earners			
no earners	$9,952	$16,765	$15,452
one earner	24,368	35,830	34,104
two earners or more	48,865	69,522	68,106
work experience of the householder			
all civilian householders	$33,565	$44,517	$42,228
worked	39,526	55,618	53,002
worked year-round full-time	42,570	60,783	58,608
did not work	16,780	22,192	20,887

SOURCE: U.S. Bureau of the Census, <u>Current Population Reports: Income 2001</u>; "(Table) 1. Median Income of Households by Selected Characteristics, Race, and Hispanic Origin of Householder: 2001, 2000 and 1999"; "(Table) H-17. Households by Total Money Income, Race, and Hispanic Origin of Householder: 1967 to 2001"; published September 2002.

NOTES: 'Total' includes other races and ethnic groups not shown separately. Number of households as of March of the <u>following</u> year. 'Occupation of the householder' represents the longest job held by the householder.

UNITS: Number of households in thousands; mean and median income in current dollars.

Table 8.03 Money Income of Households by Type of Hispanic Origin, 2000 and 2002

	Mexican	Puerto Rican	Cuban	Central/ South American	Other Hispanic	Total Hispanic
All households	100.0%	100.0%	100.0%	100.0%	100.0%	100.0%
2000						
percent with incomes of:						
$1 to $2,499 or loss	1.8	3.7	1.6	2.9	2.9	2.3
$2,500 to $4,999	1.6	2.7	2.5	1.2	1.4	1.7
$5,000 to $9,999	7.1	12.5	12.8	5.8	8.9	8.0
$10,000 to $14,999	10.1	8.9	12.0	7.9	9.1	9.7
$15,000 to $19,999	10.5	9.7	6.7	8.6	8.6	9.8
$20,000 to $24,999	9.7	7.9	6.7	8.6	8.3	9.1
$25,000 to $34,999	16.1	12.9	13.1	18.0	14.7	15.8
$35,000 to $49.999	16.7	17.1	12.2	18.3	15.9	16.7
$50,000 to $74,999	15.9	13.6	13.3	13.7	15.4	15.2
$75,000 and over	10.4	10.9	19.1	14.9	14.7	12.0
2002						
percent with incomes of:						
$1 to $2,499 or loss	2.4	2.8	3.1	3.1	2.9	2.6
$2,500 to $4,999	1.2	2.6	1.5	0.7	1.0	1.3
$5,000 to $9,999	6.0	11.1	11.1	4.4	8.7	6.7
$10,000 to $14,999	8.4	9.3	10.6	7.5	5.8	8.3
$15,000 to $19,999	9.4	9.4	10.7	8.0	9.4	9.2
$20,000 to $24,999	8.5	10.0	7.7	7.0	6.4	8.2
$25,000 to $34,999	16.0	13.2	15.0	15.7	14.0	15.4
$35,000 to $49.999	18.4	13.6	12.1	17.9	15.1	17.3
$50,000 to $74,999	16.5	15.4	12.3	18.1	17.3	16.5
$75,000 and over	13.3	12.7	15.9	17.5	19.6	14.4

SOURCE: U.S. Bureau of the Census, Current Population Reports: The Hispanic Population of the United States, 2000; "(Table) 12.1. Total Money Income in 1999 of Households by Type, Hispanic Origin and Race of Householder: March 2000"; published March 6, 2001; 2002; "Table 12.1 Total Money Income in 2001 of Households by Type, and by Hispanic Origin, and Race of Householder: March 2002"; "Table 12.2 Total Money Income in 2001 of Households by Type, and by Hispanic Origin Type of Householder: March 2002"; Internet Release date: 18 June 2003.

NOTES: Total population includes other races and ethnic groups not shown separately. 'Other Hispanic origin' includes persons from Spain and persons identifying themselves generally as Hispanic, Spanish, Spanish-American, Hispano, Latino, etc.

UNITS: Percent as a percent of total shown (100.0%).

Table 8.04 Money Income of Families, 1980 - 2003

	Hispanic	White	Total
Median income			
1980	$29,943	$44,569	$42,776
1985	29,855	45,742	43,518
1990	30,772	48,480	46,429
1995	28,341	49,191	46,843
1996	29,407	50,275	47,516
1997	30,951	51,421	49,017
1998	32,112	53,168	50,689
1999	33,633	54,411	51,996
2000	35,403	54,509	52,148
2001	34,490	54,067	51,407
2002*	34,185	54,633	51,680
2003*	34,272	55,768	52,680
Mean income			
1980	$35,842	$50,744	$48,781
1985	36,327	53,937	51,692
1990	38,494	58,484	56,015
1995	37,665	61,821	59,234
1996	39,981	63,127	60,295
1997	41,555	65,536	62,582
1998	43,086	67,659	64,628
1999	44,496	69,272	66,533
2000	47,092	70,386	67,609
2001	45,229	69,856	66,863
2002*	46,213	69,803	66,970
2003*	46,002	71,770	68,563

SOURCE: U.S. Bureau of the Census, Current Population Reports: Historical Income Tables - Families, "(Table) F-23. Families by Total Money Income, Race, and Hispanic Origin of Householder: 1967 to 2003;" published September 2003.

U.S. Bureau of the Census, Current Population Reports: Income 2003; "(Table) FINC-01. Selected Characteristics of Families by Total Money Income in 2003"

NOTES: 'Total' includes other races and ethnic groups not shown separately. '*' indicates year in which 'White' as shown is equivalent to 'White Alone' that refers to people who reported 'White' and did not report any other race category.

UNITS: Median and mean money income in 2001 CPI-U-RS 28/ adjusted dollars, as shown except for 2002 and 2003.

Table 8.05 Money Income of Families, by Selected Family Characteristic, 1985

	Hispanic	White	Total
Families			
Number of families	4,206	54,991	63,558
percent of families with incomes:			
under $2,500	2.9%	1.6%	1.9%
$2,500-$4,499	5.4	2.1	2.9
$5,000-$7,499	8.5	3.6	4.2
$7,500-$9,999	8.5	3.9	4.3
$10,000-$12,499	8.1	4.8	5.2
$12,500-$14,999	6.8	4.9	5.0
$15,000-$19,999	12.1	10.3	10.5
$20,000-$24,999	11.3	10.4	10.3
$25,000-$34,999	16.0	19.2	18.6
$35,000-$49,999	12.5	19.7	18.8
$50,000 and over	8.1	19.6	18.3
median income	$19,027	$29,152	$27,735
mean income	$23,152	$34,375	$32,944
Median family income by:			
type of family			
married couple families	$22,269	$31,602	$31,100
wife in paid labor force	28,132	36,992	36,431
wife not in paid labor force	17,116	25,307	24,556
male householder,			
no wife present	19,773	24,190	22,622
female householder,			
no husband present	8,792	15,825	13,660

continued on the next page

Table 8.05 continued

Mean family income by:	Hispanic	White	Total
type of income			
wages and salaries	$22,566	$31,277	$30,258
non-farm self-employment	14,628	14,565	14,420
farm self employment	na	4,593	4,557
property income	1,483	3,486	3,327
- interest income	1,017	2,440	2,328
transfer payments and all other income	5,347	7,776	7,469
- social security or railroad retirement income	6,014	7,684	7,488
-public assistance and supplemental income	4,458	3,416	3,498

SOURCE: U.S. Bureau of the Census, <u>Current Population Reports: Money Income of Households Families and Persons in the United States; March 1985,</u> Series P-60, #156, pp. 26-29, tables 9, 10; pp. 40-46, tables 13, 14; pp. 56-64, table 17; pp. 86-88, table 25. C3.186:P-60/156
U.S. Bureau of the Census, <u>Statistical Abstract of the United States, 1987,</u> p. 437, table 734, (data from *the Current Population Survey*). C 3.134:987

NOTES: 'Total' includes other races and ethnic groups not shown separately. Number of families as of March of the <u>following</u> year. 'Occupation of the householder' represents the longest job held by the householder. 'Property income' includes interest, dividends, net rental income, income from trusts and estates, and net royalty income.

UNITS: Number of families and families with income, in thousands of families; percent as a percent as shown; mean income in current dollars.

Table 8.06 Money Income of Families, by Selected Family Characteristic, 1990

	Hispanic	White	Total
Families			
Number of families	4,981	58,803	66,322
percent of families with			
current dollar incomes of:			
under $5,000	6.3%	2.5%	3.6%
$5,000-$9,999	12.3	4.7	5.8
$10,000-$14,999	12.6	7.0	7.5
$15,000-$24,999	21.7	16.0	16.4
$25,000-$34,999	16.6	16.5	16.2
$35,000-$49,999	15.7	20.8	20.0
$50,000-$74,999	10.0	19.3	18.2
$75,000-$99,999	2.9	7.3	6.9
$100,000 and over	1.9	5.9	5.4
mean income	$29,311	$44,532	$42,652
median income	$23,341	$36,915	$35,353
Median income by:			
type of residence			
nonfarm	$23,402	$36,974	$35,376
farm	na	34,476	34,171
inside metropolitan area	23,898	40,086	37,893
outside metropolitan area	19,061	29,693	28,272
type of family			
married couple families	$27,996	$40,331	$39,895
wife in paid labor force	34,778	47,247	46,777
wife not in paid labor force	21,168	30,781	30,265
male householder, no wife present	21,744	30,570	29,046
female householder,			
no husband present	11,914	19,528	16,932

continued on the next page

Table 8.06 continued

	Hispanic	White	Total
Median income by:			
age of householder			
15-24 years old	$13,009	$18,234	$16,219
25-34 years old	20,439	33,457	31,497
35-44 years old	27,350	42,632	41,061
45-54 years old	29,908	49,249	47,165
55-64 years old	30,839	40,416	39,035
65 years old and over	17,962	25,864	25,049
size of family			
two persons	$19,230	$31,734	$30,428
three persons	22,778	38,858	36,644
four persons	25,808	43,352	41,451
five persons	25,727	41,037	39,452
six persons	24,786	40,387	38,379
seven or more persons	30,549	39,845	35,363
number of earners			
no earners	$ 8,858	$17,369	$15,047
one earner	16,795	27,670	25,878
two earners or more	33,704	46,261	45,462

SOURCE: U.S. Bureau of the Census, <u>Current Population Reports: Money Income of Households, Families, and Persons in the United States: March 1990</u>, Series P-60, #174, pp. 52-55, table 13; p. 56, table 14. C3.186/2:990

NOTES: 'Total' includes other races and ethnic groups not shown separately. Number of families as of March of the <u>following</u> year.

UNITS: Number of families and families with income, in thousands of families; percent as a percent as shown; mean and median income in current dollars.

Table 8.07 Money Income of Families, by Selected Family Characteristic, 2003

	Hispanic	White	Total
Families			
Number of families with current dollar incomes of:	9,274	62,620	76,232
under $5,000	395	1,382	2,151
$5,000-$9,999	418	1,302	2,095
$10,000-$14,999	715	2,234	3,120
$15,000-$24,999	1,693	6,610	8,489
$25,000-$34,999	1,494	7,049	8,657
$35,000-$49,999	1,552	9,366	11,443
$50,000-$74,999	1,537	12,936	15,352
$75,000-$99,999	734	8,784	10,157
$100,000 and over	734	12,953	14,768
median income	34,272	55,768	52,680
mean income	46,002	71,770	68,563
Median income by:			
type of residence			
inside metropolitan area	34,554	59,846	56,200
outside metropolitan area	31,574	44,492	42,532
type of family			
married couple families	40,390	63,038	62,281
wife in paid labor force	52,468	76,259	75,170
wife not in paid labor force	28,323	41,334	41,122
male householder, no wife present	32,120	39,286	38,032
female householder, no husband present	21,136	29,120	26,550

continued on the next page

Table 8.07 continued

	Hispanic	White	Total
Median income by:			
age of householder			
15-24 years old	24,780	29,188	26,198
25-34 years old	30,990	49,844	46,554
35-44 years old	37,122	61,956	59,122
45-54 years old	42,926	74,163	70,149
55-64 years old	42,887	62,455	60,976
65 years old and over	25,355	36,121	35,310
size of family			
two persons	28,696	47,353	45,254
three persons	33,281	58,693	54,664
four persons	36,963	68,480	65,093
five persons	37,777	63,889	60,422
six persons	37,235	60,723	58,263
seven or more persons	45,228	61,422	59,858
number of earners			
no earners	10,777	24,183	21,878
one earner	23,813	39,127	36,661
two earners or more	51,026	75,142	73,483

SOURCE: U.S. Bureau of the Census, <u>Current Population Reports: Income 2003</u>; "(Table) FINC-01. Selected Characteristics of Families by Total Money Income in 2003".

NOTES: 'Total' includes other races not shown separately. Number of families as of March of the <u>following</u> year. 'White' as shown is equivalent to 'White Alone' that refers to people who reported 'White' and did not report any other race category.

UNITS: Number of families and families with income, in thousands of families; mean and median income in current dollars.

Table 8.08 Money Income of Families, by Type of Hispanic Origin, 2000 and 2002

	Mexican	Puerto Rican	Cuban	Central/ South American	Other Hispanic	Total Hispanic
All families	100.0%	100.0%	100.0%	100.0%	100.0%	100.0%
2000						
percent with incomes of:						
$1 to $2,499 or loss	2.1	3.3	1.8	3.0	2.2	2.3
$2,500 to $4,999	1.8	3.6	1.8	1.3	1.9	1.9
$5,000 to $9,999	5.6	8.6	4.6	4.5	6.2	5.7
$10,000 to $14,999	8.9	9.4	11.2	7.7	9.5	8.9
$15,000 to $19,999	10.8	11.3	7.1	9.4	9.0	10.3
$20,000 to $24,999	10.1	7.4	6.3	9.2	7.9	9.4
$25,000 to $34,999	16.2	13.2	15.6	17.9	13.3	15.9
$35,000 to $49.999	16.8	17.4	12.0	17.0	17.6	16.7
$50,000 to $74,999	16.9	13.7	16.7	13.8	14.7	15.9
$75,000 and over	10.9	12.3	22.9	16.2	17.7	12.8
2002						
percent with incomes of:						
$1 to $2,499 or loss	2.9	2.6	2.9	3.0	2.8	2.9
$2,500 to $4,999	1.1	2.5	0.8	1.2	1.0	1.2
$5,000 to $9,999	4.4	8.7	5.0	3.2	6.2	4.8
$10,000 to $14,999	8.1	10.2	8.0	7.0	5.0	7.9
$15,000 to $19,999	9.6	9.0	9.5	7.6	9.7	9.2
$20,000 to $24,999	8.8	10.1	7.5	7.0	6.6	8.4
$25,000 to $34,999	17.1	12.9	16.1	15.9	13.4	16.2
$35,000 to $49.999	17.8	14.2	15.1	18.6	14.9	17.3
$50,000 to $74,999	16.6	15.1	14.3	18.1	19.1	16.8
$75,000 and over	13.6	14.8	20.9	18.4	21.2	15.3

SOURCE: U.S. Bureau of the Census, <u>Current Population Reports: The Hispanic Population of the United States, 2000</u>; "Table 13.1. Total Money Income in 1999 of Families by Type, Hispanic Origin and Race of Householder: March 2000", published March 6, 2001; <u>2002</u>; Internet Release date: 18 June 2003; "Table 13.1 Total Money Income in 2001 of Families by Type, and by Hispanic Origin, and Race of Householder: March 2002"; "Table 13.2 Total Money Income in 2001 of Families by Type, and by Hispanic Origin Type of Householder: March 2002".

NOTES: 'Other Hispanic origin' includes persons from Spain and persons identifying themselves generally as Hispanic, Spanish, Spanish-American, Hispano, Latino, etc. Income from the previous year.

UNITS: Percent as a percent of total shown (100.0%)

Table 8.09 Median Weekly Earnings of Families, by Type of Family and Number of Earners, 1985, 1990 and 1993

	Hispanic	White	Total
1985			
All families with earners	na	$543	$522
married couple families	na	589	582
with one earner	na	395	385
with two or more earners	na	723	715
families maintained by women	na	311	297
families maintained by men	na	475	450
1990			
All families with earners	$496	$681	$653
married couple families	555	745	732
with one earner	322	473	455
with two or more earners	716	892	880
families maintained by women	326	382	363
families maintained by men	468	539	514
1993			
All families with earners	$505	$739	$707
married couple families	566	816	804
with one earner	334	492	481
with two or more earners	744	984	973
families maintained by women	353	415	393
families maintained by men	432	547	523

SOURCE: U.S. Department of Labor, Bureau of Labor Statistics, <u>Handbook of Labor Statistics, 1989</u>; p. 200, table 44 (data from the Current Population Survey). L 2.3/5:989

U.S. Department of Labor, Bureau of Labor Statistics, *Employment and Earnings*, <u>January, 1991</u>; p. 219, table 52; <u>January, 1994</u>; p. 239, table 52 (data from the Current Population Survey). L 2.41/2:37/1:(year)

NOTES: 'Total' includes other races and ethnic groups not shown separately. Data excludes families in which there is no wage or salary earner, or in which the husband, wife, or other person maintaining the family is either self-employed or in the armed forces.

UNITS: Median weekly earnings in dollars.

Table 8.10 Median Income of Year-Round, Full-Time Workers, by Sex, 1980 - 2003

	Hispanic		White		Total	
	male	female	male	female	male	female
1980	$23,113	$16,500	$32,658	$19,224	$31,729	$19,088
1985	22,233	17,037	32,678	20,596	31,548	20,372
1990	20,542	16,823	31,002	21,521	29,711	21,278
1995	20,553	17,855	33,515	24,264	32,199	23,777
1996	21,265	19,272	34,741	25,358	33,538	24,935
1997	21,799	19,676	36,118	26,470	35,248	26,029
1998	22,505	19,817	37,196	27,304	36,252	26,855
1999	23,342	20,052	39,331	28,023	37,574	27,370
2000	25,041	21,026	40,350	29,659	39,020	28,823
2001	25,271	21,973	40,790	30,849	40,136	30,420
2002	26,137	22,355	41,375	31,400	40,507	30,970
2003	26,414	23,062	42,142	32,192	41,503	31,653

SOURCE: U.S. Bureau of the Census, <u>Current Population Reports: Money Income of Households, Families, and Persons in the United States: March 1992</u>, Series P-60, #184; p. B 36, table B-17; <u>1996</u>, Series P-60, #197, pp.28-29, table 7. C3.186/2:(year)

U.S. Bureau of the Census, <u>Current Population Reports: Income Poverty, and Valuation of Noncash Benefits: 1994</u>, Series P-60, #189, pp. 15-16, table 5. C3.186/2:994

U.S. Bureau of the Census, <u>Current Population Reports: Money Income in the United States: 1999</u>, Series P-60, #209, pp. 30-31, table 7. <www.census.gov>

U.S. Bureau of the Census, <u>Current Population Reports: Income 2001</u>; "(Table) 7. Median Income of People by Selected Characteristics: 2001, 2000, and 1999;" published September 2002.

U.S. Bureau of the Census and Bureau of Labor Statistics, <u>Annual Demographic Survey, March Supplement, 2002</u>, "(Table) PINC-01 Selected Characteristics of People 15 Years and Over, by Total Money Income in 2002, Work Experience in 2002, Race, Hispanic Origin, and Sex";<u>2003</u>; <u>2004</u>.

NOTES: 'Total' includes other races/ethnic groups not shown separately. Data covers the earnings of wage and salary workers who usually worked 35 or more hours per week for 50 to 52 weeks during the year. Data prior to 1989 are for civilian workers only.

UNITS: Median money earnings.

Table 8.11 Money Income of Persons 15 Years Old and Older, by Selected Characteristic, 1985

	Hispanic		White		Total	
	male	female	male	female	male	female
Number of persons	6,232	6,366	76,617	82,345	88,474	96,354
persons with incomes:						
under $2,000	444	957	5,180	14,024	6,304	15,848
$2,000-$2,999	199	370	1,808	4,420	2,297	5,425
$3,000-$3,999	264	371	2,190	4,856	2,671	5,958
$4,000-$4,999	203	390	2,095	4,635	2,642	5,693
$5,000-$5,999	368	328	2,169	4,201	2,595	4,848
$6,000-$6,999	301	311	2,278	3,992	2,708	4,648
$7,000-$8,499	416	406	3,402	5,006	4,132	5,855
$8,500-$9,999	325	228	2,896	3,779	3,353	4,288
$10,000-$12,499	599	422	5,895	6,579	6,859	7,576
$12,500-$14,999	392	241	4,527	4,672	5,245	5,339
$15,000-$17,499	431	241	4,940	4,359	5,739	5,012
$17,500-$19,999	281	175	3,869	2,980	4,423	3,432
$20,000-$24,999	468	206	7,521	4,839	8,410	5,513
$25,000-$29,999	349	98	6,374	2,759	7,018	3,194
$30,000-$34,999	221	59	5,324	1,437	5,767	1,633
$35,000-$49,999	267	29	7,730	1,450	8,211	1,585
$50,000-$74,999	71	8	3,421	484	3,588	509
$75,000 and over	224	4	1,603	169	1,669	177
median income	$11,434	$ 6,020	$17,111	$ 7,357	$16,311	$ 7,217
mean income	$14,490	$ 8,178	$21,523	$10,317	$20,652	$10,173

Mean income by:

occupation

	Hispanic		White		Total	
	male	female	male	female	male	female
managerial, professional specialty	$27,148	$17,471	$34,711	$17,763	$34,201	$17,857
technical, sales, administrative support	17,692	10,461	24,050	10,988	23,293	11,076
service occupations	11,712	5,879	13,161	5,935	12,549	6,104
farming, forestry, fishing	7,451	na	8,241	3,865	8,024	3,762

continued on the next page

Table 8.11 continued

	Hispanic		White		Total	
	male	female	male	female	male	female
Mean income by:						
occupation - continued						
precision production,						
craft, repair	$16,015	$11,217	$20,593	$12,998	$20,277	$12,595
operators, fabricators,						
laborers	13,289	9,649	16,378	9,528	15,971	$9,548
work experience						
worked at full time jobs	$16,297	$11,616	$24,531	$14,556	$23,767	$14,364
worked 50-52 weeks	19,666	14,576	28,140	17,249	27,414	17,028
type of income						
wages and salaries	$14,689	$ 9,557	$21,848	$11,295	$21,056	$11,239
non-farm self-employment	14,026	7,818	16,083	5,885	15,834	5,867
farm self employment	na	na	4,234	1,654	4,184	1,695
property income	877	866	1,866	2,021	1,794	1,937
- interest income	541	605	1,305	1,454	1,254	1,395
transfer payments and all						
other income	4,313	3,686	6,812	4,428	6,572	4,318
- social security or						
railroad retirement	4,793	3,733	5,803	4,330	5,701	4,261
-public assistance and						
supplemental income	3,010	3,696	2,526	2,881	2,560	2,919

SOURCE: U.S. Bureau of the Census, <u>Current Population Reports: Money Income of Households in the United States; March 1985</u>, Series P-60, #156, pp. 107-109, table 31; pp. 135-138, table 35; pp. 141-143, table 37; pp. 160-163, tables 40, 41. C3.186:P-60/156

NOTES: 'Total' includes other races and ethnic groups not shown separately. Number of persons as of March of the <u>following</u> year. Data is based on persons living in households. Persons with incomes under $2,000 includes those with a loss. Occupation represents the longest job held by the person during the year. Educational attainment covers persons 25 years old and older; income covers persons 15 years old and older. 'Property income' includes interest, dividends, net rental income, income from trusts and estates, and net royalty income.

UNITS: Number of persons and persons by income in thousands of persons; median and mean income in dollars.

Table 8.12 Money Income of Persons 15 Years Old and Older, by Selected Characteristic, 1990

	Hispanic		White		Total	
	male	female	male	female	male	female
Number of persons	7,502	7,559	79,555	85,012	92,240	100,680
persons with incomes:						
under $5,000	1,053	2,059	8,539	22,062	10,820	26,337
$5,000-$9,999	1,353	1,502	9,249	16,358	11,312	19,563
$10,000-$14,999	1,298	901	9,529	11,652	11,253	13,566
$15,000-$24,999	1,572	892	16,679	15,162	19,166	17,516
$25,000-$34,999	776	346	12,707	7,547	14,185	8,707
$35,000-$49,999	459	149	10,531	3,895	11,604	4,457
$50,000-$74,999	184	43	5,973	1,382	6,433	1,535
$75,000 and over	72	12	3,274	509	3,446	565
median income	$13,470	$ 7,532	$21,170	$10,317	$20,293	$10,070
mean income	$17,452	$10,587	$27,142	$14,138	$26,041	$13,913

Mean income by:

work experience

worked at full-time jobs	$19,414	$14,750	$30,498	$19,269	$29,524	$19,010
worked 50-52 weeks	22,859	17,760	34,300	22,198	33,334	21,977

educational attainment

less than 8 years of school	$13,448	$ 8,269	$15,057	$ 8,598	$14,914	$ 8,602
high school graduates	20,400	13,212	25,520	13,955	24,727	13,999
1-3 years of college	25,468	17,852	31,235	17,148	30,340	17,188
4 or more years of college	32,398	20,061	45,709	25,230	44,864	25,388

age

15-24 years old	$ 9,257	$ 6,444	$ 8,915	$ 7,161	$ 8,693	$ 6,998
25-34 years old	17,895	11,262	25,442	15,317	24,365	14,955
35-44 years old	22,419	14,015	35,723	17,724	34,468	17,667
45-54 years old	22,624	13,393	38,632	17,845	37,182	17,831
55-64 years old	21,618	10,117	33,396	14,159	31,899	13,834
65 years old and over	12,280	6,496	20,918	11,864	20,011	11,441

continued on the next page

Table 8.12 continued

	Hispanic		White		Total	
	male	female	male	female	male	female
Mean income by:						
marital status						
single	$12,286	$10,149	$16,902	$14,504	$16,112	$13,656
married	20,462	10,711	32,362	13,828	31,488	13,858
spouse present	21,316	10,896	32,627	13,805	31,888	13,883
spouse absent	13,428	9,700	25,396	14,255	23,158	13,508
widowed	11,504	9,337	18,528	13,822	17,440	13,190
divorced	22,070	14,471	26,830	19,448	25,787	19,058

SOURCE: U.S. Bureau of the Census, Current Population Reports: Money Income of Households, Families, and Persons in the United States: March 1990, Series P-60, #174, pp. 104-105, table 24; p. 108, table 25; pp. 112-119, table 26; pp. 124-127, table 28; pp. 128-149, table 29; pp. 160-163, table 31. C3.186/2:990

NOTES: 'Total' includes other races and ethnic groups not shown separately. Number of persons as of March of the following year. Data is based on persons living in households. Persons with incomes under $5,000 includes those with a loss. Occupation represents the longest job held by the person during the year. Educational attainment covers persons 25 years old and older; income covers persons 15 years old and older.

UNITS: Number of persons and persons with income, in thousands of persons; percent as a percent as shown; mean and median income in current dollars.

Table 8.13 Money Income of Persons 15 Years Old and Older, by Selected Characteristic, 2003

	Hispanic		White		Total	
	male	female	male	female	male	female
Total with income persons with incomes:	12,753	10,175	84,405	83,852	100,769	102,713
$1-$2,499 or loss	598	1,160	4,144	8,679	5,233	10,431
$2,500-$4,999	403	790	2,197	4,713	2,937	5,903
$5,000-$7,499	697	1,049	2,983	6,800	3,987	8,585
$7,500-$9,999	587	837	3,008	6,064	3,861	7,570
$10,000-$12,499	1,081	972	4,470	6,398	5,391	7,838
$12,500-$14,999	766	612	3,584	4,557	4,263	5,571
$15,000-$17,499	1,047	828	4,196	4,866	5,062	6,042
$17,500-$19,999	766	467	3,242	3,417	3,946	4,201
$20,000-$22,499	1,027	581	4,213	4,248	5,142	5,284
$22,500-$24,999	563	328	2,865	3,110	3,416	3,764
$25,000-$27,499	763	421	3,815	3,664	4,607	4,581
$27,500-$29,999	341	237	2,206	2,372	2,612	2,897
$30,000-$32,499	789	367	4,377	3,548	5,167	4,315
$32,500-$34,999	211	120	1,789	1,713	2,072	2,066
$35,000-$37,499	456	249	3,182	2,682	3,767	3,243
$37,500-$39,999	188	108	1,729	1,494	2,037	1,820
$40,000-$42,499	434	204	3,409	2,291	4,108	2,807
$42,500-$44,999	123	87	1,422	1,167	1,623	1,369
$45,000-$47,499	277	104	2,317	1,413	2,744	1,677
$47,500-$49,999	98	65	1,263	920	1,467	1,121
$50,000-$52,499	270	98	2,742	1,445	3,210	1,778
$52,500-$54,999	79	41	1,108	700	1,267	819
$55,000-$57,499	144	53	1,672	760	1,900	911
$57,500-$59,999	49	17	796	407	903	467

continued on the next page

Table 8.13   continued

	Hispanic		White		Total	
	male	female	male	female	male	female
$60,000-$62,499	177	67	2,002	879	2,317	1,041
$62,500-$64,999	33	21	760	371	845	469
$65,000-$67,499	69	45	1,126	544	1,311	669
$67,500-$69,999	59	17	640	320	708	384
$70,000-$72,499	78	32	1,196	590	1,379	682
$72,500-$74,999	26	11	481	190	554	233
$75,000-$77,499	39	19	1,045	368	1,177	451
$77,500-$79,999	15	7	449	192	513	236
$80,000-$82,499	59	14	891	292	1,034	355
$82,500-$84,999	23	8	370	162	415	199
$85,000-$87,499	31	18	625	229	725	253
$87,500-$89,999	16	5	314	127	350	151
$90,000-$92,499	41	13	653	174	761	212
$92,500-$94,999	14	8	276	85	324	102
$95,000-$97,499	19	5	339	129	368	155
$97,500-$99,999	15	2	194	77	223	87
$100,000 and over	282	92	6,317	1,694	7,044	1,964
median income	$21,053	$13,642	$30,732	$17,422	$29,931	$17,259
mean income	$27,725	$18,852	$43,030	$24,897	$41,483	$24,630

SOURCE: U.S. Bureau of the Census and Bureau of Labor Statistics, <u>Annual Demographic Survey, March Supplement, 2003</u>; "(Table) PINC-01 Selected Characteristics of People 15 Years and Over, by Total Money Income in 2003, Work Experience in 2003, Race, Hispanic Origin, and Sex".

NOTES: 'Total' includes other races and ethnic groups not shown separately. Number of persons as of March of the <u>following</u> year.

UNITS: Number of persons with income, in thousands of persons; mean and median income in current dollars.

Table 8.14 Earnings of Persons, by Sex and Type of Hispanic Origin, 2002

	Mexican	Puerto Rican	Cuban	Central/ South American	Other Hispanic	Total Hispanic
Males	100.0%	100.0%	100.0%	100.0%	100.0%	100.0%
Percent with incomes of:						
$1 to $2,499 or loss	0.8	0.6	-	0.3	0.4	0.7
$2,500 to $4,999	0.3	0.5	0.5	0.7	-	0.4
$5,000 to $9,999	2.6	3.3	2.1	4.4	3.6	3.0
$10,000 to $14,999	14.4	6.6	9.8	11.5	8.3	12.9
$15,000 to $19,999	18.9	9.5	9.6	14.4	12.6	16.8
$20,000 to $24,999	16.6	12.2	11.9	16.7	13.2	16.0
$25,000 to $34,999	19.7	25.5	25.2	20.4	19.1	20.4
$35,000 to $49.999	14.0	19.0	20.1	15.3	17.2	15.0
$50,000 to $74,999	8.8	15.2	14.0	10.4	15.0	10.0
$75,000 and over	3.8	7.7	6.8	5.8	10.6	4.9
Females	100.0%	100.0%	100.0%	100.0%	100.0%	100.0%
percent with incomes of:						
$1 to $2,499 or loss	0.6	0.6	-	1.4	0.9	0.7
$2,500 to $4,999	0.6	0.4	-	1.6	0.7	0.8
$5,000 to $9,999	7.5	4.2	3.3	3.9	5.4	6.2
$10,000 to $14,999	19.1	12.6	14.9	20.9	12.1	18.0
$15,000 to $19,999	18.2	17.3	13.2	17.9	18.6	17.9
$20,000 to $24,999	16.2	18.0	17.7	14.9	17.5	16.3
$25,000 to $34,999	20.0	20.6	26.2	17.7	21.1	20.0
$35,000 to $49.999	11.2	13.8	14.9	12.6	14.5	12.1
$50,000 to $74,999	4.6	8.8	7.4	6.4	7.3	5.7
$75,000 and over	2.1	3.8	2.4	2.8	1.8	2.4

SOURCE: U.S. Bureau of the Census, <u>Current Population Reports: The Hispanic Population of the United States, 2002</u>; Internet Release date: 18 June 2003; "Table 11.1 Earnings of Full-Time, Year-Round Workers 15 Years and Over in 2001 by Sex, Hispanic Origin, and Race: March 2002"; "Table 11.2 Earnings of Full-Time, Year-Round Workers 15 Years and Over in 2001 by Sex and Hispanic Origin Type: March 2002".

NOTES: 'Other Hispanic origin' includes persons from Spain and persons identifying themselves generally as Hispanic, Spanish, Spanish-American, Hispano, Latino, etc. Full-time, year-round workers 15 years old and older. '-' represents or rounds to zero.

UNITS: Percent as a percent of total shown (100.0%), mean earnings in current dollars.

Table 8.15 Per Capita Money Income, 1985 - 1997

	Hispanic	White	Total
1985	$ 9,864	$17,409	$16,427
1986	10,251	18,088	17,090
1987	10,813	18,569	17,507
1988	10,794	18,853	17,804
1989	10,860	19,281	18,193
1990	10,345	18,745	17,667
1991	10,207	18,277	17,225
1992	9,828	18,058	16,985
1993	9,808	18,660	17,524
1994	10,218	19,073	17,929
1995	9,794	19,277	18,143
1996	10,279	19,621	18,552
1997	10,773	20,425	19,241

SOURCE: U.S. Bureau of the Census, <u>Current Population Reports: Measuring 50 Years of Economic Change</u>, Series P-60, #203; p. C-6, table C-3.

NOTES: 'Total' includes other races and ethnic groups not shown separately.

UNITS: Income in 1997 CPI-U adjusted dollars.

Table 8.16   Families Below the Poverty Level, 1980 – 2003

	Hispanic	White	Total
Number below the poverty level			
1980	751	4,195	6,217
1985	1,074	4,983	7,223
1990	1,244	4,622	7,098
1995	1,695	4,994	7,532
2000	na	na	6,400
2001	na	na	6,813
2002	na	na	7,229
2003*	na	na	7,607
Percent below the poverty level			
1980	23.2%	8.0%	10.3%
1985	25.5	9.1	11.4
1990	25.0	8.1	10.7
1995	27.0	8.5	10.8
2000	na	na	8.7
2001	na	na	9.2
2002	na	na	9.6
2003*	na	na	10.0

SOURCE: U.S. Bureau of the Census, <u>Current Population Reports: Poverty in the United States, 1999</u>; Series P-60, #210, pp. B-11 - B-17, table B-3; <u>2002</u>; "Table B-2. People and Families in Poverty by Selected Characteristics: 2001 and 2002".

U.S. Bureau of the Census, <u>Current Population Reports: Income, Poverty, and Health Insurance Coverage in the United States: 2003</u>; Series P-60, #226; Table B-3; issued August 2004.

NOTES: 'Total' includes other races and ethnic groups not shown separately. Families as of March of the following year. '*' indicates the year in which White as shown is equivalent to White Alone that refers to people who reported White and not any other race category.

UNITS: Number below the poverty level in thousands of families; percent as a percent of all families, by race, as shown.

Table 8.17 Families Below the Poverty Level by Type of Family and Presence of Related Children, 2002 and 2003

	Hispanic	White	Total
2002			
Total Families	9,094	62,313	75,616
Families below poverty level	1,792	4,862	7,229
Married-couple families	927	2,510	3,052
Male householder, no wife present	148	349	564
Female householder, no husband present	717	2,004	3613
Total families with children under 18 years	6,329	30,501	38,846
Families below poverty level	1,527	3,488	5,397
Married-couple families	752	1,494	1,831
Male householder, no wife present	118	250	395
Female householder, no husband present	657	1,744	3,171
2003			
Total Families	9,274	62,620	76,232
Families below poverty level	1,925	5,058	7,607
Married-couple families	976	2,504	3,115
Male householder, no wife present	157	383	636
Female householder, no husband present	792	2,171	3,856
Total families with children under 18 years	6,453	30,443	39,029
Families below poverty level	1,629	3,698	5,772
Married-couple families	789	1,499	1,885
Male householder, no wife present	127	287	470
Female householder, no husband present	713	1,912	3,416

SOURCE: U.S. Bureau of the Census, <u>Current Population Reports: Poverty in the United States: 2002</u>; "Table POV44: Region, Division and Type of Residence – Poverty Status for Families by Family Structure: 2002, Below 100% of Poverty"; "Table POV45: Region, Division and Type of Residence – Poverty Status for Families With Related Children Under 18 by Family Structure: 2002, Below 100% of Poverty"; <u>2003</u>.

NOTES: 'Total' includes other races not shown separately. 'White' as shown is equivalent to 'White Alone' that refer to people who reported 'White' and did not report any other race category.

UNITS: Number in thousands of families

Table 8.18   Poverty Status of Families, by Type of Hispanic Origin, 2002

	Mexican	Puerto Rican	Cuban	Central/ South American	Other Hispanic	Total Hispanic
Total Families						
Total	5,441	834	358	1,275	608	8,516
Below poverty level	1,110	202	47	191	99	1,649
Married Couple						
Total	3,818	436	268	854	401	5,778
Below poverty level	605	47	22	91	33	799
Male householder, no spouse present						
Total	544	79	28	119	46	817
Below poverty level	91	16	1	23	9	139
Female householder, no spouse present						
Total	1,078	319	62	301	161	1,922
Below poverty level	414	139	24	77	57	711

SOURCE: U.S. Bureau of the Census, <u>Current Population Reports: The Hispanic Population of the United States, 2002</u>; Internet Release date: 18 June 2003; "Table 15.1 Poverty Status of Families in 2001 by Family Type, and Hispanic Origin, and Race of Householder: March 2002"; "Table 15.2 Poverty Status of Families in 2001 by Family Type, and Hispanic Origin Type of Householder: March 2002".

NOTES: 'Other Hispanic origin' includes persons from Spain and persons identifying themselves generally as Hispanic, Spanish, Spanish-American, Hispano, Latino, etc.

UNITS: Number in thousands of families.

Table 8.19   Persons Below the Poverty Level, 1980 – 2003

	Hispanic	White	Total
Number below the poverty level			
1980	3,491	19,699	29,272
1985	5,236	22,860	33,064
1990	6,006	22,326	33,585
1995	8,574	24,423	36,425
1996	8,697	24,650	36,529
1997	8,308	24,396	35,574
1998	8,070	23,454	34,476
1999	7,439	21,922	32,258
2000	7,155	21,291	31,139
2001	7,997	22,739	32,907
2002*	8,555	23,466	34,570
2003*	9,051	24,272	35,861
Percent below the poverty level			
1980	25.7%	10.2%	13.0%
1985	29.0	11.4	14.0
1990	28.1	10.7	13.5
1995	30.3	11.2	13.8
1996	29.4	11.2	13.7
1997	27.1	11.0	13.3
1998	25.6	10.5	12.7
1999	22.8	9.8	11.8
2000	21.2	9.4	11.3
2001	21.4	9.9	11.7
2002*	21.8	10.2	12.1
2003*	22.5	10.5	12.5

SOURCE: U.S. Bureau of the Census, Current Population Reports: Poverty in the United States, 2001; P60-219, pp. 21-24, table A-1; 2002; "Table 1. Number in Poverty and Poverty Rate by Race and Hispanic Origin: 2001 and 2002". U.S. Bureau of the Census, Current Population Reports: Income, Poverty, and Health Insurance Coverage in the United States: 2003; Series P-60, #226; Table B-1; issued August 2004.

NOTES: 'Total' includes other races and ethnic groups not shown separately. '*' indicates the year in which 'White' as shown is equivalent to 'White Alone' that refers to people who reported 'White' and did not report any other race category.

UNITS: Number below the poverty level in thousands of persons; percent as a percent of all persons, by race, as shown.

Table 8.20   Children Below the Poverty Level, 1980 - 2003

	Hispanic	White	Total
Number below the poverty level			
1980	1,749	7,181	11,543
1985	2,606	8,253	13,010
1990	2,865	8,232	13,431
1995	4,080	8,981	14,665
1996	4,237	9,044	14,623
1997	3,972	8,990	14,113
1998	3,837	8,443	13,467
1999	3,506	7,568	12,109
2000	3,330	7,328	11,633
2001	3,570	7,527	11,733
2002	3,782	7,549	12,133
2003	4,077	7,985	12,866
Percent below the poverty level			
1980	33.2%	13.9%	18.3%
1985	40.3	16.2	20.7
1990	38.4	15.9	20.6
1995	40.0	16.2	20.8
1996	40.3	16.3	20.5
1997	36.8	16.1	19.9
1998	34.4	15.1	18.9
1999	30.3	13.5	16.9
2000	28.0	13.0	16.2
2001	28.0	13.4	16.3
2002	28.6	13.6	16.7
2003	29.7	14.3	17.6

SOURCE: U.S. Bureau of the Census, <u>Current Population Reports: Poverty in the United States, 2000;</u> Series P-60, #214 pp. 23-25, table A-2; <u>2001</u>; pp. 26-30, table A-2.
U.S. Bureau of the Census, <u>Current Population Reports: Income, Poverty, and Health Insurance Coverage in the United States: 2003</u>; Series P-60, #226; Table B-2; issued August 2004.

NOTES: 'Total' includes other races not shown separately.

UNITS: Number below the poverty level in thousands of children; percent as a percent of all children under 18 years, by race, as shown.

Table 8.21 Persons 65 Years Old and Over Below the Poverty Level, 1970 - 2003

	Hispanic	White	Total
Number below the poverty level			
1970	na	4,011	4,793
1985	219	2,698	3,456
1990	245	2,707	3,658
1995	342	2,572	3,318
1996	370	2,667	3,428
1997	384	2,569	3,376
1998	356	2,555	3,386
1999	358	2,409	3,167
2000	353	2,601	3,359
2001	413	2,656	3,414
2002	439	2,739	3,576
2003	406	2,666	3,552
Percent below the poverty level			
1970	na %	22.6%	24.6%
1985	23.9	11.0	12.6
1990	22.5	10.1	12.2
1995	23.5	9.0	10.5
1996	24.4	9.4	10.8
1997	23.8	9.0	10.5
1998	21.0	8.9	10.5
1999	20.4	8.3	9.7
2000	18.8	8.7	10.2
2001	21.8	8.9	10.1
2002	21.4	9.1	10.4
2003	19.5	8.8	10.2

SOURCE: U.S. Bureau of the Census, Statistical Abstract of the United States, 1994; p. 476, table 731; 2000; p. 476, table 757; 2001, p. 443, table 682; 2002; p. 442, table 671. C 3.134:9:(year)
U.S. Bureau of the Census, Current Population Reports: Income, Poverty, and Health Insurance Coverage in the United States: 2003; Series P-60, #226; Table B-2; issued August 2004.

NOTES: 'Total' includes other races not shown separately.

UNITS: Number below the poverty level in thousands of persons; percent as a percent of all persons, by race, as shown.

Table 8.22 Income of Persons from Specified Sources, 2003

	Hispanic	White	Total
All persons, 15 years and over	22,928	168,257	203,482
Number with income from:			
Earnings	19,071	125,350	151,880
Unemployment compensation	1,032	6,647	8,219
Workers' compensation	273	1,659	2,022
Social Security	2,380	35,066	40,632
SSI (Supplemental Security Income)	738	3,438	5,444
Public assistance (total)	512	1,432	2,428
Veterans' benefits	96	1,938	2,323
Survivors benefits	79	2,397	2,649
Disability benefits	143	1,265	1,642
Pensions	533	14,041	15,809
Interest	5,461	86,898	98,565
Dividends	1,185	32,494	35,947
Rents, royalties, estates or trusts	673	10,118	11,255
Educational assistance	826	6,554	8,466
Child support	556	4,202	5,443
Alimony	22	378	401
Mean income, total from:	$23,787	$33,993	$32,222
Earnings	25,496	37,282	36,323
Unemployment compensation	3,946	4,518	4,493
Workers' compensation	7,509	6,587	6,573
Social Security	8,095	10,185	9,977
SSI (Supplemental Security Income)	5,118	5,444	5,417
Public assistance (total)	3,814	3,054	3,154
Veterans' benefits	10,457	9,068	9,516
Survivors benefits	12,717	11,835	11,719
Disability benefits	9,201	11,220	10,825
Pensions	12,205	15,157	14,987
Interest	780	1,575	1,507
Dividends	2,207	2,558	2,484
Rents, royalties, estates or trusts	3,676	5,783	5,650
Educational assistance	5,062	5,094	5,129
Child support	4,632	4,828	4,616
Alimony	na	11,722	11,498

SOURCE: U.S. Bureau of the Census and Bureau of Labor Statistics, <u>Annual Demographic Survey, March Supplement, 2003</u>; "(Table) PINC-09. Source of Income in 2003-- Number With Income and Mean Income of Specified Type in 2003 of People 15 Years Old and Over, by Race, Hispanic Origin and Sex".

NOTES: 'Total' includes other races and ethnic groups not shown separately. Persons 15 years old and older as of March the following year

UNITS: Number of persons in thousands

Table 8.23   Income of Households from Specified Sources, 1992

	Hispanic	White	Total
All households	6,626	82,083	96,391
one or more members received:			
Social Security	16.8%	28.5%	27.7%
AFDC or other non-SSI cash assistance	12.1	3.7	5.2
SSI	6.9	3.2	4.1
food stamps	18.7	6.6	8.8
housing assistance	7.9	3.3	4.6
free or reduced-price school lunches	21.8	5.5	7.4
employer subsidized health insurance	43.5	54.3	52.9
Medicare	16.5	26.6	25.9
Medicaid	28.5	10.1	12.8
Mean household income from:			
Social Security	$7,306	$8,980	$8,708
AFDC or other non-SSI cash assistance	4,513	3,444	3,489
SSI	4,336	3,651	3,666
food stamps	1,713	1,430	1,564
housing assistance	2,297	1,957	2,022
free or reduced-price school lunches	605	547	553
employer subsidized health insurance	3,231	3,163	3,139
Medicare	3,116	3,652	3,511
Medicaid	1,558	1,696	1,595

SOURCE: U.S. Bureau of the Census, <u>Current Population Reports: Measuring the Effect of Benefits and Taxes on Income and Poverty: 1992</u>, Series P60-186RD, pp. 52-54, table 7. C 3.186/P-60/186RD

NOTES: 'Total' includes other races/ethnic groups not shown separately.

UNITS: Number of households in thousands. Percent as a percent of all households, 100.0%. Mean amount of income from specified source per household receiving that source.

Table 8.24 Child Support Payments Agreed to or Awarded Custodial Parents, 2001

	Hispanic	White	Total
All Custodial Parents	1,921	9,535	13,383
Child support agreed to or awarded	984	5,915	7,916
Supposed to receive child support	856	5,212	6,924
Received payments	613	4,032	5,119
Full Payments	366	2,472	3,099
Partial Payments	247	1,560	2,020
Did not receive payments	242	1,180	1,804
All Custodial Mothers	1,689	7,843	11,291
Child support agreed to or awarded	884	5,258	7,110
Supposed to receive child support	755	4,624	6,212
Received payments	550	3,622	4,639
Full Payments	339	2,222	2,821
Partial Payments	211	1,401	1,818
Did not receive payments	205	1,002	1,573
All Custodial Fathers	232	1,692	2,092
Child support agreed to or awarded	101	657	807
Supposed to receive child support	101	588	712
Received payments	63	410	480
Full Payments	27	251	278
Partial Payments	36	159	202
Did not receive payments	38	178	232

SOURCE: U.S. Bureau of the Census, <u>Current Population Reports: Custodial Mothers and Fathers and Their Child Support: 2001</u>, Series P-60, #225, "Table 4. Child Support Payments Agreed to or Awarded Custodial Parents by Selected Characteristics and Sex: 2001", published in October 2003. C3.186:P-60/003

NOTES: 'Total' includes other races/ethnic groups not shown separately.

UNITS: Numbers in thousands.

Chapter 9: Crime & Corrections

Table 9.01 Victimization Rates for Personal Crimes, 2001 and 2002

	Hispanic victims	White victims	All Victims
2001			
crimes of violence	29.5	24.5	25.1
rape/sexual assault	1.1*	1.0	1.1
robbery	5.3	2.6	2.8
assault	23.1	20.8	21.2
personal theft	0.7*	0.8	0.8
2002			
crimes of violence	23.6	22.8	23.1
rape/sexual assault	0.7*	0.8	1.1
robbery	3.2	1.9	2.2
assault	19.7	20.0	19.8
personal theft	0.4*	0.7	0.7

SOURCE: U.S. Department of Justice, Office of Justice Programs, <u>Criminal Victimization 2001</u>; p. 6, table 2; p.3, table 1; <u>2002</u>; p. 5, table 3; p. 8, table 6 (data from the *National Crime Victimization Survey*).

NOTES: 'Victims of Total' includes victims of other races not shown separately. Personal crimes include completed and attempted rape, robbery, assault, and larceny, but exclude homicide.
The National Crime Victimization Survey has been redesigned. Comparisons of estimates of crime based on previous survey procedures (before 1993) are not recommended. * Based on 10 or fewer sample cases.

UNITS: Rates per 1,000 persons, 12 years old and over.

Table 9.02 Victimization Rates for Personal Crimes, by Type of Crime, 2002

	Hispanic	White	Total
All personal crimes	24.0	23.5	23.7
Crimes of violence	23.6	22.8	23.1
completed	8.7	7.4	7.6
attempted/threatened	14.9	15.4	15.5
rape/sexual assault	0.7*	0.8	1.1
rape/attempted rape	0.6*	0.5	0.7
- rape	0.2*	0.3	0.4
- attempted rape	0.3*	0.2	0.3
sexual assault	0.1	0.3	0.3
robbery	3.2	1.9	2.2
completed/property taken	2.4	1.4	1.7
- with injury	0.5*	0.6	0.7
- without injury	1.8	0.8	0.9
attempted to take property	0.8*	0.5	0.5
- with injury	0.1*	0.2	0.2
- without injury	0.7*	0.3	0.4
assault	19.7	20.0	19.8
aggravated	6.1	4.1	4.3
- with injury	2.3	1.4	1.4
- threatened with weapon	3.8	2.7	2.9
simple	13.7	15.9	15.5
- with minor injury	3.7	4.0	3.9
- without injury	10.0	11.9	11.6
purse snatching/pocket picking	0.4*	0.7	0.7

SOURCE: U.S. Department of Justice, Bureau of Justice Statistics, <u>Sourcebook of Criminal Justice Statistics 2002</u>; table 3.8, table 3.9. J 29.9/2:002

NOTES: NOTES: 'Total' includes other races and ethnic groups not shown separately. *Based on 10 or fewer sample cases. The National Crime Victimization Survey has been redesigned. Comparisons of estimates of crime based on previous survey procedures (before 1993) are not recommended.

UNITS: Rates per 1,000 persons, 12 years old and over.

Table 9.03 Victimization Rates for Property Crimes, by Type of Crime, 2002

	Hispanic households	White households	Total households
All property crimes	210.1	157.6	159.0
Household burglary	30.3	26.0	27.7
completed	26.6	22.6	23.5
- forcible entry	12.8	7.9	9.2
- unlawful entry without force	13.8	14.7	14.3
attempted forcible entry	3.7	3.4	4.2
Theft	162.1	124.1	122.3
completed	157.8	119.9	118.2
- less than $50.	35.4	39.6	37.9
- $50-$249	61.6	40.3	40.4
- $250 or more	45.7	30.0	29.6
- amount not available	15.1	10.0	10.2
attempted	4.3	4.1	4.1
Motor vehicle theft	17.7	7.5	9.0
completed	14.9	6.0	7.1
attempted	2.8*	1.6	1.9

SOURCE: U.S. Department of Justice, Bureau of Justice Statistics, <u>Sourcebook of Criminal Justice Statistics 2002</u>; table 3.25, table 3.26. J29.9/2:002

NOTES: 'Total households' includes households of other races not shown separately.
The National Crime Victimization Survey has been redesigned. Comparisons of estimates of crime based on previous survey procedures (before 1993) are not recommended.

UNITS: Rates per 1,000 households.

Table 9.04 Criminal History Profile of Prisoners Under Sentence of Death, 2003

	Hispanic	White	Total
U.S. Total	369	1,541	3,374
Prior felony convictions			
Yes	200	879	2,007
No	141	544	1,103
Not reported	na	na	264
Prior homicide convictions			
Yes	25	125	272
No	339	1,387	3,032
Not reported	na	na	70
Legal status at time of capital offense			
Charges pending	17	120	239
Probation	38	132	327
Parole	72	199	501
Prison escapee	6	23	42
Prison inmate	8	52	95
Other status	2	7	17
None	191	850	1,809
Not reported	na	na	344

SOURCE: U.S. Department of Justice, Bureau of Justice Statistics, <u>Capital Punishment 2003</u>; p. 8, table 8; issued November 2004, revised February 2005. NCJ 201848

NOTES: 'Total' includes other races and ethnic groups not shown separately.

UNITS: Number of jail inmates.

Table 9.05 Prisoners Under Jurisdiction of Federal and State Correctional Authorities, 1994 – 1997, 2000 – 2002

	Hispanic	White	Total
December 31, 1994			
total	156,908	464,167	1,054,774
federal institutions	25,226	58,403	95,034
state institutions	131,682	405,764	959,740
December 31, 1995			
total	174,292	455,021	1,126,287
federal institutions	27,559	60,261	100,250
state institutions	146,733	394,760	1,026,037
December 31, 1996			
total	186,761	478,308	1,180,524
federal institutions	30,003	61,885	105,544
state institutions	156,758	416,423	1,074,980
December 31, 1997			
total	198,673	505,513	1,240,962
federal institutions	33,110	65,539	112,973
state institutions	165,563	439,974	1,127,989
June 30, 2000			
total	203,700	453,300	1,305,253
federal institutions	33,200	29,800	110,974
state institutions	151,810	395,637	1,101,202
December 31, 2001			
total	na	na	1,404,032
federal institutions	na	na	156,993
state institutions	na	na	1,247,039
December 31, 2002			
total	na	na	1,440,655
federal institutions	na	na	163,528
state institutions	na	na	1,277,127

SOURCE: U.S. Department of Justice, Bureau of Justice Statistics, <u>Sourcebook of Criminal Justice Statistics, 1995</u>; p. 562, table 6.26; <u>1996</u>; p. 524, table 6.26; <u>1998</u>; p. 498, table 6.44; <u>1999</u>; p. 510, table 6.34; <u>2001</u>; p. 496, table 5.25; <u>2002</u>; table 6.24, table 6.28.
J 29.9/6:(year)

NOTES: 'Total' includes other races and ethnic groups not shown separately. 'White' excludes Hispanic persons.

UNITS: Number of prisoners under jurisdictional authority.

Table 9.06 Jail Inmates, 1990 - 2004

	Hispanic	White	Total
1990	14.3%	41.8%	100%
1991	14.2	41.1	100
1992	14.5	40.1	100
1993	15.1	39.3	100
1994	15.4	39.1	100
1995	14.7	40.1	100
1996	15.6	41.6	100
1997	15.7	40.6	100
1998	15.5	41.3	100
1999	15.5	41.3	100
2000	15.1	41.9	100
2001	14.7	43.0	100
2002	14.7	43.8	100
2003	15.4	43.6	100
2004	15.2	44.4	100

SOURCE: U.S. Department of Justice, Bureau of Justice Statistics, <u>Prison and Jail Inmates 2001</u>; p. 9, table 11; <u>2004</u>; p. 8, table 10.

NOTES: 'Total' includes other races and ethnic groups not shown separately. 'White' excludes Hispanic persons.

UNITS: Percent of local jail inmates.

Table 9.07   Prisoners Under Sentence of Death, by State, 2004

	Hispanic	White	Total
United States	354	1,591	3,487
Alabama	2	103	197
Arizona	19	93	130
Arkansas	1	16	39
California	126	248	635
Colorado	1	0	3
Connecticut	1	4	8
Delaware	3	9	19
Florida	33	219	381
Georgia	3	56	114
Idaho	0	20	20
Illinois	1	5	10
Indiana	0	27	39
Kansas	0	5	7
Kentucky	1	28	36
Louisiana	2	27	92
Maryland	0	4	11
Mississippi	0	32	70
Missouri	0	34	58
Montana	0	4	4
Nebraska	1	5	7
Nevada	9	42	87
New Hampshire	0	0	0
New Jersey	0	9	16
New Mexico	0	2	2
New York	0	2	4
North Carolina	4	74	203
Ohio	2	100	210
Oklahoma	3	54	102
Oregon	2	25	31
Pennsylvania	18	69	235
South Carolina	0	40	75
South Dakota	0	4	4
Tennessee	1	58	104
Texas	120	143	454
Utah	1	6	10
Virginia	0	12	26
Washington	0	6	11
Wyoming	0	2	2

SOURCE: U.S. Department of Justice, Bureau of Justice Statistics, <u>Sourcebook of Criminal Justice Statistics, 2004</u>; table 6.77. Data from NAACP Legal Defense and Educational Fund.   J 29.9/6: (year)

NOTES: 'Total' includes other races and ethnic groups not shown separately.

UNITS: Number prisoners under sentence of death.

Table 9.08   Chances of Going to State or Federal Prison, 1997

	Hispanic	White	Total
For the first time, by age			
20	1.5%	0.4%	1.1%
25	3.6	0.9	2.4
30	5.2	1.4	3.3
35	6.3	1.7	4.0
40	7.5	2.0	4.4
45	8.2	2.1	4.7
50	8.8	2.3	4.9
55	9.1	2.4	5.0
65	9.4	2.5	5.1
Lifetime	9.4	2.5	5.1
At some time during the rest of life, by age			
birth	9.4%	2.5%	5.1%
20	8.7	2.3	4.5
25	6.4	1.7	3.1
30	4.9	1.2	2.1
35	3.8	0.9	1.4
40	2.3	0.6	0.9
45	1.6	0.4	0.6

SOURCE: U.S. Department of Justice, Bureau of Justice Statistics, <u>Lifetime Likelihood of Going to State or Federal Prison</u>, March 1997, pp. 2-3, tables 1, 2 .
J 29.11/8:997

NOTES: Chances of going to State or Federal Prison for the first time are cumulative percents. These estimates were obtained by sequentially applying age-specific first-incarceration rates and mortality rates for each group to a hypothetical population of 100,000 births. Changes of going to State or Federal Prison at some time are for persons not previously incarcerated. These estimates were obtained by subtracting the cumulative percent first incarcerated for each age from the lifetime likelihood of incarceration. 'White' and 'Black' exclude persons of Hispanic origin.

UNITS: Percent of all resident population.

Table 9.09   Attitudes Toward the Police, 2002

Question: Do you think the police in your community treat Total fairly or do they tend to treat one or more of these groups unfairly?

	Hispanic	White	Total
Treat Total fairly	41%	61%	57%
Treat one or more groups unfairly	56	27	33
Don't know	3	10	9

Question: Are you sometimes afraid that the police will stop and arrest you when you are completely innocent, or not?

	Hispanic	White	Total
Yes, sometimes afraid	39%	16%	21%
No, not afraid	61	84	78

SOURCE:	U.S. Department of Justice, Bureau of Justice Statistics, <u>Sourcebook of Criminal Justice Statistics, 2002</u>; table 2.24, table 2.25. J 29.9/6:002
NOTES:	Table constructed by SOURCEBOOK staff from data provided by Louis Harris and Associates, Inc.
UNITS:	Percent of persons taking survey who answered with given response.

Table 9.10 Attitudes Toward the Death Penalty, 2003

Question: "Are you in favor of the death penalty for a person convicted of murder?"

	Non-White	White	Total
Yes, in favor	50%	75%	70%
No, not in favor	46	23	28
Don't know / refused	4	2	2

Question: "Generally speaking, do you believe the death penalty is applied fairly or unfairly in this country today?"

	Non-White	White	Total
Applied fairly	44%	65%	60%
Applied unfairly	54	32	37
Don't know / refused	2	3	3

SOURCE: U.S. Department of Justice, Bureau of Justice Statistics, <u>Sourcebook of Criminal Justice Statistics, 2002</u>; table 2.50, table 2.52. J 29.9/6:002

NOTES: Table constructed by <u>Sourcebook</u> staff from data provided by The Gallup Organization, Inc.

UNITS: Percent of persons taking survey who answered with given response.

Table 9.11   Inmates Ever Tested for HIV and Results – 1996, 1997, and 2002

	<u>Hispanic</u>	<u>White</u>	<u>Total</u>
1996			
Local jails			
number	45,759	110,023	289,991
percent HIV positive	3.2%	1.4%	2.2%
1997			
State prisons			
number	123,725	257,919	790,128
percent HIV positive	2.5%	1.4%	2.2%
Federal prisons			
number	18,466	21,128	70,902
percent HIV positive	0.7%	0.3%	0.6%
2002			
State prisons			
number	55,938	136,069	374,711
percent HIV positive	2.9%	0.8%	1.3%

SOURCE: U.S. Department of Justice, Bureau of Justice Statistics, <u>HIV in Prisons and Jails, 1996</u>; p. 14, table 8. <www.ojp.usurlobj.gov/bjs/pub/pdf/hivpj96.pdf> Accessed October 11, 1999; <u>2002</u>; p. 8, table 9; NCJ 205333.

NOTES: 'Total' includes other races/ethnic groups not shown separately.

UNITS: Percent of inmates tested for HIV (Human Immunodeficiency Virus) and reporting the results.

Table 9.12 Persons Stalked During Their Lifetime, 1996

	Hispanic	White	Total
Male	3.3%	2.1%	2.2%
Female	7.6	8.2	8.1

SOURCE: U.S. Department of Justice, Bureau of Justice Statistics, <u>Sourcebook of Criminal Justice Statistics, 1998</u>; p. 191, table 3.37. J 29.9/2:998

NOTES: 'Total' includes other races/ethnic groups not shown separately. Stalking is defined as a course of Conduct directed at a specific person that involves repeated visual or physical proximity, nonconsensual communication, or verbal, written or implied threats that would cause a reasonable person fear.

UNITS: Rates per 1,000 persons, 12 years old and over.

Chapter 10: Vital Statistics & Health

Table 10.01   AIDS (Acquired Immunodeficiency Syndrome) Cases, by Sex and Age, 1985 - 2003

	Hispanic	White	Total
All years*			
children under 13 years old	1,714	1,613	8,939
persons over 13 years old			
male	112,101	333,873	708,452
female	24,997	33,766	156,837
1985			
children under 13 years old	18	26	131
persons over 13 years old			
male	992	4,746	7,504
female	98	143	524
1990			
children under 13 years old	169	157	725
persons over 13 years old			
male	4,743	20,825	36,179
female	726	1,228	4,544
1995			
children under 13 years old	135	117	745
persons over 13 years old			
male	9,111	26,028	56,689
female	2,236	3,042	12,978

continued on the next page

Table 10.01   continued

	Hispanic	White	Total
2000			
children under 13 years old	30	32	189
persons over 13 years old			
male	5,275	11,314	30,135
female	1,462	1,859	9,958
2001			
children under 13 years old	26	30	170
persons over 13 years old			
male	5,318	11,054	30,663
female	1,543	1,993	10,617
2002			
children under 13 years old	24	23	150
persons over 13 years old			
male	5,543	11,221	31,644
female	1,561	1,930	10,951
2003			
children under 13 years old	34	23	153
persons over 13 years old			
male	6,344	11,831	32,781
female	1,776	1,923	11,297

SOURCE: U.S. Department of Health and Human Services, <u>Health United States, 2004</u>, p. 208, table 52 (data from Centers for Disease Control and Prevention, National Center for HIV, STD, and TB Prevention, Division of HIV/AIDS). HE 20.6223: (year)

NOTES: 'Total Races' includes other races/ethnic groups not shown separately. 'White' excludes white Hispanics. Data excludes residents of U.S. Territories. Historic data is revised continually on an ongoing basis. Data for all years have been updated through June 30, 1999. * 'all years' includes cases prior to 1985. Data for all years have been updated through June 30, 2000, to include temporarily delayed case reports and may differ from previous editions of Health, United States.

UNITS: Number of cases known to the Centers for Disease Control, by year of report; percent distribution as a percent of total (100.0%).

Table 10.02   Death rates for Human Immunodeficiency Virus (HIV) infection, 1987 - 2002

	Hispanic		White		Total	
	Male	female	male	female	male	female
1987	18.8	2.1	8.7	0.6	10.4	1.1
1990	28.8	3.8	15.7	1.1	18.5	2.2
1995	40.8	8.8	20.4	2.5	27.3	5.3
1997	14.0	3.3	5.9	1.0	9.6	2.6
1998	10.2	2.8	4.5	0.8	7.6	2.2
1999	10.9	3.0	4.9	1.0	8.2	2.5
2000	10.6	2.9	4.6	1.0	7.9	2.5
2002	9.1	2.6	4.3	0.9	7.4	2.5

SOURCE: U.S. Department of Health and Human Services, <u>Health United States, 2004</u>, pp. 187-188, table 42 (Centers for Disease Control and Prevention, National Center for Health Statistics).   HE 20.6223: (year)

NOTES: 'Total' includes other races/ethnic groups not shown separately. Data shown only for states with a Hispanic origin item their death certificates. Age-adjusted rates for all years differ from those shown in previous editions of Health, United States. Age-adjusted rates are calculated using the year 2000 standard population starting with Health, United States, 2001.

UNITS: Number of deaths known to the Centers for Disease Control, by year of report.

Table 10.03   AIDS (Acquired Immunodeficiency Syndrome) Cases, by Transmission Category, 1990 - 2001

	Hispanic	White	Total
All years*			
all transmission categories	118,012	335,375	758,434
men who have sex with men	45,316	226,714	357,583
injecting drug use	38,185	40,591	184,247
men who have sex with men and			
injecting drug use	5,930	25,427	48,132
hemophilia/coagulation disorder	434	3,939	5,171
heterosexual contact	13,524	17,445	79,769
sex with injecting drug user	5,106	6,675	28,368
transfusion	978	5,034	8,698
undetermined	13,645	16,225	74,834
1990			
all transmission categories	5,476	22,062	40,740
men who have sex with men	2,449	16,474	23,658
injecting drug use	2,010	2,054	9,270
men who have sex with men and			
injecting drug use	331	1,646	2,943
hemophilia/coagulation disorder	28	279	347
heterosexual contact	375	650	2,253
sex with injecting drug user	279	349	1,484
transfusion	82	505	770
undetermined	201	454	1,499

continued on the next page

Table 10.03   continued

	Hispanic	White	Total
2000			
all transmission categories	6,764	13,242	40,230
men who have sex with men	2,093	7,239	13,648
injecting drug use	1,552	1,852	8,099
men who have sex with men and			
injecting drug use	215	765	1,587
hemophilia/coagulation disorder	8	73	98
heterosexual contact	1,007	1,121	6,562
sex with injecting drug user	210	354	1,490
transfusion	45	95	297
undetermined	1,844	2,097	9,939
2001, January - June			
all transmission categories	3,026	6,168	19,002
men who have sex with men	970	3,277	6,241
injecting drug use	506	799	3,169
men who have sex with men and			
injecting drug use	70	316	657
hemophilia/coagulation disorder	2	38	48
heterosexual contact	376	477	2,757
sex with injecting drug user	78	142	611
transfusion	7	38	96
undetermined	1,095	1,223	6,034

SOURCE: U.S. Department of Health and Human Services, <u>Health United States, 2002</u>, p. 183, table 55 (data from Centers for Disease Control and Prevention, National Center for Health Statistics, National Center for HIV, STD, and TB Prevention, Division of HIV/AIDS). HE 20.6223:002

NOTES: 'Total' includes other races/ethnic groups not shown separately. 'White' excludes White Hispanics. Data excludes cases of residents of U.S. Territories. 'Hemophilia' includes coagulation disorders. 'Heterosexual' includes persons who have had heterosexual contact with a person with AIDS, or at risk of AIDS, and persons without other identified risks who were born in countries where heterosexual transmission is believed to play a major role although precise means of transmission have not yet been fully determined. * 'All years' includes cases prior to 1985. Data for all years have been updated through June 30, 2001, to include temporarily delayed case reports and may differ from previous editions of Health, United States.

UNITS: Number of cases known to the Centers for Disease Control, by year of report.

Table 10.04   Vaccinations of Children 19-35 Months of Age for Selected Diseases, 2000 and 2003

	Hispanic	White	Total
2000			
combined series (4:3:1:3)	73%	79%	76%
DTP (4 doses or more)	79	84	82
Polio (3 doses or more)	88	91	90
Measles-containing	90	92	91
Hib (3 doses or more)	91	95	93
Hepatitis B (3 doses or more)	88	91	90
Varicella	70	66	68
2003			
combined series (4:3:1:3)	79%	84%	81%
DTP (4 doses or more)	82	88	85
Polio (3 doses or more)	90	93	92
Measles-containing	93	93	93
Hib (3 doses or more)	93	95	94
Hepatitis B (3 doses or more)	91	93	92
Varicella	86	84	85

SOURCE: U.S. Department of Health and Human Services, <u>Health United States, 2004,</u> (Centers for Disease Control and Prevention, National Center for Health Statistics) pp. 250-251, table 72 (Data from the National Immunization Survey). HE 20.6223: (year)

NOTES: 'Total' includes other races/ethnic groups not shown separately. 'White' excludes White Hispanics. Data excludes cases of residents of U.S. Territories.   The 4:3:1:3 combined series consists of 4 doses of diphtheria-tetanus-pertussis (DTP) vaccine, 3 doses of polio vaccine, 1 dose of a measles-containing vaccine, and 3 doses of Haemophilus influenza type b (Hib) vaccine. DPT is the Diphtheria-tetanus-pertussis vaccine. Hib is the Haemophilus influenza type b (Hib) vaccine.

UNITS: Percent of children 19-35 months of age.

Table 10.05   Health Insurance Coverage, 1990 - 2003

	Hispanic	White	Total
Not covered by private or government health insurance			
total, 1990	28.2%	12.0%	12.9%
total, 1997	34.2%	15.0%	16.1%
total, 2000	32.0%	12.9%	14.0%
children under 18 years	24.9	10.9	11.6
total, 2001	33.2%	13.6%	14.6%
children under 18 years	24.1	11.0	11.7
total, 2002	32.4%	14.2%	15.2%
children under 18 years	22.7	11.1	11.6
total, 2003*	32.7%	14.6%	15.6%
children under 18 years	21.0	7.4	11.4

SOURCE: U.S. Bureau of the Census, <u>Current Population Reports: Household Economic Studies - Health Insurance Coverage: 1987-1990</u>, Series P-70, #29; p. 19, table 1 C 3.186/P-70/29.

U.S. Bureau of the Census, <u>Current Population Reports: Health Insurance Coverage: 1997</u>; Series P60-202; p. 2, figure 2; p. 3, figure 5; <u>2000</u>; Series P60-215; p. 5, figure 2; p. 8, figure 4; <u>2001</u>; Series P60-220; p. 6, figure 2; p. 9, figure 4; <u>2002</u>; p. 6, figure 2; p.8, figure 4 (issued September 2003).

U.S. Bureau of the Census, <u>Current Population Reports: Income, Poverty, and Health Insurance Coverage in the United States: 2003</u>; Series P-60, #226; p. 15, table 5; p.19, figure 7; issued August 2004.

NOTES: 'Total' includes other races and ethnic groups not shown separately. '*' indicates year in which 'White' as shown is equivalent to 'White Alone' that refers to people who reported 'White' and did not report any other race category.

UNITS: Percent as a percent of all persons in households, 100.0%.

Table 10.06   Health Care Coverage for Persons Under 65 Years of Age, by Type of Coverage, 1984 - 2002

	Hispanic	White	Total
1984			
Private insurance	57.1%	80.1%	77.1%
Private insurance obtained through workplace	52.9	72.0	69.2
Medicaid or other public assistance	12.2	4.6	6.7
not covered	29.1	13.4	14.3
1995			
Private insurance	48.0%	74.7%	71.6%
Private insurance obtained through workplace	44.6	68.5	65.6
Medicaid or other public assistance	19.8	8.8	11.3
not covered	31.5	15.3	15.9
2000			
Private insurance	49.0%	75.8%	71.7%
Private insurance obtained through workplace	46.1	70.8	67.0
Medicaid or other public assistance	14.2	7.2	9.4
not covered	35.4	15.2	16.8
2001			
Private insurance	47.6%	75.2%	71.5%
Private insurance obtained through workplace	45.0	70.3	67.0
Medicaid or other public assistance	16.0	8.1	10.3
not covered	34.8	14.7	16.2
2002			
Private insurance	46.1%	73.5%	69.7%
Private insurance obtained through workplace	43.4	68.8	65.2
Medicaid or other public assistance	18.9	9.5	11.8
not covered	33.8	15.3	16.6

SOURCE: U.S. Department of Health and Human Services, Health United States, 2004; pp. 345-346, table 129; pp. 348, table 130; pp. 350, table 131. HE 20.6223: (year)

NOTES: 'Total' includes other races not shown separately. Medicaid includes persons receiving AFDC (Aid to Families with Dependent Children) or SSI (Supplemental Security Income), or those with a current Medicaid card. Not covered includes those persons not covered by private insurance, Medicaid, Medicare, and military plans. Data **are** age-adjusted. The questionnaire changed in 1997 compared with previous years.

UNITS: Percent of the population.

Table 10.07   Health Care Coverage for Persons 65 Years of Age and Over, by Type of Coverage, 1995 - 2002

	Hispanic	White	Total
1995			
Private insurance	39.8%	78.3%	74.5%
Private insurance obtained through workplace	18.4	40.4	38.9
Medicaid or other public assistance	32.7	7.4	9.6
Medicare fee-for-service only	23.6	13.5	14.8
Medicare HMO	-	-	-
2000			
Private insurance	23.4%	66.9%	63.1%
Private insurance obtained through workplace	15.1	37.2	35.6
Medicaid or other public assistance	29.6	5.6	7.6
Medicare fee-for-service only	20.8	15.5	16.8
Medicare HMO	25.0	15.2	15.2
2001			
Private insurance	24.0%	66.4%	62.7%
Private insurance obtained through workplace	16.2	37.4	36.0
Medicaid or other public assistance	30.1	6.2	8.1
Medicare fee-for-service only	23.9	16.5	17.9
Medicare HMO	20.1	13.0	12.9
2002			
Private insurance	23.1%	64.0%	60.6%
Private insurance obtained through workplace	16.3	35.9	34.7
Medicaid or other public assistance	28.6	6.3	8.0
Medicare fee-for-service only	na	na	na
Medicare HMO	22.1	11.7	11.9

SOURCE: U.S. Department of Health and Human Services, <u>Health United States, 2004</u>, (Centers for Disease Control and Prevention, National Center for Health Statistics) pp. 352-354, table 132 (data from the National Health Interview Survey). HE 20.6223: (year)

NOTES: 'Total' includes other races/ethnic groups not shown separately. Medicaid includes persons receiving AFDC (Aid to Families with Dependent Children) or SSI (Supplemental Security Income), or those with a current Medicaid card. Medicare fee-for-service only includes persons who are not covered by private insurance, Medicaid or a Medicare HMO. Data are age-adjusted.
The questionnaire changed in 1997 compared with previous years.

UNITS: Percent of the population.

Table 10.08 Selected Characteristics of Live Births, 1990 - 2002

	Hispanic births	White births	Total births
1990			
birth weight under 2,500 grams	6.06%	5.70%	6.97%
birth weight under 1,500 grams	1.03	0.95	1.27
mother under 18 years old	6.6	3.6	4.7
mother 18-19 years old	10.2	7.3	8.1
births to unmarried mothers	36.7	20.4	28.0
mother with less than 12 years of school	53.9	22.4	23.8
mother with 16 years or more of school	5.1	19.3	17.5
prenatal care began in 1st trimester	60.2	79.2	75.8
prenatal care began in 3rd trimester or no prenatal care	12.0	4.9	6.1
2000			
birth weight under 2,500 grams	6.41%	6.55%	7.57%
birth weight under 1,500 grams	1.14	1.14	1.43
mother under 18 years old	6.3	3.5	4.1
mother 18-19 years old	9.9	7.1	7.7
births to unmarried mothers	42.7	27.1	33.2
mother with less than 12 years of school	48.9	21.4	21.7
mother with 16 years or more of school	7.6	26.3	24.7
prenatal care began in 1st trimester	74.4	85.0	83.2
prenatal care began in 3rd trimester or no prenatal care	6.3	3.3	3.9

continued on the next page

Table 10.08   continued

	Hispanic births	White births	Total births
2001			
birth weight under 2,500 grams	6.47%	6.68%	7.68%
birth weight under 1,500 grams	1.14	1.16	1.44
mother under 18 years old	5.8	3.3	3.8
mother 18-19 years old	9.7	6.9	7.5
births to unmarried mothers	42.5	27.7	33.5
mother with less than 12 years of school	48.8	21.7	21.7
mother with 16 years or more of school	7.9	26.7	25.2
prenatal care began in 1st trimester	75.7	85.2	83.4
prenatal care began in 3rd trimester or no prenatal care	5.9	3.2	3.7
2002			
birth weight under 2,500 grams	6.55%	6.80%	7.82%
birth weight under 1,500 grams	1.17	1.17	1.46
mother under 18 years old	5.6	3.1	3.6
mother 18-19 years old	9.3	6.6	7.1
births to unmarried mothers	43.5	28.5	34.0
mother with less than 12 years of school	48.1	21.6	21.5
mother with 16 years or more of school	8.3	27.3	25.9
prenatal care began in 1st trimester	76.7	85.4	83.7
prenatal care began in 3rd trimester or no prenatal care	5.5	3.1	3.6

SOURCE: U.S. Department of Health and Human Services, <u>Health United States, 2003</u>; (Centers for Disease Control and Prevention, National Center for Health Statistics) p. 103, table 6; p. 106, table 8; p. 107, table 9; p. 108, table 10; p. 110, table 12; <u>2004</u>; p. 113, table 6; p. 116, table 8; p. 117, table 9; p. 118, table 10; p. 120, table 12.   HE 20.6223: (year)

NOTES: Data based on race of the mother. Data on Hispanic-origin available in 48 states plus Washington, DC.

UNITS: Percent, as a percent of all live births, 100.0%.

Table 10.09   Projected Fertility Rates, Women 10-49 Years Old, 2000 and 2010

	Hispanic women	White women	All women
2000			
Total fertility rate	3,108	2,114	2,130
birth rates			
10-14 years old	1.9	0.6	0.9
15-19 years old	94.4	43.6	48.5
20-24 years old	184.6	107.9	112.3
25-29 years old	170.8	124.3	121.4
30-34 years old	109.0	97.4	94.1
35-39 years old	48.7	40.7	40.4
40-44 years old	11.6	7.8	7.9
45-49 years old	0.6	0.4	0.5
2010			
Total fertility rate	2,818	2,098	2,123
birth rates			
10-14 years old	2.3	0.9	1.3
15-19 years old	95.7	54.3	43.6
20-24 years old	175.2	112.6	107.9
25-29 years old	146.7	118.5	124.3
30-34 years old	91.6	90.0	97.4
35-39 years old	41.9	36.6	40.7
40-44 years old	9.9	7.1	7.8
45-49 years old	0.6	0.3	0.4

SOURCE: U.S. Bureau of the Census, <u>Statistical Abstract of the United States, 2002</u>; p. 62, table 72; <u>2003</u>; p. 75, table 89; <u>2004</u>; p. 63, table 76. C 3.134(year)

NOTES: 'All women' includes women of other races and ethnic groups not shown separately. The total fertility rate is the number of births that 1,000 women would have in their lifetime if, at each year of age they experienced the birth rates occurring in the specified year. Projections are based on middle fertility assumptions.

UNITS: Total fertility rate and birth rate in births per 1,000 women.

Table 10.10   Births and Birth Rates, by Age of the Mother, 2002 and 2003

	Hispanic	White	Total
2002			
Live births	876,642	3,174,760	4,021,726
Fertility rate	94.4	64.8	64.8
Birth rate per 1,000 women, by age group			
10-14 years old	1.4	0.5	0.7
15-19 years old	83.4	39.4	43.0
20-24 years old	164.3	101.6	103.6
25-29 years old	139.4	117.4	113.6
30-34 years old	95.1	95.5	91.5
35-39 years old	47.8	42.4	41.4
40-44 years old	11.5	8.2	8.3
45-49 years old	0.7	0.5	0.5
2003			
Live births	912,256	3,227,755	4,091,063
Fertility rate	96.9	66.2	66.1
Birth rate per 1,000 women, by age group			
10-14 years old	1.3	0.5	0.6
15-19 years old	82.2	38.3	41.7
20-24 years old	163.4	100.6	102.6
25-29 years old	144.4	119.6	115.7
30-34 years old	102.0	99.4	95.2
35-39 years old	50.8	44.8	43.8
40-44 years old	12.2	8.7	8.7
45-49 years old	0.7	0.5	0.5

SOURCE: U.S. Department of Health and Human Services, <u>National Vital Statistics Report: Births: Final Data for 2002, Volume 52, No. 10, December 17, 2003</u>; p. 31, table 2; p. 32, table 3; p. 38, table 6; p. 41, table 8; <u>2003, Volume 53, No. 9, November 23, 2004</u>; p. 10, table 2; p. 11, table 3. HE 20.6217: (year)

NOTES: 'Total' includes other races and ethnic groups not shown separately. Data based on race of the mother. Fertility rate is the total number of births, regardless of age of mother, per 1,000 women aged 15-44 years.

UNITS: Live births in number of births; rates as shown.

Table 10.11   Birth Rates for Women 15-44 Years of Age, by Live Birth Order, 2000 and 2003

	Hispanic mothers	White mothers	All mothers
2000 (preliminary)			
All live births	105.9	66.7	67.6
first child	39.5	26.9	27.1
second child	32.3	22.0	22.0
third child	19.9	11.2	11.3
fourth child and over	14.2	6.6	7.2
2002			
All live births	94.4	64.8	64.8
first child	34.6	25.7	25.8
second child	29.0	21.5	21.1
third child	17.9	11.0	10.9
fourth child and over	12.9	6.5	7.0
2003			
All live births	96.9	66.2	66.1
first child	35.4	26.7	26.7
second child	30.1	21.9	21.5
third child	18.6	11.1	11.0
fourth child and over	12.7	6.5	6.8

SOURCE: U.S. Department of Health and Human Services National Vital Statistics Report: Births: Preliminary Data for 2000, Volume 49, No. 5, July 24, 2001; p. 10, table 3. HE 20.6217:001

U.S. Department of Health and Human Services, National Vital Statistics Report: Births: Final Data for 2002, Volume 52, No. 10, December 17, 2003; p. 32, table 3; p. 41, table 8; 2003, Volume 53, No. 9, November, 2004; p. 11, table 3. HE 20.6217: (year)

NOTES: 'All mothers' includes mothers of other races and ethnic groups not shown separately. Data based on race of the mother.

UNITS: Live births per 1,000 women 15-44 years of age.

Table 10.12   Use of Selected Substances by Persons 12 Years Old and Older, 2000 and 2003

	Hispanic	White	Total
2000			
any illicit drug	5.3%	6.4%	6.3%
marijuana	3.6	4.9	4.8
psychotherapeutic drug*	1.7	1.8	1.7
alcohol	39.8	50.7	46.6
binge alcohol	22.7	21.2	20.6
any tobacco	22.2	31.0	29.3
cigarettes	20.7	25.9	24.9
cigars	3.5	5.0	4.8
2003			
any illicit drug	8.0%	8.3%	8.2%
marijuana	4.9	6.4	6.2
psychotherapeutic drug*	3.0	2.8	2.7
alcohol	41.5	54.4	50.1
binge alcohol	24.2	23.6	22.6
any tobacco	23.7	30.0	29.8
cigarettes	21.4	25.9	25.4
cigars	4.9	7.2	5.4

SOURCE: U.S. Department of Health and Human Services, <u>Health United States, 2004</u>, pp. 228-229, table 63.   HE 20.6223: (year)

NOTES: 'Total' includes other races not shown separately. Both 'Black' and 'White' exclude Hispanic persons. Use of selected substances in the past month by person 12 years of age and over.

Any illicit drug includes marijuana/hashish, cocaine, heroin, hallucinogens, or any psychotherapeutic drug for nonmedical use.

*Psychotherapeutic drug for nonmedical use includes prescription-type pain relievers, tranquilizers, stimulants, or sedatives; does not include over-the-counter drugs.

Binge Alcohol: Five or more drinks on the same occasion at least once in the past month.

UNITS: Percent as a percent of population by selected substance.

Table 10.13   Death Rates for Malignant Neoplasms of the Breast, for Females, by Age, 1990 and 2002

	Hispanic women	White women	All Women
1990			
All ages, age adjusted rate	19.5	33.2	33.3
All ages, crude rate	11.5	35.9	34.0
35-44 years old	11.7	17.1	17.8
45-54 years old	32.8	44.3	45.4
55-64 years old	45.8	78.5	78.6
65-74 years old	64.8	113.3	111.7
75-84 years old	67.2	148.2	146.3
85 years old and over	102.8	198.0	196.8
2002			
All ages, age adjusted rate	15.5	25.0	25.6
All ages, crude rate	9.2	29.5	28.3
35-44 years old	7.8	10.7	12.0
45-54 years old	21.6	29.4	31.4
55-64 years old	33.5	55.0	56.2
65-74 years old	48.7	84.6	84.4
75-84 years old	73.1	126.5	125.9
85 years old and over	105.3	192.6	191.5

SOURCE: U.S. Department of Health and Human Services, Health United States, 2004, (Centers for Disease Control and Prevention, National Center for Health Statistics); pp. 182-183, table 40. HE 20.6223: (year)

NOTES: 'All Women' includes women of other races/ethnic groups not shown separately. Data excludes deaths of nonresidents of the United States. *Indicates data based on fewer than 20 deaths. Age-adjusted rates for all years differ from those shown in previous editions of Health, United States. Age-adjusted rates are calculated using the year 2000 standard population starting with Health, United States, 2001.

UNITS: Rate is the number of deaths per 100,000 resident female population, by age group.

Table 10.14   Death Rates for Motor Vehicle Accidents, by Sex and Age, 2000 and 2002

	Hispanic		White		Total	
	male	female	male	female	male	female
2000						
All ages, age adjusted	21.3	7.9	21.8	9.8	21.7	9.5
All ages, crude	20.1	7.2	21.6	10.0	21.3	9.7
under 1 year	*	*	4.2	3.5	4.6	4.2
1-14 years old	4.4	3.9	4.8	3.7	4.9	3.7
15-24 years old	34.7	10.6	39.6	17.1	37.4	15.9
25-34 years old	24.9	6.5	25.1	8.9	25.5	8.8
35-44 years old	21.6	7.3	21.8	8.9	22.0	8.8
45-64 years old	21.7	8.3	19.7	8.7	20.2	8.7
65 years old and over	28.9	13.4	29.4	16.2	29.5	15.8
2002						
All ages, age adjusted	22.2	8.1	22.4	9.8	22.1	9.6
All ages, crude	21.3	7.4	22.4	10.1	21.9	9.8
under 1 year	*	*	2.9	2.2	3.3	2.8
1-14 years old	5.1	3.2	4.5	3.2	4.6	3.3
15-24 years old	38.9	12.4	41.9	17.9	39.3	16.6
25-34 years old	26.4	7.2	26.6	9.0	26.5	8.8
35-44 years old	22.6	7.3	22.3	9.4	22.3	9.3
45-64 years old	19.9	8.4	20.6	8.7	20.7	8.7
65 years old and over	30.7	13.1	29.8	16.3	29.8	15.7

SOURCE: U.S. Department of Health and Human Services, <u>Health United States, 2004</u>, (Centers for Disease Control and Prevention, National Center for Health Statistics) pp. 190-193, table 44. HE 20.6223: (year)

NOTES: 'Total' includes other races and ethnic groups not shown separately. Excludes deaths of nonresidents of the United States. *Indicates data based on fewer than 20 deaths. Age-adjusted rates for all years differ from those shown in previous editions of Health, United States. Age-adjusted rates are calculated using the year 2000 standard population starting with Health, United States, 2001.

UNITS: Rate is the number of deaths per 100,000 resident population.

Table 10.15   Death Rates for Assault (Homicide), by Sex and Age, 2000 and 2002

	Hispanic		White		Total	
	male	female	male	female	male	female
2000						
All ages, age adjusted	11.8	2.8	5.2	2.1	9.0	2.8
All ages, crude	13.4	2.8	5.2	2.1	9.3	2.8
under 1 year	6.6	7.4	8.2	5.0	10.4	7.9
1-14 years old	1.7	1.0	1.2	0.8	1.5	1.1
15-24 years old	28.5	3.7	9.9	2.7	20.9	3.9
25-44 years old	17.2	3.7	7.4	2.9	13.3	4.0
45-64 years old	9.1	2.9	4.1	1.8	6.0	2.1
65 years old and over	4.4	2.4	2.5	1.6	3.3	1.8
2002						
All ages, age adjusted	11.6	2.5	5.3	2.0	9.4	2.8
All ages, crude	13.2	2.6	5.4	2.0	9.6	2.7
under 1 year	6.6	5.9	6.2	4.6	7.9	7.1
1-14 years old	1.6	1.2	1.0	0.9	1.5	1.3
15-24 years old	29.6	3.8	10.6	2.5	21.5	3.8
25-44 years old	16.5	3.4	7.7	2.8	14.2	4.0
45-64 years old	8.6	2.3	4.2	1.9	6.2	2.2
65 years old and over	4.4	*	2.6	1.4	3.2	1.6

SOURCE: U.S. Department of Health and Human Services, Health United States, 2003; pp. 184-186, table 45; 2004; pp. 194-196, table 45. (Centers for Disease Control and Prevention, National Center for Health Statistics) HE 20.6223: (year)

NOTES: 'Total' includes other races/ethnic groups not shown separately. Excludes deaths of nonresidents of the United States. *Based on fewer than 20 deaths. Age-adjusted rates for all years differ from those shown in previous editions of Health, United States. Age-adjusted rates are calculated using the year 2000 standard population starting with Health, United States, 2001.

UNITS: Rate is the number of deaths per 100,000 resident population

Table 10.16   Death Rates for Suicide, by Sex and Age, 2000 and 2002

	Hispanic		White		Total	
	male	female	male	female	male	female
2000						
All ages, age adjusted	10.3	1.7	19.1	4.3	17.7	4.0
All ages, crude	8.4	1.5	18.8	4.4	17.1	4.0
15-24 years old	10.9	2.0	17.9	3.1	17.1	3.0
25-44 years old	11.2	2.1	22.9	6.0	21.3	5.4
45-64 years old	12.0	2.5	23.2	6.9	21.3	6.2
65 years old and over	19.5	*	33.3	4.3	31.1	4.0
2002						
All ages, age adjusted	9.9	1.8	20.0	4.7	18.4	4.2
All ages, crude	8.3	1.6	19.9	4.8	17.9	4.3
15-24 years old	10.6	2.1	17.7	3.1	16.5	2.9
25-44 years old	10.9	2.0	24.0	6.6	22.2	5.8
45-64 years old	11.9	2.5	25.9	7.5	23.5	6.7
65 years old and over	17.5	1.9	34.2	4.3	31.8	4.1

SOURCE: U.S. Department of Health and Human Services, <u>Health United States, 2003</u>; pp. 187-189, table 46; <u>2004</u>, pp. 197-199, table 46. (Centers for Disease Control and Prevention, National Center for Health Statistics) HE 20.6223: (year)

NOTES: 'Total' includes other races and ethnic groups not shown separately. Excludes deaths of nonresidents of the United States. *Indicates data based on fewer than 20 deaths. Age-adjusted rates for all years differ from those shown in previous editions of Health, United States. Age-adjusted rates are calculated using the year 2000 standard population starting with Health, United States, 2001.

UNITS: Rate is the number of deaths per 100,000 resident population.

Table 10.17 Dental Visits in the Past Year by Poverty Status, 2000 and 2002

	Hispanic	White	Total
2000			
Poor			
2-17 years old	53.9%	63%	61.8%
18-64 years old	38.1	52.1	46.7
65 years old and over	31.4	34.4	30.3
Non-Poor			
2-17 years old	69.1%	82.5%	80.1%
18-64 years old	61.3	73.8	72.0
65 years old and over	54.3	68.3	66.7
2002			
Poor			
2-17 years old	59.9%	69.4%	64.4%
18-64 years old	39.0	48.8	44.6
65 years old and over	38.1	38.2	35.0
Non-Poor			
2-17 years old	68.3%	82.7%	79.6%
18-64 years old	58.5	71.1	69.0
65 years old and over	61.3	66.4	64.6

SOURCE: U.S. Department of Health and Human Services, <u>Health United States, 2002,</u> (Centers for Disease Control and Prevention, National Center for Health Statistics); pp. 235-236, table 80 (data from the National Health Interview Survey); <u>2004</u>; pp. 265-266, table 79.   HE 20.6223: (year)

NOTES: 'Total' includes other races and ethnic groups not shown separately. 'White' excludes white Hispanics. Data excludes residents of U.S. Territories. Poor persons are defined as below the poverty threshold. Non-poor persons have incomes of 200 percent or greater than the poverty threshold.

UNITS: Percent of persons with a dental visit in the past year.

Table 10.18   Abortions, 1992 - 2001

	Hispanic	White	Total
1992	30.7	23.6	33.5
1993	28.9	23.1	33.4
1994	27.8	21.7	32.1
1995	26.5	20.4	31.1
1996	27.6	20.2	31.4
1997	26.8	19.4	30.6
1998*	27.3	18.9	26.4
1999*	26.1	17.7	25.6
2000*	22.5	16.7	24.5
2001*	23.0	16.5	24.6

SOURCE: U.S. Department of Health and Human Services, <u>Health, United States, 2004,</u> (data from Centers for Disease Control and Prevention, National Center for Health Statistics) p. 126, table 16. HE 20.6223:003

NOTES: 'Total' includes women of other races not shown separately. 1989 and later, "White" includes women of Hispanic ethnicity. CA, AK, NH, OK did not report abortion data in 1998*.

UNITS: Abortions per 100 live births.

Table 10.19   Maternal Mortality Rates, by Age of the Mother, 1995 - 2002

	Hispanic mothers	White mothers	mothers of Total
1990			
All persons	47	177	343
All ages, age adjusted rate	7.4	5.1	7.6
1995			
All persons	43	129	277
All ages, age adjusted rate	5.4	3.6	6.3
1999			
All persons	67	214	391
All ages, age adjusted rate	7.9	5.5	8.3
2000			
All persons	81	240	396
All ages, age adjusted rate	9.0	6.2	8.2
2001			
All persons	81	228	399
All ages, age adjusted rate	8.8	6.5	8.8
2002			
All persons	62	190	357
All ages, age adjusted rate	6.0	4.8	7.6

SOURCE: U.S. Department of Health and Human Services, Health United States, 2004, p. 189, table 43. HE 20.6223: (year)

NOTES: 'Mothers of Total' include mothers of other races not show separately. Data for maternal mortality for complications of pregnancy, childbirth and the puerperium. Rates for women 35 years old and over computed by relating deaths to live births to women in this age group. *Indicates data based on fewer than 20 deaths.

UNITS: Rate is the number of deaths of mothers per 100,000 live births.

Table 10.20   Work-Loss Days, 1998 and 2002

	<u>Hispanic</u>	<u>White</u>	<u>Total</u>
1998			
All persons	19,982	147,652	197,304
bed days in the past 12 months	86,697	678,508	928,891
Days per person	4.4	4.6	4.8
All employed persons	14,381	106,575	142,153
work-loss days in the past 12 months	52,755	480,483	647,934
Days per person	3.7	4.6	4.6
2002			
All persons	22,691	166,362	205,825
bed days in the past 12 months	71,693	735,923	947,246
Days per person	3.2	4.5	4.7
All employed persons	16,335	118,761	147,474
work-loss days in the past 12 months	60,321	500,148	638,545
Days per person	3.7	4.3	4.4

SOURCE: U.S. Department of Health and Human Services, <u>Vital and Health Statistics</u>, Series 10; #209 (1998); pp. 46-48, table 17; #222 (2002); pp. 48-49, table 17 (data from the National Health Interview Survey).

NOTES: 'Total' includes other races not shown separately. Respondents were asked how many times in the last 12 months an injury or illness caused them to miss a day of work or had kept them in bed more than half a day.

UNITS: Number of work-loss days per 100 persons 18 years old and over, currently employed.

Table 10.21   Limitation of Activity, 1998 and 2002

	Hispanic	White	Total
1998			
Total with any limitation of activity	24.0%	33.6%	31.9%
very difficult or unable to			
walk a quarter of a mile	4.6	7.1	7.0
stand or be one's feet for 2 hours	5.9	8.4	8.2
stoop, bend or kneel	5.9	8.1	7.8
climb up to 10 steps without resting	4.1	5.1	5.2
sit for 2 hours	3.0	2.8	2.9
reach over one's head	2.4	2.5	2.6
use fingers to grasp or handle	1.6	1.6	1.6
small objects			
lift or carry a heavy object*	4.2	4.3	4.5
push or pull large objects	6.0	7.5	7.4
2002			
Physical activities that are very difficult or			
cannot be done at all			
any physical difficulty	12.4%	13.6%	14.0%
walk a quarter of a mile	5.6	6.2	6.5
climb up to 10 steps without resting	5.4	4.5	4.9
stand or be one's feet for 2 hours	7.3	8.1	8.5
sit for 2 hours	2.9	3.0	3.1
stoop, bend or kneel	7.7	7.9	8.2
reach over one's head	2.4	2.3	2.4
use fingers to grasp or handle	2.2	1.6	1.7
small objects			
lift or carry a heavy object*	5.2	3.6	4.0
push or pull large objects	6.6	5.7	6.0

SOURCE: U.S. Department of Health and Human Services, <u>Vital and Health Statistics</u>, Series 10; #207 (1998); pp. 52-54, table 19; #222 (2002); pp. 53-54, table 19 (data from the National Health Interview Survey).

NOTES: 'Total' includes other races not shown separately. *Heavy object is defined as something as heavy as 10 pounds (such as a full bag of groceries).

UNITS: Percent as a percent of the population of 18 years of age and over.

Table 10.22   Medical Injury or Poisoning Episodes, 1998 and 2003

	Hispanic	White	Total
1998			
all persons	31,033	193,384	269,007
all episodes	2,501	27,144	34,020
fall	793	8,433	10,523
struck by person or object	289	3,925	4,886
transportation	495	3,213	4,459
over exertion	222	4,046	4,679
cutting / piercing instrument	216	2,305	2,837
other causes	385	3,924	4,983
poisoning	101	1,298	1,654
2003			
all persons	39,735	233,582	286,010
all episodes	2,067	20,975	23,782
fall	653	7,056	8,002
struck by person or object	281	2,546	2,990
transportation	397	3,094	3,775
over exertion	221	3,071	3,369
cutting / piercing instrument	157	1,729	1,881
other causes	277	2,809	3,043
poisoning	*81	670	722

SOURCE: U.S. Department of Health and Human Services, <u>Vital and Health Statistics</u>, Series 10; #<u>207</u> (1998); pp. 32-34, table 9 and 10; #<u>220</u> (2002); pp.22-25, table 9 and 10; #<u>224</u> (2005); pp.25-27, table 8 and 9 (data from the National Health Interview Survey).

NOTES: 'Total' includes other races not shown separately. Based on a question in survey that asked all respondents whether they had been poisoned and/or injured seriously enough in the past 3 months to seek medical advice or treatment. '*' represents estimates that do not meet standard of reliability or precision.

UNITS: Number of persons or incidents in thousands.

Table 10.23   Injuries, by Selected Characteristic, 2003

	Hispanic	White	Total
2003			
all persons	39,735	233,582	286,010
by activity engaged			
- driving	*311	2,217	2,744
- working at paid job	291	2,835	3,335
- working around house or yard	159	3,138	3,376
- attending school	*87	402	510
- sports	239	2,839	3,206
- leisure activities (non-sports)	426	4,634	5,182
by place of occurrence			
- at home inside	487	5,445	5,926
- at home outside	316	4,454	4,949
- at school/childcare center	221	1,077	1,261
- at hospital	na	320	392
- on a street or highway	409	3,135	3,832
- at a recreational center	206	2,711	3,039
- at an industrial place	*102	1,010	1,089
- at a service area	152	880	1,082

SOURCE: U.S. Department of Health and Human Services, <u>Vital and Health Statistics</u>, Series 10; #<u>224</u> (2005); pp. 28-29,table 8, table 11; pp. 32-33, table 11 (data from the National Health Interview Survey).

NOTES: 'Total' includes other races not shown separately. *Figure does not meet standard of reliability or precision.

UNITS: Number of persons who had a medically attended injury episode in thousands.

Table 10.24   Selected Characteristics of Persons With a Work Disability, 2003

	Hispanic	White	Total
Persons with a work disability by age			
Total	1,998	13,541	18,058
persons 16-24 years old	185	962	1,395
persons 25-34 years old	334	1,516	2,173
persons 35-44 years old	408	2,752	3,708
persons 45-54 years old	515	3,739	5,010
persons 55-64 years old	557	4,572	5,772
Work Disabled as a percent of total population, by age			
Total	na	na	na
persons 16-24 years old	3.1	3.4	3.9
persons 25-34 years old	4.5	4.9	5.6
persons 35-44 years old	6.9	7.8	8.5
persons 45-54 years old	14.1	11.3	12.5
persons 55-64 years old	26.5	19.6	21.1
Percent of work disabled:			
Receiving Social Security Income	27.2	34.7%	33.4%
Receiving Food Stamps	21.8	14.5	17.1
covered by Medicaid	56.6	69.1	65.7
Residing in public housing	8.9	4.9	6.9
Residing in subsidized housing	4.5	3.1	3.9

SOURCE: U.S. Bureau of the Census, <u>Statistical Abstract of the United States, 2004</u>, p. 355, table 539 (data from the Current Population Survey).
C 3.134: (year)

NOTES: 'Total' includes other races and ethnic groups not shown separately. Covers the civilian noninstitutional population and members of the armed forces living off post or with members of their families on post. Persons are classified as having a work disability if they (1) have a health problem or disability which prevents them from or which limits the kind or amount of work they can do; (2) have a service disability or ever retired or left a job for health reasons; (3) did not work in survey reference week or previous year because of long-term illness or disability; or, (4) are under age 65 and are covered by Medicare or receive Supplemental Security Income.

UNITS: Persons with a work disability in thousands of persons; work disabled as a percent of total population in percent; percent of the work disabled by characteristic as a percent of the work disabled.

Table 10.25   Percentage of Adults Engaging in Leisure-Time Physical Activity, 1997 - 2003

	Hispanic	White	Total
1997			
no participation in physical activity	36.6%	27.6%	29.5%
participates in regular, sustained activity	17.1	20.3	19.6
participates in regular, vigorous activity	8.6	14.0	12.9
1998			
no participation in physical activity	38.4%	26.7%	28.7%
participates in regular, sustained activity	17.4	21.6	20.8
participates in regular, vigorous activity	11.4	14.0	13.6
2000			
persons who are physically inactive	41.0%	24.2%	27.6%
persons with insufficient activity	37.9	48.3	46.2
persons who meet recommended activity	21.1	27.5	26.2
2003			
persons who are physically inactive	36.0%	20.9%	24.3%
persons not meeting recommended activity	62.5	51.0	54.0
persons who meet recommended activity	37.5	49.0	46.0

SOURCE: U.S. Bureau of the Census, <u>Statistical Abstract of the United States, 1999</u>; p. 157, table 248; <u>2000</u>; p. 145, table 232; <u>2002</u>; p. 127, table 191; <u>2004</u>; p. 129, table 195 (data from National Center for Chronic Disease Prevention and Health Promotion), C 3.134(year)

NOTES: 'Total' includes other races not shown separately. 'Regular, sustained activity' is any type or intensity of activity that occurs 5 or more times per week and 30 minutes or more per occasion. 'Regular, vigorous activity' is rhythmic contraction of large muscle groups performed 3 times per week or more for at least 20 minutes per occasion.
'Recommended activity' is physical activity at least 5 times/week x 30 minutes/time or vigorous physical activity for 20 minutes at a time at least 3 times/week.

UNITS: Percent of persons 18 years of age and over.

Table 10.26   Health Status for Children, 2003

	Hispanic children	White children	All children
Respondent-assessed health status			
All children under 18	13,464	56,545	72,973
Excellent	6,109	32,175	39,979
Very good	3,850	15,843	20,675
Good	3,101	7,638	11,004
Fair/poor	392	840	1,253
Selected measures of health care access			
All children under 18	13,464	56,545	72,973
Uninsured for health care	2,699	5,360	7,086
Unmet medical need	402	1,212	1,613
Delayed care due to cost	530	2,080	2,643
No usual place of care	1,445	2,608	3,438
Two or more visits to the emergency room in the past 12 months	995	3,550	5,108

SOURCE: U.S. Department of Health and Human Services, <u>Vital and Health Statistics</u>, Series 10; <u>Summary Health Statistics for U.S. Children: National Health Interview Survey, 2003</u>; #223; pp. 16-17, table 5; pp. 39-40, table 15.

NOTES: 'Total' includes other races and ethnic groups not shown separately. '*' indicates year in which 'White' as shown is equivalent to 'White Alone' that refers to people who reported 'White' and did not report any other race category.

UNITS: Number in thousands of children under 18 years of age.

Chapter 11: Special Topics

Table 11.01   Selected Characteristics of Farms and Farm Operators, 2002

	Hispanic farms	All farms
Characteristics of farms		
Farms and land in farms		
farms (number)	50,592	2,128,982
land in farms (acres)	20,770,712	938,279,056
harvested cropland (acres)	na	302,697,252
Farms by size		
1-9 acres	8,390	179,346
10-49 acres	16,061	563,772
50-179 acres	13,088	658,705
180-499 acres	7,047	388,617
500 acres or more	6,006	338,542
Owned and rented land in farms		
owned land in farms		
farms	46,755	1,979,140
acres	13,942,460	584,963,623
rented or leased land in farms		
farms	13,942	700,846
acres	6,828,252	353,315,433
2002 Market value of agricultural products sold, (in thousands of dollars)		
total	$4,669,572	$200,646,355
average per farm	92,299	94,245
crops (including nursery and greenhouse crops)	3,072,961	95,151,954
livestock, poultry and their products	1,596,611	105,494,401
Farms by value of sales		
less than $1,000	$12,591	$430,953
$1,000-$2,499	7,818	307,368
$2,500-$4,999	6,208	243,026
$5,000-$9,999	5,857	246,624
$10,000-$24,999	6,447	272,333
$25,000-$49,999	3,557	163,521
$50,000 or more	8,114	465,157

continued on the next page

Table 11.01   continued

	Hispanic farms	All farms
Farms by North American Industry Classification System		
oilseed and grain farming (1111)	3,365	37,540,988
vegetable and melon farming (11112)	1,532	13,145,448
fruit and tree nut farming (1113)	7,739	13,489,154
greenhouse, nursery, and floriculture production (1114)	2,236	15,065,589
other crop farming (1119)	8,101	14,548,102
tobacco farming (11191)	298	1,506,953
cotton farming (11192)	477	3,789,565
sugarcane farming, hay farming, and all other crop farming (11193, 11194, 11199)	7,326	8,315,743
beef cattle ranching and farming (112111)	17,756	19,755,572
cattle feedlots (112112)	903	22,895,343
dairy cattle and milk production (11212)	982	22,737,525
hog and pig farming (1122)	552	12,337,959
poultry and egg production (1123)	744	24,410,930
sheep and goat farming (1124)	1,587	445,366
animal aquaculture and other animal production (1125, 1129)	5,095	4,274,380

Operator characteristics

	Hispanic farms	All farms
Total operators	72,349	2,128,982
Residence		
on farm operated	49,313	1,680,160
not on farm operated	23,036	448,822
Principal occupation		
farming	40,094	1,224,246
other	32,255	904,736
Days of work off farm		
none	32,349	962,200
any	40,000	1,166,782
1-49 days	5,343	122,248
50-99 days	3,403	66,306
100-199 days	5,572	145,880
200 days or more	25,682	832,348

continued on the next page

Table 11.01 continued

	Hispanic farms	All farms
Characteristics of the farm operator - continued		
Years on present farm		
2 years or less	5,037	74,754
3 or 4 years	8,200	143,599
5 to 9 years	17,024	374,756
10 years or more	42,088	1,535,873
average years on present farm	na	20.7
Age		
under 25 years old	1,554	16,962
25-34 years old	5,189	106,097
35-44 years old	14,884	366,306
45-54 years old	19,974	572,664
55-64 years old	15,444	509,123
65 years old and over	15,304	557,830
average age	52.6	55.3
Sex		
male	55,744	1,891,163
female	16,605	237,819
Principal operator is a hired manager		
farms	2,781	55,372
acres	5,037,926	103,135,293

SOURCE: U.S. Bureau of the Census, <u>2002 Census of Agriculture</u>, Vol. 1 Geographic Area Series, Part 51, U.S. Summary and State Data; p. 8, table 2; p. 16, table 9; p. 52, table 50; pp. 214-226, table 61; p. 51, table 49; p. 56, table 54. C 3.31/4:002/v. 1/ pt. 51

NOTES: 'All farms' includes farms owned/operated by persons of Total/ethnic groups.

UNITS: Farms, farms by size, farms by organization, farms by value of sales, farms by Standard Industrial Classification, in number of farms; land in farms and harvested crop lands in acres; market value of agricultural products sold in thousands of dollars. Characteristics of farm operators in number of farm operators.

Table 11.02   Summary of Results of the 2000 Consumer Expenditure Survey

	Hispanic consumer units	White consumer units	All consumer units
Number of consumer units	9,473	96,137	109,367
income before taxes	$34,891	$46,260	$44,649
Average number in consumer unit:			
persons	3.4	2.5	2.5
children under 18 years old	1.2	.6	.7
persons 65 and over	.2	.3	.3
earners	1.6	1.4	1.4
vehicles	1.6	2.0	1.9
percent homeowner	47%	68%	66%
Average annual expenditures			
Total	$32,735	$39,406	$38,045
food	5,362	5,304	5,158
food at home	3,496	3,066	3,021
- cereals and bakery products	491	462	453
- meats, poultry, fish, and eggs	1,036	780	795
- dairy products	359	336	325
- fruits and vegetables	670	530	521
- other food at home	940	959	927
food away from home	1,865	2,238	2,137
alcoholic beverages	285	394	372
housing	10,850	12,651	12,319
shelter	6,437	7,312	7,114
- owned dwellings	2,949	4,877	4,602
- rented dwellings	3,307	1,923	2,034
- other lodging	181	512	478
utilities, fuels and public services	2,170	2,478	2,489
household operations	465	714	684
housekeeping supplies	474	507	482
household furnishings and equipment	1,303	1,640	1,549
apparel and services	2,076	1,878	1,856

continued on the next page

Table 11.02   continued

	Hispanic consumer units	White consumer units	All consumer units
transportation	$6,719	$7,721	$7,417
- vehicle purchases	3,146	3,574	3,418
- gasoline and motor oil	1,244	1,337	1,291
- other vehicle expenses	1,945	2,361	2,281
- public transportation	385	448	427
health care	1,243	2,198	2,066
entertainment	1,186	1,980	1,863
personal care products and services	564	555	564
reading	59	157	146
education	363	666	632
tobacco products and smoking supplies	173	329	319
miscellaneous	602	804	776
cash contributions	645	1,260	1,192
personal insurance and pensions	2,608	3,510	3,365
- life and other personal insurance	189	404	399
- pensions and Social Security	2,420	3,105	2,966

SOURCE: U.S. Department of Labor, Bureau of Labor Statistics, <u>Consumer Expenditure Survey, 2000</u>, table 7, accessed 4 March 2003.
<ftp://ftp.bls.gov/pub/special.requests/cc/standard/2000/tenracar.txt>

NOTES: 'All consumer units' includes consumer units of Total and ethnic groups.

UNITS: Number of consumer units in thousands; average numbers as shown; average annual expenditures by category, averages in current dollars.

Table 11.03   Summary of Results of the 2002 Consumer Expenditure Survey

	Hispanic consumer units	White consumer units	All consumer units
Number of consumer units	10,500	98,553	112,108
income before taxes	$37,360	$51,177	$49,430
Average number in consumer unit:			
persons	3.3	2.5	2.5
children under 18 years old	1.1	.6	.7
persons 65 and over	.2	.3	.3
earners	1.6	1.	1.4
vehicles	1.7	2.1	2.0
percent homeowner	48%	69%	66%
Average annual expenditures			
Total	$34,742	$42,135	$40,677
food	5,666	5,542	5,375
food at home	3,643	3,159	3,099
- cereals and bakery products	498	459	450
- meats, poultry, fish, and eggs	1,057	789	798
- dairy products	385	342	328
- fruits and vegetables	720	565	552
- other food at home	982	1,004	970
food away from home	2,023	2,383	2,276
alcoholic beverages	301	402	376
housing	11,841	13,633	13,283
shelter	7,372	8,043	7,829
- owned dwellings	3,567	5,432	5,165
- rented dwellings	3,645	2,065	2,160
- other lodging	161	546	505
utilities, fuels and public services	2,413	2,673	2,684
household operations	407	733	706
housekeeping supplies	471	578	545
household furnishings and equipment	1,179	1,606	1,518
apparel and services	2,097	1,756	1,749

continued on the next page

Table 11.03   continued

	Hispanic consumer units	White consumer units	All consumer units
transportation	$6,769	$8,077	$7,759
- vehicle purchases	3,130	3,836	3,665
- gasoline and motor oil	1,261	1,278	1,235
- other vehicle expenses	2,062	2,553	2,471
- public transportation	317	411	389
health care	1,366	2,490	2,350
entertainment	1,409	2,211	2,079
personal care products and services	492	531	526
reading	60	148	139
education	488	792	752
tobacco products and smoking supplies	186	336	320
miscellaneous	628	818	792
cash contributions	612	1,327	1,277
personal insurance and pensions	2,827	4,072	3,899
- life and other personal insurance	196	419	406
- pensions and Social Security	2,631	3,653	3,493

SOURCE: U.S. Department of Labor, Bureau of Labor Statistics, <u>Consumer Expenditure Survey, 2002</u>, table 7, issued February 2004.

NOTES: 'All consumer units' includes consumer units of Total.

UNITS: Number of consumer units in thousands; average numbers as shown; average annual expenditures by category, averages in current dollars.

Table 11.04   Occupied Housing Units, by Tenure, 1980, 1999 and 2003

	Hispanic householder	White householder	All householders
1980			
All households	4,008	68,810	80,390
owner occupied			
number	1,739	46,671	51,795
percent	43.4%	67.8%	64.4%
renter occupied	2,269	22,139	28,595
1999			
All households	9,041	83,624	102,803
owner occupied			
number	4,087	60,041	68,796
percent	45.2%	71.8%	66.9%
renter occupied	4,955	23,583	34,007
2003			
All households	11,039	87,512	105,867
owner occupied			
number	5,106	63,141	72,254
percent	46.3%	72.2%	68.2%
renter occupied	5,933	24,370	33,614

SOURCE: U.S. Bureau of the Census, <u>Statistical Abstract of the United States, 1999</u>; p. 730, table 1214; <u>2001</u>; p. 606, table 955; <u>2002</u>; p. 599, table 938; <u>2004</u>; p. 611, table 950.   C 3.134:(year)

NOTES: 'Total' includes persons of Total/ethnic groups. Persons of Hispanic origin can be of any race.

UNITS: Number of housing units; percent as a percent of total as shown.

Table 11.05   Housing Affordability, Families, 1995

	Hispanic	White	Total
Percent that cannot afford a median priced home in their region using conventional, fixed rate, 30 year financing			
All families	80.8%	47.4%	52.2%
married couples	73.3	39.9	42.2
male householder (no wife present)	87.5	69.2	73.2
female householder (no husband present)	95.7	79.4	84.5
Percent that cannot afford a median priced home in their region using FHA, fixed rate, 30 year financing			
All families	80.3%	46.1%	51.0%
married couples	72.3	38.3	40.6
male householder (no wife present)	87.5	69.6	73.2
female householder (no husband present)	95.9	79.4	84.6

continued on the next page

Table 11.05   continued

	Hispanic	White	Total
Percent that cannot afford a modestly priced home in their region using conventional, fixed rate, 30 year financing			
All families	74.7%	39.6%	44.4%
married couples	65.3	32.2	34.2
male householder (no wife present)	82.5	59.6	64.1
female householder (no husband present)	93.1	72.0	77.7
Percent that cannot afford a modestly priced home in their region using FHA, fixed rate, 30 year financing			
All families	72.6%	37.2%	42.1%
married couples	62.4	29.3	31.4
male householder (no wife present)	82.5	58.2	62.8
female householder (no husband present)	92.6	71.3	77.0

SOURCE: U.S. Bureau of the Census, <u>Current Housing Reports: Who Can Afford to Buy A House in 1995?</u>, table 2-2; table 3-2.   C 3.215:H121/99-1

NOTES: 'Total' includes families of Total/ethnic groups.

UNITS: Percent as a percent of families as shown.

Table 11.06   General Mobility, 1999-2000, and 2002-2003

	Hispanic	White	Total
1999-2000			
Total	32,103	221,703	270,219
non-movers	25,347	187,810	226,831
moved to			
same county	4,254	18,811	24,399
different county, same state	1,006	7,135	8,814
different state, same region	335	2,992	4,062
different division, same region	217	1,076	1,261
different region	318	2,633	3,105
abroad	626	1,247	1,746
2002-2003			
Total	38,680	228,198	282,556
non-movers	31,727	197,953	242,463
moved to			
same county	4,434	17,418	23,468
different county, same state	1,059	6,111	7,728
different state, same region	464	2,873	3,752
different division, same region	141	931	1,181
different region	351	2,135	2,695
abroad	504	777	1,269

SOURCE: U.S. Bureau of the Census, Current Population Survey, <u>Geographic Mobility: March 1999 to March 2000</u>, pp. 1-6, table 2; <u>Geographic Mobility: March 2002 to March 2003</u>, table 2.

NOTES: 'Total' includes persons of Total/ethnic groups. Persons of Hispanic origin can be of any race. Mobility data from March 1999 to March 2000, and from March 2002 to March 2003.

UNITS: Number of persons one year old and over in thousands.

Table 11.07   Hispanic Owned Firms, by Major Industry Group, 1992, 1997

	all firms		firms with paid employees			
	firms	sales & receipts	firms	sales & receipts	employees	annual payroll
1992						
All industries	771,708	$72,824,270	115,364	$57,187,370	691,056	$10,768,112
agricultural services, forestry and fishing	31,600	1,464,572	3,985	935,079	19,174	233,781
mining	1,327	304,926	194	250,485	1,527	33,555
construction	97,476	8,212,208	20,192	6,447,317	76,882	1,417,290
manufacturing	18,461	6,157,555	5,209	5,827,194	65,920	1,280,030
transportation and public utilities	47,797	3,702,744	5,100	2,373,189	35,484	606,617
wholesale trade	17,727	12,489,034	5,434	11,687,451	37,547	859,658
retail trade	107,846	17,730,517	27,641	15,116,613	197,626	2,001,152
finance, insurance, and real estate	49,231	4,831,923	5,087	2,774,196	23,177	472,149
services	347,297	16,787,257	40,863	11,558,361	231,977	3,836,093
industries not classified	52,945	1,143,533	1,660	217,485	1,743	27,787
1997						
All industries	1,199,896	$186,274,582	211,884	$158,674,537	1,388,746	$29,830,028
agricultural services, forestry and fishing	40,040	2,279,397	5,925	1,309,733	25,955	416,702
mining	1,909	429,446	325	367,442	3,569	97,854
construction	152,573	21,923,384	31,478	19,146,212	168,873	4,218,419
manufacturing	25,552	28,684,759	10,173	27,719,404	171,738	4,549,598
transportation and public utilities	84,554	8,293,935	12,735	5,605,332	79,682	1,587,106
wholesale trade	31,480	40,386,625	14,125	38,746,137	94,281	2,388,988
retail trade	155,061	32,280,310	48,713	28,599,447	324,474	3,892,182
finance, insurance and real estate	56,629	6,644,826	9,944	4,728,312	34,783	949,006
services	500,449	39,177,767	70,838	30,406,573	463,889	11,297,362
industries not classified	151,931	6,174,133	7,909	2,045,945	21,502	432,812

SOURCE: U.S. Bureau of the Census, 1992 Economic Censuses MB92-2 Survey of Minority-Owned Business Enterprises: Hispanic, pp. 13-14, table 1. C 3.258:92-2
1997 Economic Censuses Survey of Minority-Owned Business Enterprises: Hispanic, pp. 17-18, table 1. EC97CS-4

NOTES: Data from the 1992 and 1997 Economic Censuses.

UNITS: Firms in number of firms; sales and receipts in thousands of dollars; employees in number of employees; annual payroll in thousands of dollars.

Glossary

ACUTE CONDITION see **CONDITION (HEALTH).**

AGE ADJUSTMENT
Age adjustment, using the direct method, is the application of the age specific rates in a population of interest to a standardized age distribution in order to eliminate the differences in observed rates that result from age differences in population composition. This adjustment is usually done when comparing two or more populations at one point in time, or one population at two or more points in time.

AGGRAVATED ASSAULT see **CRIME.**

ARSON see **CRIME.**

AVERAGE see **MEAN; MEDIAN.**

BED (HOSPITAL; NURSING HOME)
Any bed that is staffed for use by inpatients is counted as a bed in a facility.

BED-DISABILITY DAY see **DISABILITY DAY.**

BIRTH see **LIVE BIRTH.**

BURGLARY see **CRIME.**

CAUSE OF DEATH
For the purpose of national mortality statistics, every death is attributed to one underlying condition, based on information reported on the death certificate and utilizing the international rules (International Classifications of Disease) for selecting the underlying cause of death from reported conditions. Selected causes of death are shown on tables.

CHRONIC CONDITION see **CONDITION (HEALTH).**

CIVILIAN LABOR FORCE
All persons (excluding members of the Armed Forces) who are either employed or unemployed. (The experienced civilian labor force is a subgroup of the civilian labor force, composed of all persons, employed and unemployed, that have worked before.)
Employed persons are those persons 16 years old and over who were either a) "at work"- those who did any work at all as paid employees, or in their own business or profession, or on their own farm, or worked 15 or more hours as unpaid workers on a family farm or in a family business; or b) "with a job but not at work"- those who did not work during the reference period but had jobs or businesses from which they were temporarily absent due to illness, bad weather, industrial dispute, vacation, or other personal reasons. Excluded from the employed are persons whose only activity consisted of work around the house or volunteer work for religious, charitable, and similar organizations.

Employed persons are classified as either **full-time workers**, those who worked 35 hours or more per week; or **part-time workers**, those who worked less than 35 hours per week.

Unemployed persons are those who were neither "at work" nor "with a job, but not at work" <u>and</u> who were a) looking for work, and b) available to accept a job. Also included as unemployed are persons who are waiting to be called back to a job from which they have been laid off. The unemployed are divided into four groups according to reason for unemployment:

--**job losers** (including those who have been laid off)
--**job leavers** who have left their job voluntarily
--**reentrants**, persons who have worked before and are reentering the labor force
--**new entrants** to the labor force looking for work

CIVILIAN NONINSTITUTIONAL POPULATION see **POPULATION.**

CIVILIAN POPULATION see **POPULATION.**

COLLEGE

A postsecondary school which offers a general or liberal arts education, usually leading to an associate, bachelor's, master's, doctor's, or first professional degree. Junior colleges and community colleges are included. See also **Institution of Higher Education; University.**

COMMUNITY HOSPITAL

All non-federal short term hospitals, excluding hospital units of institutions, whose services are available to the public. **Short term hospitals** are those where the average length of stay is less than 30 days.

CONDITION (HEALTH)

A health condition is a departure from a state of physical or mental well-being. Based on duration, there are two categories of conditions: acute and chronic.

An **acute condition** is one that has lasted less than three months, and has involved either a physician visit (medical attention) or restricted activity.

A **chronic condition** is any condition lasting three months or more, or is one classified as chronic regardless of the time of onset. See also **Health Limitation of Activity.**

CONSOLIDATED METROPOLITAN STATISTICAL AREA (CMSA)

A geographic area concept introduced in June, 1984, which, in combination with Metropolitan Statistical Area (MSA), and Primary Metropolitan Statistical Area (PMSA), replace the Standard Metropolitan Statistical Area (SMSA) concept. CMSAs are designated in accordance with criteria established by the federal Office of Management and Budget (OMB). In general CMSAs are MSAs with a population of one million or more, and which have component PMSAs. See also **Metropolitan Statistical Area.**

CONSUMER EXPENDITURE SURVEY

A survey of current consumer expenditures reflecting the buying habits of American consumers. Begun in 1979 and conducted jointly by the U.S. Bureau of Labor Statistics and the U.S. Bureau of the Census, the survey consists of two parts: an interview panel survey in which the expenditures of consumer units are obtained in five interviews conducted every three months, and a diary or record keeping survey completed by the participating households for two consecutive one-week periods. See also **Consumer Unit.**

The Consumer Expenditure Survey, which collects data on expenditures, should not be confused with the Consumer Price Index, which measures the average change in prices of consumer goods and services.

CONSUMER UNIT

An entity used as the basis of the Consumer Expenditure Survey. A consumer unit comprises either

--all the members of a particular household who are related by blood, marriage, adoption, or other legal arrangements; or

--a person living alone or sharing a household with others, or living as a roomer in a private home or lodging house or in a permanent living quarters in a hotel or motel, but who is financially independent; or

--two or more persons living together who pool their income to make joint expenditure decisions.

A consumer unit may or may not be a household.

CRIME

A crime is an action which is prohibited by law. Their are two major statistical programs which measure crime in the United States. The first is the Uniform Crime Reporting (UCR) program, administered by the FBI. The Bureau receives monthly and annual reports from most police agencies around the country (covering approximately 97% of the population). These reports contain information on eight major types of crime (called collectively, serious crime), which are known to police. Serious crime consists of four violent crimes (murder and non-negligent manslaughter, which includes willful felonious homicides and is based on police investigations rather than determinations of a medical examiner; forcible rape, which includes attempted rape; robbery, which includes stealing or taking anything of value by force or violence, or by threat of force or violence, and includes attempted robbery; and aggravated assault which includes intent to kill), and four property crimes (burglary, which includes any unlawful entry to commit a felony or theft and includes attempted burglary and burglary followed by larceny; larceny, which includes theft of property or articles of value without use of force, violence, or fraud, and excludes embezzlement, con games, forgery, etc.; motor vehicle theft, which includes all cases where vehicles are driven away and abandoned, but excludes vehicles taken for temporary use and returned by the taker; and arson, which includes any willful or malicious burning or attempt to burn, with or without the intent to defraud, of a dwelling house, public building, motor vehicle, aircraft, or personal property of another.)

The second approach to the measurement of crime is through the National Crime Survey (NCS) administered by the Bureau of Justice Statistics. The survey is based on a representative sample of approximately 49,000 households, inhabited by about 102,000 persons age 12 and over. Although the categories of crime are similar to those used by the FBI in the UCR, the NCS is based on reports of victimization directly by victims, as opposed to crimes reported to police as in the UCR. As might be imagined, not all crimes are reported or known to police, therefore NCS estimates of crime tend to be significantly higher than UCR figures. The NCS also differs from the UCR in that only crimes whose victims can be interviewed are included (hence there are no homicide statistics), and only victims who are 12 years old or older are counted. The two central concepts in the NCS are victimization, which is the specific criminal act as it affects a single victim, and a criminal incident, which is a specific criminal act involving one or more victims. Thus in regard to personal crime, there are more victimizations, than incidents.

DEATH see **CAUSE OF DEATH; INFANT MORTALITY.**

DISABILITY

The presence of a physical, mental, or other health condition which has lasted six or more months and which limits or prevents a particular type of activity. See also **Work Disability.**

DISABILITY DAY

A day on which a person's usual activity is reduced because of illness or injury. There are four types of disability days (which are not mutually exclusive). They are

--a **restricted-activity day**, a day on which a person cuts down on his or her usual activities because of illness or an injury.

--a **bed-disability day,** a day on which a person stays in bed more than half of the daylight hours (or normal waking hours) because of a specific illness or injury. All hospital days are bed-disability days. Bed disability days may also be work-loss days or school loss days.

--a **work-loss day**, a day on which a person did not work at his or her job or business for at least half of his or her normal workday because of a specific illness or injury. Work loss days are determined only for employed persons.

--a **school-loss day**, a day on which a child did not attend school for at least half of his or her normal schoolday because of a specific illness or injury. School-loss days are determined only for children 6 to 16 years of age.

DISPOSABLE INCOME see **INCOME.**

EMPLOYED PERSONS see **CIVILIAN LABOR FORCE.**

EMPLOYMENT STATUS see **LABOR FORCE STATUS.**

ENROLLMENT

The total number of students registered in a given school unit at a given time, generally in the fall of the year. See also **Full-Time Enrollment; Part-Time Enrollment.**

EVER MARRIED PERSONS see MARITAL STATUS.

EXPERIENCED CIVILIAN LABOR FORCE

That portion of the Civilian Labor Force, both employed and unemployed, that have worked before. Excludes new entrants to the Civilian Labor Force. See also **Civilian Labor Force.**

EXPERIENCED WORKER see **EXPERIENCED CIVILIAN LABOR FORCE.**

FAMILY

A type (subgroup) of household in which there are two or more persons living together (including the householder) who are related by birth, marriage, or adoption. All such related persons in one housing unit are considered as members of one family. (For example, if the son or daughter of the family householder and that son's or daughter's spouse and/or children are members of the household, they are all counted as part of the householder's family.) However, non-family members who are not related to the householder (such as a roomer or boarder and his or her spouse, or a resident employee and his or her spouse who are living in), are not counted as family members but as unrelated individuals living in a family household. Thus for Census purposes, a housing unit can contain only one household, and a household can contain only one family. See also **Family Type; Household; Householder; Unrelated Individual.**

FAMILY INCOME see **INCOME.**

FAMILY TYPE

Families are classified by type according to the sex of the householder and the presence of a spouse and children. The three main types of households are: **Married Couples,** in which a husband and wife live together (with or without other persons in the household); **Male Householder, No Wife Present,** in which a male householder lives together with other members of his family but without a wife; and **Female Householder, No Husband Present,** in which a female householder lives together with other members of her family but without a husband. See also **Family; Family Household; Household.**

FARM

As defined by the Bureau of the Census (and adopted by the Department of Agriculture), a farm is any place from which $1,000 or more of agricultural products were sold, or would have been sold during a given year. Control of the farm may be exercised through ownership or management, or through a lease, rental or cropping arrangement. In the case of landowners who have one or more tenants or renters, the land operated by each is counted as a separate farm. This definition has been in effect since 1974.

FARMLAND

All land under the control of a farm operator, including land not actually under cultivation or not used for pasture or grazing. Rent free land is included as part of a farm only if the operator has sole use of it. Land used for pasture or grazing on a per head basis that is neither owned nor leased by the farm operator is not included except for grazing lands controlled by grazing associations leased on a per acre basis.

FARM INCOME

Gross farm income comprises cash receipts from farm marketings of crops and livestock, federal government payments made directly to farmers for farm-related activities, rental value of farm homes, value of farm products consumed in farm homes, and other farm-related income such as machine hire and custom work.

FULL-TIME ENROLLMENT (HIGHER EDUCATION)

The number of students enrolled in higher education courses with a total credit load equal to at least 75% of the normal full-time course load.

FULL-TIME WORKERS see CIVILIAN LABOR FORCE.

HEALTH LIMITATION OF ACTIVITY

A characteristic of persons with chronic conditions. Each person identified as having a chronic condition is classified as to the extent to which his or her activities are limited by the condition as follows:

--persons unable to carry on a major activity (that is the principal activity of a person of his or her age-sex group: for persons 1-5 years of age, it refers to ordinary play with other children; for persons 6-16 years of age, it refers to school attendance; for persons 17 years of age and over, it usually refers to a job, housework, or school attendance.)

--persons limited in the amount or kind of major activity performed.

--persons not limited in major activity, but otherwise limited.

--persons not limited in activity.

See also **Condition (Health).**

HEALTH MAINTENANCE ORGANIZATION (HMO)

A prepaid health plan delivering comprehensive care to members through designated providers, having a fixed monthly payment for health care services, and requiring members to be in the plan for a specified period of time (usually one year). HMOs are distinguished by the relationship of the providers to the plan. HMO model types are: **Group** -- an HMO that delivers health services through a physician group controlled by the HMO, or an HMO that contracts with one or more independent group practices to provide health services; **Individual Practice Association (IPA)** -- an HMO that contracts directly with physicians in independent practice, and/or contracts with one or more associations of physicians in independent practice, and/or contracts with one or more multi-specialty group practices (but the plan is predominantly organized around solo-single specialty practices).

HIGHER EDUCATION see INSTITUTION OF HIGHER EDUCATION.

HISPANIC ORIGIN
An aspect of a person's ancestry. The Bureau of the Census in many of its survey asks persons if they are of Hispanic origin. There are four main subcategories of Hispanic origin: Mexican, Puerto Rican, Cuban, and other Hispanic. Hispanic origin is not a racial classification. Persons may be of any race and of Hispanic origin. Hispanic origin is used interchangeably with Spanish and Spanish origin.

HOME OWNERSHIP see **TENURE.**

HOSPITAL see **COMMUNITY HOSPITAL.**

HOSPITAL DAY
A hospital day is a night spent in a hospital by a person admitted as an inpatient.

HOUSEHOLD
The person or persons occupying a housing unit. There are two main types of households: family households, which consist of two or more persons related by birth, marriage, or adoption living together (see also **Family; Family Type**); and non-family households, which consist of a person living alone, or together with unrelated individuals (see Unrelated Individuals). See also **Householder.**

HOUSEHOLD INCOME see **INCOME.**

HOUSEHOLD TYPE see **HOUSEHOLD.**

HOUSEHOLDER
The person in whose name a housing unit is rented or owned.

HOUSING UNIT
A house, apartment, mobile home or trailer, group of rooms, or single room occupied as a separate living quarter, or, if vacant, intended for occupancy as a separate living quarter. Separate living quarters are those in which the occupants live and eat separately from any other persons in the building and which have direct access from the outside of the building or through a common hall.

Both occupied and vacant housing units are counted in many surveys; however, recreational vehicles, boats, caves, tents, railroad cars, and the like are only included if they are occupied as someone's usual place of residence. Vacant mobile homes are included if they are intended for occupancy on the site where they stand. Vacant mobile homes on dealer's sales lots, at the factory, or in storage yards are excluded.

Most housing unit data is for year-round housing units which comprises all occupied housing units plus vacant housing units intended for year round use. Vacant units held for seasonal use or migratory labor are excluded. See also **Occupancy Status, Rooms, Specified Owner-Occupied Housing Units, Tenure, Value (Housing).**

HOUSING TENURE see **TENURE.**

INCIDENT see **CRIME.**

INCOME

The term income has different definitions depending on how it is modified and in what situation it is used. Like many government statistical terms, income can be viewed hierarchically.

Personal income is the current income received by persons from all sources, minus their personal contributions for social insurance. Persons include individuals (including owners of unincorporated firms), non-profit institutions serving individuals, private trust funds, and private non-insured welfare funds. Personal income includes transfers (payments not resulting from current production) from government and business such as Social Security benefits, public assistance, etc., but excludes transfers among persons. Also included are certain non-monetary types of income, chiefly estimated net rental value to owner-occupants of their homes, the value of services furnished without payment by financial intermediaries, and food and fuel produced and consumed on farms.

Disposable personal income is personal income less personal tax and non-tax payments. It is income available to persons for spending and saving. Personal tax and non-tax payments are tax payments (net of refunds) by persons (excluding contributions for social insurance) that are not chargeable to business expenses, and certain personal payments to general government that are treated like taxes. Personal taxes include income, estate and gift, personal property, and motor vehicle licenses. Non-tax payments include passport fees, fines and penalties, donations, tuition and fees paid to schools and hospitals mainly operated by the government.

Money income is a smaller less inclusive category than personal income. Money income is the sum of the amounts received from wages and salaries, self-employment income (including losses), Social Security, Supplemental Security Income, public assistance, interest, dividends, rents, royalties, estate or trust income, veterans payments, unemployment and workers' compensation payments, private and government retirement and disability pensions, alimony, child support, and any other source of money income which was regularly received. Capital gains or losses and lump-sum or one-time payments, such as life insurance settlements, are excluded. Also excluded are non-cash benefits such as food stamps, health benefits, housing subsidies, rent-free housing, and the goods produced and consumed on farms. Money income is reported for households and various household types as well as for unrelated individuals. (In regard to family money income it should be noted that only the amount received by all family members 15 years old and over is counted, and excludes income received by household members not related to the householder.) It is reported in aggregate, median, mean, and per capita amounts. Money income is also used for determining the poverty status of families and unrelated individuals.

INFANT MORTALITY

The deaths of live-born children who do not reach their first birthday. Infant mortality is usually expressed as a rate per 1,000 live births.

INPATIENT DAYS (HOSPITALS)

The number of adult and pediatric days of care rendered during a given period. See also Hospital Day.

INSTITUTION OF HIGHER EDUCATION

An institution which offers programs of study beyond the secondary school level terminating in an associate, baccalaureate, or higher degree. See also **College; University.**

JAIL

A facility, usually operated by a local law enforcement agency, holding persons detained pending adjudication and/or persons committed after adjudication to a sentence of one year or less.

LABOR FORCE STATUS

A term which refers to whether or not a person is in the labor force, and, if in the labor force, whether he or she is employed or unemployed, a full-time worker or a part-time worker, etc. Persons are in the labor force if they are in the civilian labor force or in the Armed Forces.

The civilian labor force consists of both employed and unemployed persons, full-time and part-time workers. Generally, persons outside the labor force consist of full-time homemakers, students who do not work, retired persons, and inmates of institutions. "Discouraged workers," those who do not have a job and have not been seeking one, are also considered to be not in the labor force. See also **Civilian Labor Force.**

LARCENY see CRIME.

LIMITATION OF ACTIVITY see HEALTH LIMITATION OF ACTIVITY.

LIVE BIRTH

The live birth of an infant, defined as the complete expulsion or extraction from its mother of a product of conception, irrespective of the duration of the pregnancy, which, after such separation, breathes or shows any evidence of life such as heartbeat, umbilical cord pulsation, or definite movement of voluntary muscles, whether or not the umbilical cord has been cut or the placenta is attached. Each such birth is considered live born.

MARITAL STATUS

All persons 15 years of age and older are classified by the Bureau of the Census according to marital status. The Bureau defines two broad categories of marital status: **Single** - all those persons who have never been married (including persons whose marriage has been annulled), and **Ever married** - which is composed of the now married, the widowed, and the divorced. **Now married** persons are those who are legally married (as well as some persons who have common law marriages, along with some unmarried couples who live together and report their marital status as married), and whose marriage has not ended by widowhood or divorce. The now married are sometimes further subdivided: married, spouse present; separated; married, spouse absent; married, spouse absent, other. **Married, spouse present** covers married couples living together. **Separated** includes those persons legally separated or otherwise absent from their spouse because of marital discord (such as persons who have been deserted or who have parted because they no longer want to live together but who have not obtained a divorce). Separated includes persons with a limited divorce. **Married, spouse absent** covers those households where the both the husband and the wife were not counted as members of the same household, (or where both husband and wife lived together in group quarters). **Married, spouse absent, other**, includes those married persons whose spouse was not counted as a member of the same household, besides those who are separated. Included are persons whose spouse was employed and living away from home, absent in the armed forces, or was an inmate of an institution. **Widowed** includes widows and widowers who have not remarried. **Divorced** includes persons who are legally divorced and have not remarried.

MARRIED COUPLES see **FAMILY TYPE.**

MARRIED PERSONS see **MARITAL STATUS.**

MEAN

    The arithmetic average of a set of values. It is derived by dividing the sum of a group of numerical items by the total number of items. Mean income (of a population), for example, is defined as the value obtained by dividing the total or aggregate income by the population. Thus, the mean income for families is obtained by dividing the aggregate of all income reported by persons in families by the total number of families. See also **Median.**

MEDIAN

    In general, a value that divides the total range of values into two equal parts. For example, to say that the median money income of families in the United States in 1985 was $27,735 indicates that half of all families had incomes larger than that value, and half had less. See also **Mean.**

MEDICAID

    A federally funded but state administered and operated program which provides medical benefits to certain low income persons in need of medical care. The program, authorized in 1965 by Title XIX of the Social Security Act, categorically covers participants in the Aid to Families with Dependent Children (AFDC) program, as well as some participants in the Supplemental Security Income (SSI) program, along with those other people deemed medically needy in each participating state. Each state determines the benefits covered, rates of payment to providers, and methods of administering the program.

MEDICARE

    A federally funded nationwide health insurance program providing health insurance protection to people 65 years of age and over, people eligible for social security disability payments for more than two years, and people with end-state renal disease, regardless of income. The program was enacted July 30, 1965, as title XVIII, Health Insurance for the Aged, of the Social Security Act, and became effective on July 1, 1966. It consists of two separate but coordinated programs: hospital insurance (Part A), and supplementary medical insurance (Part B).

METROPOLITAN AREA see **CONSOLIDATED METROPOLITAN STATISTICAL AREA; METROPOLITAN STATISTICAL AREA; PRIMARY METROPOLITAN STATISTICAL AREA; STANDARD CONSOLIDATED STATISTICAL AREA; STANDARD METROPOLITAN STATISTICAL AREA**

METROPOLITAN STATISTICAL AREA (MSA)

A geographic concept introduced in June, 1984, to replace the Standard Metropolitan Statistical Area (SMSA). In general, an MSA is a geographic area consisting of a large population nucleus, together with adjacent communities that have a high degree of economic and social integration with that nucleus. MSAs are designated in accordance with a detailed 16 section criteria established by the federal Office of Management and Budget (OMB). In general, MSAs are a county based concept which must include a city that, with contiguous, densely settled territory, constitutes a Census Bureau defined urbanized area having at least 50,000 population. (However, if an MSA's largest city has less than 50,000 population, the MSA as a whole must have a total population of at least 100,000). Adjacent MSAs are consolidated into a single MSA if certain conditions relating to commuting to work, size, and geographic proximity are met. See also **Consolidated Metropolitan Statistical Area; New England County Metropolitan Area; Primary Metropolitan Statistical Area.**

NEW ENGLAND COUNTY METROPOLITAN AREA (NECMA)

A geographic concept developed for the New England states (Massachusetts, Connecticut, Rhode Island, Maine, New Hampshire, Vermont) to present data that is only available on a county-level basis . Unlike the rest of the country, Metropolitan Statistical Areas (MSAs) in the New England states are officially defined in terms of cities and towns instead of counties. As a result New England MSA data may not be directly comparable to MSA data in the rest of the country. NECMAs are county-based geographic areas (which follow the same general guidelines of MSAs in other parts of the country) and thus provide a basis of comparison with other states. NECMAs do not replace the MSAs in New England, but supplement them.

MOBILE HOME see **HOUSING UNIT.**
MONEY INCOME see **INCOME.**

MURDER see **CRIME.**

NATIONAL CRIME SURVEY

A twice yearly survey of 49,000 households comprising over 102,000 inhabitants 12 years of age and older. Administered by the Bureau of Justice Statistics, the survey measures criminal victimization by surveying victims directly. It differs from the FBI Uniform Crime Report (UCR) which is based on crimes reported to police. See also **Crime.**

NURSING HOME

A facility with three or more beds providing adults with nursing care and/or personal care (such as help with bathing, eating, using toilet facilities, or dressing) and/or supervision over such activities as money management, walking, and shopping.

OCCUPANCY STATUS (HOUSING)

The classification of all housing units as either occupied or vacant. **Occupied housing units** are those that have one or more persons living in them as their usual residence, and include units whose usual occupants are temporarily absent (e.g., on vacation). **Vacant housing units** are those that have no one living in them as their usual residence. Also classified as vacant are housing units that are temporarily occupied solely by persons who have a usual residence elsewhere, newly constructed units completed to the point where all exterior windows and doors are installed and final usable floors are in place, and vacant mobile homes or trailers intended to be occupied on the site on which they stand.

OCCUPATION

The kind of work a person does at a job or business. Occupation is reported for a given survey period, (most frequently the period covered by the survey, the reference period, is the week including March 12). If the person was not at work during the reference period, occupation usually refers to the person's most recent job or business. Persons working at more than one job are asked to identify the job at which he or she works the most hours, which is then counted as his or her occupation.

Occupations are classified according to the Standard Occupational Classification system (SOC), a system promulgated by the federal Office of Management and Budget.

OWNER OCCUPIED HOUSING UNIT see **TENURE**.

PART-TIME ENROLLMENT (HIGHER EDUCATION)

The number of students enrolled in higher education courses with a total credit load of less than 75% of the normal full-time credit load.

PART-TIME WORKERS see **CIVILIAN LABOR FORCE**.

PERSONAL INCOME see **INCOME**.

POPULATION

The number of inhabitants of an area. The total population of the United States is the sum of all persons living within the United States, plus all members of the Armed Forces living in foreign countries, Puerto Rico, Guam, and the U.S. Virgin Islands. Other Americans living abroad (e.g., civilian federal employees and dependents of members of the Armed Forces or other federal employees are not included).

The **resident population of the United States**, is the population living within the geographic United States. This includes members of the Armed Forces stationed in the United States and their families as well as foreigners working or studying here. It excludes foreign military, naval, and diplomatic personnel and their families located here and residing in embassies or similar quarters, as well as Americans living abroad. Resident population is often the denominator when calculating birth and death rates, incidence of disease, and other rates.

The **civilian population** is the resident population excluding members of the Armed Forces. However, families of members of the Armed Forces are included.

The **civilian non-institutional population** is the civilian population not residing in institutions. Institutions include, correctional institutions; detention homes and training schools for juvenile delinquents; homes for the aged and dependent (e.g., nursing homes and convalescent homes); homes for dependent and neglected children; homes and schools for the mentally and physically handicapped; homes for unwed mothers; psychiatric, tuberculosis, and chronic disease hospitals; and residential treatment centers.

POVERTY STATUS

Although the term poverty connotes a complex set of economic, social, and psychological conditions, the standard statistical definition provides for only estimates of economic poverty. These are based on the receipt of money income before taxes and exclude the value of government payments and transfers such as food stamps or Medicare; private transfers, such as health insurance premiums paid by employers; gifts; the depletion of assets; and borrowed money. Thus the term poverty as used by government agencies, classifies persons and families in relation to being above or below a specified income level, or poverty threshold. Those below this threshold are said to be in poverty, or more accurately, as below the poverty level. Poverty thresholds vary by size of family, number of children, and age of householder and are updated annually. Poverty status is also determined for unrelated individuals living in households, but not for those living in group quarters nor for persons in the Armed Forces. The poverty threshold is revised each year according to formula based on the Consumer Price Index.

PRIMARY METROPOLITAN STATISTICAL AREA (PMSA)

This geographic concept, introduced in June, 1984, combines with Metropolitan Statistical Area (MSA) and Consolidated Metropolitan Statistical Areas (CMSA), to replace the Standard Metropolitan Statistical Area (SMSA) concept. PMSAs are designated according to criteria established by the federal Office of Management and Budget. In general PMSAs are those counties with populations of at least 100,000 (60% must be urban), in which less than 50% of its resident workers commute to jobs outside the county. PMSAs are parts of Consolidated Metropolitan Statistical Areas (CMSAs).

PRISON

A confinement facility having custodial authority over adults sentenced to confinement for a period of more than one year. Prisons are usually run by State or federal authorities.

PRIVATE SCHOOL see **SCHOOL**.

PROPERTY CRIME see **CRIME**.

PUBLIC SCHOOL see **SCHOOL**.

RACE

The Bureau of the Census in many of its surveys (most notably in the decennial censuses of population) asks all persons to identify themselves according to race. The concept of race as used by the Bureau reflects the self-identification of the respondents. It is not meant to denote any clear cut scientific or biological definition.

Although it is often reported with racial categories, **Hispanic origin**, or Spanish origin, is not a racial category. Persons may be of any race and of Hispanic origin. Those who describe themselves as Hispanic (or Mexican, Cuban, Chicano, etc.) in response to a question about race, are included by the Bureau in the racial classification, "other." See also **Hispanic Origin.**

RAPE see **CRIME.**

REFERENCE PERSON

Most frequently, the person who responds to a government survey. Most surveys done by the federal government are based on households and begin by asking the initial respondent the name of the person in whose name the housing unit is owned or rented (this person is designated as the householder). Usually the householder is the reference person. Other household members are defined in relation to the householder.

REGION

The Bureau of the Census has divided the United States into four regions. This division is the primary geographic subdivision of the nation for statistical reporting purposes. As a result, almost all federal agencies, along with many private data collectors, have adopted the regional subdivision and use it for presenting statistical data. The four regions are the **Northeast** (Maine, New Hampshire, Vermont, Massachusetts, Rhode Island, Connecticut, New York, New Jersey, Pennsylvania); the **Midwest** (Ohio, Indiana, Illinois, Michigan, Wisconsin, Minnesota, Iowa, Missouri, North Dakota, South Dakota, Kansas, Nebraska); the **South** (Delaware, Maryland, District of Columbia, Virginia, West Virginia, North Carolina, South Carolina, Georgia, Florida, Kentucky, Tennessee, Alabama, Mississippi, Arkansas, Louisiana, Oklahoma, Texas); and the **West** (Montana, Idaho, Colorado, Wyoming, New Mexico, Arizona, Utah, Nevada, Washington, Oregon, California, Alaska, Hawaii). In this book, all regional data conform to this definition.

REGULAR SCHOOL see **SCHOOL.**

RENTER OCCUPIED HOUSING UNIT see **TENURE.**

RESIDENT POPULATION see **POPULATION.**

RESTRICTED-ACTIVITY DAY see **DISABILITY DAY.**

ROBBERY see **CRIME.**

ROOMS (HOUSING)

The number of whole rooms intended for living purposes in both occupied and vacant housing units. These rooms include living rooms, dining rooms, kitchens, bedrooms, finished recreation rooms, enclosed porches suitable for year-round use, and lodger's rooms. Excluded are strip or Pullman kitchens, bathrooms, open porches, balconies, foyers, halls, half-rooms, utility rooms, unfinished attics or basements, or other space used for storage. A partially divided room, such as a dinette next to a kitchen or living room, is a separate room only if there is a partition from floor to ceiling, but not if the partition consists solely of shelves or cabinets.

RURAL see **URBAN/RURAL POPULATION.**

SCHOOL

Elementary and secondary schools are divisions of the school system consisting of students in one or more grade groups or other identifiable groups, organized as one unit with one or more teachers giving instruction of a defined type, and housed in a school plant of one or more buildings. More than one school may be housed in one school plant as is the case where elementary and secondary programs are housed in the same building.

Regular schools generally are those which advance a person toward a diploma or degree. They include public and private nursery schools, kindergartens, graded schools, colleges, universities, and professional schools.

Public schools are controlled and supported by local, state, or federal government agencies.

Private schools are controlled and supported mainly by religious organizations, private persons, or private organizations.

SCHOOL ENROLLMENT see **ENROLLMENT.**

SCHOOL-LOSS DAY see **DISABILITY DAY.**

SELF-EMPLOYMENT INCOME

A type of money income which comprises net income (gross receipts minus operating expenses) received by persons from an unincorporated business, profession, and/or from the operation of a farm as a farm owner, tenant, or sharecropper. See also **Money Income.**

SEPARATED PERSONS see **MARITAL STATUS.**

SERIOUS CRIME see **CRIME.**

SINGLE PERSON HOUSEHOLDS see **HOUSEHOLD.**

SINGLE PERSONS see **MARITAL STATUS.**

SPECIFIED OWNER-OCCUPIED HOUSING UNITS

Specified owner-occupied units are single family houses on less than ten acres, which have no commercial enterprise or medical practice on the property. Excluded are owner-occupied condominium housing units, mobile homes, trailers, boats, tents, or vans occupied as a usual residence as well as owner-occupied non-condominium units in multi-family buildings. See also **Housing Unit.**

STANDARD CONSOLIDATED STATISTICAL AREA (SCSA)

A large concentration of metropolitan population composed of two or more contiguous Standard Metropolitan Statistical Areas (SMSAs) which together meet certain criteria of population size, urban character, social and economic integration, and/or contiguity of urbanized areas. Each SCSA must have a population of one million or more. The SCSA concept was replaced with the new metropolitan area classifications in June, 1984. See Consolidated Metropolitan Statistical Area; Metropolitan Statistical Area; Primary Metropolitan Statistical Area.

STANDARD METROPOLITAN STATISTICAL AREA (SMSA)

A geographic area concept used until 1984. In general, an SMSA is a large population nucleus and nearby communities which have a high degree of economic and social integration within that nucleus. Each SMSA consists of one or more entire counties (or county equivalents) that meet certain criteria of population, commuting ties, and metropolitan character. In New England, towns and cities rather than counties are the basic units and count as county equivalents. An SMSA includes a city and, generally, the entire surrounding urbanized area and the remainder of the county or counties in which the urbanized area is located. An SMSA also includes those additional outlying counties which meet specified criteria relating to metropolitan character and level of commuting ties.

The SMSA concept was developed in 1949 and has been refined for each succeeding decennial census since 1950. In June, 1984, SMSAs were superseded by three new metropolitan area concepts: Metropolitan Statistical Areas (MSAs), Consolidated Metropolitan Statistical Areas (CMSAs), and Primary Metropolitan Statistical Areas (PMSAs).

TAXES

Compulsory contributions exacted by a government for public purposes (except employee and employer assessments for retirement and social insurance purposes, which are classified as insurance trust revenue). All tax revenue is classified as general revenue and comprises amounts received (including interest and penalties, but excluding protested amounts and refunds) from all taxes imposed by a government.

TENURE

A concept relating to housing units. All occupied housing units are classified as being either owner-occupied or renter occupied. A housing unit is owner-occupied if the owner or co-owner lives in the unit even if the unit is mortgaged or not fully paid for. All other housing units are considered to be renter occupied, regardless of whether or not cash rent is paid for them by a member of the household. See also **Housing Unit.**

UNEMPLOYED PERSONS see CIVILIAN LABOR FORCE.

UNEMPLOYMENT see CIVILIAN LABOR FORCE.

UNIFORM CRIME REPORTING (UCR) PROGRAM
A program administered by the FBI which collects reports from most police agencies in the nation (covering approximately 95% of the population) on serious crimes known to police (violent crime and property crime), arrests, police officers and related items. The Bureau issues monthly and annual summary reports based on the program. See also **Crime.**

UNIVERSITY
An institution of higher education consisting of a liberal arts college, a diverse graduate program, and usually two or more professional schools or faculties and empowered to confer degrees in various fields of study. See also **Higher Education.**

UNRELATED INDIVIDUAL
An unrelated individual is generally a person living in a household, and is either: 1) a householder living alone or only with persons who are not related to him or her by blood, marriage, or adoption, or; 2) a roomer, boarder, partner, roommate, or resident employee unrelated to the householder. Certain persons living in group quarters (who are not inmates of institutions) are also counted as unrelated individuals.

URBAN/RURAL POPULATION
Urban and rural are type of area concepts rather than specific areas outlined on maps. The urban population comprises all persons living in urbanized areas and in places of 2,500 or more inhabitants outside urbanized areas. The rural population consists of everyone else. Therefore, a rural classification need not imply a farm or sparsely settled areas, since a small city or town is rural when it is outside an urbanized area and has fewer than 2,500 inhabitants. The terms urban and rural are independent of metropolitan and non-metropolitan; both urban and rural areas occur inside and outside metropolitan areas. See also **Urbanized Area.**

URBANIZED AREA
A population concentration of at least 50,000 inhabitants, generally consisting of a central city and the surrounding, closely settled, contiguous territory (suburbs). The urbanized area criteria define a boundary based on a population density of at least 1,000 persons per square mile, but also include some less densely settled areas, such as industrial parks and railroad yards, if they are within areas of dense urban development. The density level of 1,000 persons per square mile corresponds approximately to the contiguously built-up area around a city or cities. The urban fringe is that part of the urbanized area outside of a central city or cities.

Typically, an entire urbanized area is included within an Standard Metropolitan Statistical Area (SMSA) or Metropolitan Statistical Area (MSA). The SMSA (or MSA) is usually much larger in terms of area and includes territory where the population density is less than 1,000. Occasionally more than one urbanized area is located within an SMSA (MSA). In some cases a small part of an urbanized area may extend beyond an SMSA (MSA) boundary, or possibly into an adjacent SMSA (MSA). Urbanized areas sometimes cross state boundaries as well.

VACANCY STATUS see **OCCUPANCY STATUS.**

VALUE (HOUSING UNITS)
In surveys done by the Bureau of the Census, the value of owner-occupied housing units is the respondent's estimate of the current dollar worth of the property; for vacant units, the value is the price asked for the property. A property is defined as the house and the land on which it stands. Respondents are asked by the Bureau to estimate the value of the house and land even if they own only the house, or own the house jointly. Statistics for value are only gathered by the Bureau for owner-occupied condominium units and for specified owner-occupied units (single family houses on less than ten acres, and with no business on the property).

VICTIMIZATION see **CRIME.**

VIOLENT CRIME see **CRIME.**

VOTING AGE POPULATION
All persons over the age of 18 (the voting age for federal elections) in a given geographic area comprise the voting age population. The voting age population does include a small number of persons who, although of voting age, are not eligible to vote (e.g. resident aliens, inmates of institutions, etc.). The voting age population is estimated in even numbered years by the Bureau of the Census.

WAGES AND SALARIES
Wages and salaries are a type (subgroup) of money income and include civilian wages and salaries, Armed Forces pay and allowances, piece-rate payments, commissions, tips, National Guard or Reserve pay (received for training periods), and cash bonuses before deductions for taxes, pensions, union dues, etc. See also **Money Income.**

WIDOWED PERSONS see **MARITAL STATUS.**

WORK DISABILITY
A health condition which limits the kind or amount of work a person can do, or prevents working at a job. A person is limited in the kind of work he or she can do if the person has a health condition which restricts his or her choice of jobs. A person is limited in amount of work if he or she is not able to work at a full-time (35 hours or more per week) job or business. See also **Condition (Health).**

WORK-LOSS DAY see **DISABILITY DAY.**

Index

abortion, 10.18

age, *see individual subject areas, e.g.,
civilian labor force, by age*

agriculture, 8.02

affordability of housing, 11.04

AIDS, 9.11, 10.01, 10.02, 10.03

alcohol use, 10.12

Associate degrees, *see higher
education*

Bachelor's degrees, *see higher
education*

birth rates, 10.10, 10.11

births, live, 10.08, 10.11

blue collar workers, *see civilian labor
force*

children
    childcare arrangements, 3.11
    enrolled in school, 4.01, 4.02,
    4.04, 4.05
    health status, 10.26
    in families, 3.06, 3.07, 3.08, 3.09,
    3.10, 3.11, 3.12
    living arrangements, 3.10
    poverty of, 8.16, 8.19
    support payments, 8.24
    vaccinations of, 10.04
    with AIDS, 10.01, 10.02, 10.03

cigarette use, 10.12

civilian labor force
    & school enrollment, 5.08, 7.17
    by age, 7.01, 7.02, 7.05, 7.10,
    7.11
    by industry, 7.08, 11.06
    by occupation, 7.07
    by sex, 7.02, 7.05, 7.07, 7.09,
    7.11, 7.12, 7.16
    employment, 7.05, 7.06, 7.07,
    7.08, 7.09, 7.22
    families, 7.22
    full-time/part-time status, 7.09
    minimum wage workers, 7.15
    participation, 7.01, 7.02, 7.03,
    7.04, 7.17
    projections, 7.04
    self-employment, 7.19, 7.21
    unemployment, 7.10, 7.11, 7.12,
    7.13, 7.14, 7.18, , 7.20
    union membership, 7.16

cocaine use, 10.12

colleges, *see higher education*

congress, members of, 6.02

crime
    attitudes toward, 9.09, 9.10
    fear of, 9.09, 9.10

criminal victimization, 9.01, 9.02, 9.03,
    9.12

death rates, 10.13, 10.14, 10.15, 10.16

death sentence, *see inmates, prison*

degrees, college *see higher education*

dental visits, 10.17

disability, work, 10.24

Doctor's degrees, *see higher education*

dropouts, *see school and schools*

drug use, 10.12

dwellings, *see housing units*

earnings, *see income*

education, *see higher education; school and schools*

educational attainment, 2.07, 2.08, 5.15, 5.16, 5.17, 5.18, 5.19
    by age, 5.16
    median school years completed, 5.15, 5.18
    years of college completed, 5.15, 5.16, 5.17, 5.18, 5.19
see also higher education; school and schools

elected officials, 6.01

elections, *see voters and voting*

employment, *see civilian labor force*

enrollment in college, *see higher education*

enrollment in school, *see school and schools*

families
    by type, 3.06, 3.07, 3.08, 3.09
    childcare arrangements of, 3.11
    employment status of, 7.22
    income of, 8.06, 8.07, 8.08
    married couples, 3.06, 3.07, 3.08
    poverty of, 8.16, 8.17, 8.18

family income, *see income*

farms and farming, 11.01

fear of crime, *see crime*
fertility rates, 10.09

firms owned by Hispanics, 11.06

first professional degrees, *see higher education*

graduates, *see higher education; school and schools*

health
    children, 10.26
    insurance, 10.05, 10.06, 10.07
    practices, 10.25, 10.17
    see also death rates

high school, *see school and schools*

high school graduates, *see educational attainment*

higher education
    Associate degrees, 5.10
    Bachelors degrees, 5.11
        by field of study, 5.11
    degrees conferred,
        by type, 5.10, 5.11, 5.12, 5.13, 5.14
    Doctors degrees, 5.13
    employment of students, 5.08, 5.20
    enrollment, 5.01, 5.02, 5.03, 5.04, 5.05, 5.06
    financial aid, 5.07
    first professional degrees, 5.14
    Masters degrees, 5.12
    private colleges, 5.06
    public colleges, 5.06
see also educational attainment

HIV, 9.11

homes, 11.02, 11.03

households, 3.01, 3.02, 3.03, 3.04, 3.05, 3.06, 3.07, 3.08, 3.09

money income, 8.01, 8.02, 8.03,
    8.04, 8.05, 8.06, 8.07, 8.08,
    8.23
net worth of, 8.23
touched by crime, 9.03
see also families

houses, 11.02, 11.03

housing affordability, 11.04

housing tenure
    families, 3.01, 3.02, 3.03, 3.04
    households, 3.06, 3.07, 3.08,
        3.09, 3.10

housing units, 11.02, 11.03

income
    child support payments, 8.26
    family income, 8.04, 8.05, 8.06,
        8.07, 8.08
    household income, 8.01, 8.02,
        8.03, 8.23
    money income per capita, 8.14
    of full-time workers, 8.10
    of persons, 8.09, 8.11, 8.12, 8.13,
    8.22
    per capita, 8.15
see also poverty

inmates, prison, 9.05, 9.06
    criminal history of, 9.04
    HIV-positive, 9.11
    under death sentence, 9.04, 9.07

interracial married couples, 2.05

jail inmates, *see inmates*

labor force, *see civilian labor force*

labor union membership, 7.16

live births, 10.08, 10.11

marijuana use, 10.12

marital status, 2.01, 2.02, 2.03, 2.04

married couples, *see families*

Master's degrees, *see higher education*

minimum wage workers, *see civilian
    labor force*

mobility, 11.05

money income, *see income*

occupations, *see civilian labor force*

parents, custodial, 3.09, 8.24

population, resident, 1.08, 1.09, 1.11,
    2.09
    of cities, 1.10

poverty, 8.18, 8.19, 8.20, 8.21
    of children, 7.18, 8.17
    of families, 8.16, 8.17
    of persons, 8.18, 8.20, 8.21

prison, chances of going to, 9.08

private colleges, *see higher education*

professionals, *see civilian labor force*

projections
    civilian labor force, 7.04
    population, 1.05, 1.06, 1.07, 1.11

public colleges, *see higher education*

public officials, 6.01

registration (to vote), *see voters and
    voting*

salaries and wages, *see civilian labor force; income*

school and schools
    computer use, 4.10
    enrollment, 4.01, 4.02, 4.04, 4.05
    elementary, 4.05
    preprimary, 4.04
    high school dropouts, 4.11
    school age population, 4.03
    student achievement, 4.08, 4.09, 4.13
    testing, 4.08, 4.09, 4.13
see also higher education

school enrollment, *see school and schools*

state data
    school enrollment, 4.05

student achievement, 4.08, 4.09, 4.13

students, *see higher education; school and schools*

suicide, 10.16

teachers, 4.06, 4.07

tenure, housing, 11.02, 11.03

test scores
    math, 4.09
    reading, 4.08
    science, 4.09

unemployment, *see civilian labor force*

union membership, *see labor unions*

universities; *see higher education; school and schools*

unmarried couples, 2.05

vaccination of children, 10.04

victimization, *see criminal victimization*

voter registration, *see voters and voting*

voters and voting
    by age, 6.04, 6.05, 6.08, 6.07, 6.08, 6.09, 6.10, 6.11, 6.12
    by educational attainment, 6.04, 6.05, 6.06, 6.07, 6.08, 6.09, 6.10, 6.11, 6.12
    by income, 6.04, 6.05, 6.08, 6.07, 6.08, 6.09, 6.10, 6.11, 6.12
    by labor force status, 6.07, 6.08, 6.09, 6.10, 6.11, 6.12
    by occupation, 6.07, 6.08, 6.09, 6.10, 6.11, 6.12
    by sex, 6.04, 6.05, 6.06, 6.07, 6.08, 6.09, 6.10, 6.11, 6.12
    registration, 6.03, 6.05, 6.08, 6.11
    voting, 6.06, 6.09, 6.12
    voting age population, 6.04, 6.07, 6.10

white collar workers, *see civilian labor force*

years of school completed, *see educational attainment*